# FAVORITE BRAND NAME
# CHRISTMAS
## COLLECTION

Publications International, Ltd.

**Pictured on the front cover:** *Top row, left:* Peanut Butter Reindeer *(page 146); Center:* Oven-Roasted Vegetables *(page 193); Right:* Chocolate Walnut Coffee Rings *(page 79). Bottom row, left:* Classic Pecan Pie *(page 202); Center:* Herbed Roast *(page 84); Right:* Apple Crumb Squares *(page 143).*

**Pictured on the back cover:** *Top row, left:* Easy Caramel Pop Corn Balls, Almond Butter Crunch Pop Corn and Rocky Road Peanut Butter Pop Corn Bars *(page 160); Center:* Peach-Glazed Virginia Ham *(page 93); Right:* Banana Crescents *(page 126). Bottom row, left:* Jammy Pinwheels *(page 151)*, Chocolate Cherry Oatmeal Fancies *(page 148)* and Southwestern Bizcochitos *(page 149); Center:* Tortelloni Wreath with Pesto Dip *(page 19); Right:* Swiss 'n' Cheddar Cheeseball *(page 151).*

**Microwave Cooking:** Microwave ovens vary in wattage. The cooking times given in this publication are approximate. Use the cooking times as guidelines and check for doneness before adding more time. Consult manufacturer's instructions for suitable microwave-safe cooking dishes.

**Preparation/Cooking Times:** The preparation times are based on the approximate amount of time required to assemble the recipe before cooking, baking, chilling or serving. These times include preparation steps such as measuring, chopping and mixing. The fact that some preparations can be done simultaneously is taken into account and a total Prep and Cook Time is given. Preparation of optional ingredients and serving suggestions are not included.

# Contents

# BEFORE YOU BEGIN

Throughout the world, wherever Christmas is celebrated, getting together with friends and family to rejoice in the holiday season is an old tradition. The wonderful aroma whirling about the kitchen in preparation of the big holiday feast brings smiles and recollections of Christmases past. In this section, you will find helpful hints such as menu planning and carving techniques designed to guide you through the holidays. So, before you begin scurrying about in anticipation of the holidays, take some time to read through the information below.

## PARTY PLANNING AND MENUS

The following are some helpful pointers to keep in mind when you are selecting recipes for an entertaining menu.

• If this is one of your first company meals, keep it on the small side. It is easier to cook and serve for eight to ten rather than twenty people.

• Do not invite more people than you can comfortably seat at your table.

• Make sure you have enough serving dishes and utensils.

• Select the entrée first, then plan the other dishes around it.

• Not every item on the menu needs to be a showstopper. Select one or two involved recipes and let the remainder be easy-to-prepare or store-bought.

• Eye appeal is an important consideration when planning a meal. Select foods with a variety of colors.

• A balanced meal offers contrasting flavors. The tart flavor of cranberries with the mild flavor of turkey make a perfect contrast.

• Choose side dishes with different shapes and sizes. Whole berry cranberry relish served along with peas and Brussels sprouts would not offer as much interest to a meal as whole berry cranberry relish served along with broccoli spears and diagonally sliced carrots.

• Pick recipes that can be made ahead of time. This leaves you more time for your guests.

• Many guests like to contribute to the festivities by bringing a side dish, dessert, appetizer or wine. Be sure to have some recommendations ready so that if you are asked, you may offer suggestions that complement the rest of the meal.

• Not all entertaining requires a full meal. Consider inviting family and friends over for just desserts or light snacks.

• Review the recipes you plan to make, then prepare a comprehensive grocery list. Those last minute dashes to the supermarket can be very stressful.

• Lastly, remember to serve hot foods hot and cold foods cold. For food safety, do not let any foods remain at room temperature for over 2 hours.

To get you started, here is a selection of holiday menus featuring the delicious recipes found in this publication. Use them as a starting point, making substitutions to suit your personal tastes.

### Family Breakfast

Orange Juice & Champagne (page 10)

French Toast Strata Pie (page 116)

Cinnamon Date Scones (page 72)

Sour Cream Coffee Cake with Chocolate and Walnuts (page 74)

fresh seasonal fruit

fresh brewed coffee and assorted juices

### Afternoon Tea by the Fire

Smoked Turkey Sandwiches (page 23)

Cranberry Raisin Nut Bread (page 80) with Cranberry-Orange Spread (page 81)

Walnut-Brandy Shortbread (page 140)

Chocolate Dipped Brandy Snaps (page 142)

assorted teas

## CARVING

Once the menu has been planned, one of the more formidable tasks when preparing a large meal is carving the roast or bird. To help you carve the main attraction like a pro, follow these helpful guidelines.

### General Guidelines

• Allow enough time before serving not only for cooking the meat, but for stand time and carving.

• A stand time of 10 to 20 minutes is recommended for large cuts of meat, such as roasts, turkeys and whole chickens. Stand time allows the meat to finish cooking. Meat is easier to carve after standing. If meat is carved immediately out of the oven, it loses more of its flavorful juices.

• The temperatures given for removing meat and poultry from the oven are 5° to 10°F lower than the standard final temperatures. This is because the temperature continues to rise during the stand time.

• During the stand time, put the finishing touches on the salad and side dishes. This is also a good time to make the gravy.

• Unless you are planning on carving at the table, place the meat on a large cutting board with a well at one end to hold the juice. Use a long, sharp carving knife to slice the meat and a long-handled meat fork to steady the meat.

### Boneless Roasts

Boneless beef, pork and lamb roasts are easy to carve. Hold the roast steady with a long-handled meat fork. With the knife held perpendicular to the cutting board, cut across the grain into thin uniform slices.

### Standing Beef Rib Roast

For added stability, cut a wedge-shaped slice from the large end of the roast so that the meat will sit flat. Insert a long-handled meat fork below the top rib. Slice across the top of roast toward the rib bone. This roast can be sliced between ½ to ¾ inch thick. With the tip of the knife, cut along the rib bone to release the slice of meat. To remove the meat slice, slide the knife blade under the cut slice of meat. Holding it steady with meat fork, lift the slice and place it on a platter.

### Roast Turkey

To remove the leg, hold the drumstick and cut the skin with a carving knife between the thigh and the body of the turkey to the joint. Pull the leg away from the body of the turkey and cut through the joint at the backbone.

To separate the drumstick from the thigh, place the leg on the cutting board skin side up. Cut through at the joint. To slice the drumstick, hold the drumstick at an angle, bony side up. Cut down into ¼-inch slices. Rotate the drumstick as you cut. Remove and discard the large tendons.

To cut the thigh into slices, turn the thigh skin side down. Cut along the length of the bone, then turn skin side up and cut the meat across the grain.

To remove the wings, insert a meat fork into the turkey to hold it steady. Cut down between the wing and the body of the turkey with a carving knife. Pull the wing out and cut through the joint.

To remove the breast meat, insert a long-handled meat fork into the turkey to hold it steady. At the base of the breast meat, make a horizontal cut across the breast to the bone. Cut the slices with straight even strokes down to the horizontal cut.

# APPETIZERS & BEVERAGES

## Pesto Cheese Wreath

Parsley-Basil Pesto* (recipe follows)
3 (8-ounce) packages cream cheese, softened
½ cup mayonnaise
¼ cup whipping cream or half-and-half
1 teaspoon sugar
1 teaspoon onion salt
⅓ cup chopped roasted red peppers** or pimiento, drained
Pimiento strips and Italian flat leaf parsley leaves (optional)
Assorted crackers and vegetables

*One-half cup purchased pesto may be substituted for Parsley-Basil Pesto.

**Look for roasted red peppers packed in cans or jars in the Italian food section of the supermarket.

Prepare Parsley-Basil Pesto; set aside. Beat cream cheese and mayonnaise in small bowl until smooth; beat in whipping cream, sugar and onion salt.

Line 5-cup ring mold with plastic wrap. Spoon half of the cheese mixture into prepared mold; spread evenly. Spread Parsley-Basil Pesto evenly over cheese; top with chopped red peppers. Spoon remaining cheese mixture over peppers; spread evenly. Cover; refrigerate until cheese is firm, 8 hours or overnight.

Uncover mold; invert onto serving plate. Carefully remove plastic wrap. Smooth top and sides of wreath with spatula. Garnish with pimiento strips and parsley leaves as shown in photo, if desired. Serve with assorted crackers and vegetables.

*Makes 16 to 24 appetizer servings*

## Parsley-Basil Pesto

2 cups fresh parsley leaves
¼ cup pine nuts or slivered almonds
2 tablespoons grated Parmesan cheese
2 cloves garlic
1 tablespoon dried basil leaves
¼ teaspoon salt
2 tablespoons olive or vegetable oil

Process all ingredients except oil in food processor or blender until finely chopped. With machine running, add oil gradually, processing until mixture is smooth.

*Makes about ½ cup*

*Clockwise from top: Holiday Appetizer Puffs (page 8), Pesto Cheese Wreath and Cheese Pinecones (page 8)*

## Cheese Pinecones

2 cups (8 ounces) shredded Swiss cheese
½ cup butter or margarine, softened
3 tablespoons milk
2 tablespoons dry sherry or milk
⅛ teaspoon ground red pepper
1 cup finely chopped blanched almonds
¾ cup slivered blanched almonds
¾ cup sliced almonds
½ cup whole almonds
   Fresh rosemary sprigs
   Assorted crackers

Beat cheese, butter, milk, sherry and red pepper in medium bowl until smooth; stir in chopped almonds.

Divide mixture into 3 equal portions; shape each into tapered ovals to resemble pinecones. Insert slivered, sliced and whole almonds into cones as shown in photo (page 6). Cover; refrigerate 2 to 3 hours or until firm.

Arrange cheese pinecones on wooden board or serving plate. Garnish tops with rosemary. Serve with assorted crackers.
*Makes 12 to 16 appetizer servings*

## Holiday Appetizer Puffs

1 sheet frozen puff pastry, thawed
   (½ of 17¼-ounce package)
2 tablespoons olive or vegetable oil
   Toppings: grated Parmesan cheese,
    sesame seeds, poppy seeds, dried
    dill weed, dried basil, paprika,
    drained capers, green olive slices

Preheat oven to 425°F. Roll pastry on lightly floured surface to 13-inch square. Cut into shapes with cookie cutters (simple shaped cutters work best). Place on ungreased baking sheets.

Brush cutouts lightly with oil. Decorate with desired toppings. Bake 6 to 8 minutes or until golden. Serve warm or at room temperature.
*Makes about 1½ dozen appetizers*

## Stone Crab Claws with Honey-Mustard Sauce

2½ pounds stone crab claws, cracked
1 cup mayonnaise
⅓ cup half-and-half
2 tablespoons honey
2 tablespoons prepared mustard
2 teaspoons ground coriander

Arrange crab claws on serving plate. Combine remaining ingredients; mix well until blended. Serve with stone crab claws.
*Makes 3 appetizer servings and 1½ cups sauce*

*Favorite recipe from **Florida Department of Agriculture and Consumer Services***

***Stone Crab Claws with Honey-Mustard Sauce***

## Sausage Filled Wontons

1 pound BOB EVANS FARMS® Original
    Recipe Roll Sausage
¼ cup chopped onion
½ cup (2 ounces) shredded American
    cheese
3 ounces cream cheese
½ teaspoon dried marjoram leaves
¼ teaspoon dried tarragon leaves
30 wonton wrappers
    Vegetable oil
    Dipping sauce, such as plum sauce or
    sweet and sour sauce (optional)

To prepare filling, crumble sausage into large skillet. Add onion. Cook over medium heat until sausage is browned, stirring occasionally. Remove from heat; drain off any drippings. Stir in American cheese, cream cheese, marjoram and tarragon. Mix until cheeses melt. Lightly dampen 1 wrapper by dipping your finger in water and wiping all the edges, making ¼-inch border around square. (To keep wonton wrappers from drying, cover remaining wrappers with damp kitchen towel while working.) Place rounded teaspoonful sausage mixture in the middle of wrapper. Fold wrapper over filling to form triangle, sealing edges and removing any air bubbles. Repeat with remaining wrappers and filling.

Heat 4 inches oil in deep fryer or heavy large saucepan to 350°F; fry wontons, a few at a time, until golden brown. Remove with slotted spoon; drain on paper towels. Reheat oil between batches. Serve hot with dipping sauce, if desired. Refrigerate leftovers. *Makes 30 appetizers*

*Hot Mulled Cider*

## Hot Mulled Cider

1 orange
1 lemon
12 whole cloves
6 cups apple cider
⅓ cup sugar
3 cinnamon sticks
12 whole allspice berries
    Additional cinnamon sticks and citrus
    strips for garnish

Pierce 6 evenly spaced holes around orange and lemon with point of wooden skewer. Insert whole cloves into the holes. Cut a slice out of the orange to include all of the cloves. Cut the remainder of orange into thin slices.

Combine orange slices, lemon slices, cider, sugar, cinnamon sticks and allspice in medium saucepan. Bring just to a simmer over medium heat. *Do not boil.* Reduce heat to low; cook 5 minutes.

Pour cider through strainer into mugs. Discard fruit and seasonings. Garnish, if desired. *Makes 6 (1-cup) servings*

*Top to bottom: Pecan Cheese Balls (variations) and Cheddar Cheese Spread*

## Pecan Cheese Ball

1 package (8 ounces) cream cheese, softened
¼ cup finely chopped fresh parsley
2 tablespoons finely chopped fresh chives
½ teaspoon Worcestershire sauce
   Dash hot pepper sauce
¾ cup finely chopped pecans
   Assorted crackers

Combine all ingredients except pecans and crackers in medium bowl. Cover; refrigerate until firm. Form cheese mixture into a ball. Roll in pecans. Store tightly wrapped in plastic wrap in refrigerator. Allow cheese ball to soften at room temperature before serving with crackers.

*Makes 1 cheese ball*

**Gift Tip:** Give Pecan Cheese Ball with an assortment of other cheeses, a wooden cheese board, a jar of imported pickles or mustard and/or a bag of pecans.

**Variations:** Form cheese mixture into 1½-inch balls. Roll in paprika, chopped herbs, such as parsley, watercress or basil, or chopped green olives instead of pecans.

## Cheddar Cheese Spread

3 ounces *each* white Cheddar, yellow Cheddar and cream cheese, cut into small pieces
6 green onions, white parts only, finely chopped
2 tablespoons butter or margarine, softened
2 tablespoons dry sherry
1 teaspoon Worcestershire sauce
1 teaspoon Dijon mustard
¼ teaspoon salt (optional)
   Dash hot pepper sauce (optional)
2 tablespoons finely chopped fresh chives
   Assorted crackers

Place all ingredients except chives and crackers in food processor or blender; process until smooth. Add chives; pulse to mix. Place in crock or gift container. Cover; refrigerate. Allow spread to soften at room temperature before serving. Serve with crackers. *Makes about 2 cups spread*

## Orange Juice & Champagne

6 teaspoons orange-flavored liqueur
1 quart orange juice, chilled
1 bottle (750 ml) champagne, chilled
   Strawberries for garnish

Pour 1 teaspoon liqueur into each of 6 wine glasses. Fill each glass two-thirds full with orange juice. Fill glasses with champagne. Garnish, if desired. Serve immediately.

*Makes 6 servings*

## Party Chicken Tarts

2 tablespoons butter or margarine
1 cup chopped fresh mushrooms
¼ cup finely chopped celery
¼ cup finely chopped onion
2 tablespoons all-purpose flour
1½ cups chopped cooked chicken
6 tablespoons sour cream
½ teaspoon garlic salt
1 package (10 ounces) flaky refrigerator
    biscuits (10 to 12 count)
Nonstick cooking spray
1 tablespoon butter or margarine,
    melted
Grated Parmesan cheese

Melt 2 tablespoons butter in large skillet
until hot. Add mushrooms, celery and
onion; cook and stir 4 to 5 minutes.
Sprinkle with flour; stir in chicken and sour
cream. Cook until thoroughly heated. Stir
in garlic salt; set aside. Cut each biscuit into
quarters; press each piece into miniature
muffin tins coated with cooking spray to
form tart shell. Brush each piece with
melted butter. Bake at 400°F 6 minutes.
Remove from oven; *reduce oven temperature
to 350°F.* Fill each tart with 1 teaspoon
chicken mixture; sprinkle with cheese. Bake
14 to 15 minutes. Serve immediately.

*Makes 40 to 48 appetizers*

**Note:** For ease in serving at party time,
prepare filling ahead and cook tarts 5
minutes. Fill and bake just before serving
for best flavor.

*Favorite recipe from **National Broiler Council***

*Party Chicken Tarts*

## Rock Shrimp Mini Quiches

½ pound cooked rock shrimp
1 package (8 ounces) refrigerator butter-
    flake rolls *or* 24 mini pastry shells
1 egg, beaten
½ cup evaporated milk
1 tablespoon cooking sherry
½ teaspoon salt
⅛ teaspoon white pepper
¼ cup grated Parmesan cheese

Finely chop shrimp. Grease two miniature
muffin tins. Divide rolls into 24 equal
pieces and press into muffin tins to form a
shell. Place 1 teaspoon chopped shrimp in
each muffin cup.

Combine egg, milk, sherry, salt and pepper.
Divide mixture evenly among muffins. Top
with ½ teaspoon Parmesan cheese. Bake at
375°F 25 minutes.

*Makes 24 hors d'oeuvres*

*Favorite recipe from **Florida Department of Agriculture and
Consumer Services***

# Batter-Fried Shark Bites

    Pesto Mayonnaise (recipe follows)
1 pound shark steaks, about 1 inch thick
¾ cup all-purpose flour
½ teaspoon salt
¼ teaspoon baking powder
½ cup milk
1 egg, beaten
1 tablespoon butter or margarine, melted
    Vegetable oil for frying

Prepare Pesto Mayonnaise.

Rinse shark and pat dry with paper towels. Remove skin from fish. Cut fish into 1-inch cubes. Place on paper towels; set aside.

Combine flour, salt and baking powder in shallow dish; make well in center. Add milk, egg and butter; beat until smooth. Heat 1 inch of oil in heavy deep skillet over medium heat to 365°F.

Dip 1 fish cube at a time into batter, coating all sides. Place as many cubes as fit at a time into hot oil without crowding; fry until golden brown. Adjust heat to maintain temperature. (Allow temperature of oil to return to 365°F between each batch.)

Remove from skillet and drain on paper towels. Serve immediately with Pesto Mayonnaise. *Makes 30 appetizers*

## Pesto Mayonnaise

½ cup mayonnaise
¼ cup prepared pesto sauce
1 tablespoon lemon juice
    Lemon zest for garnish

Combine mayonnaise, pesto sauce and lemon juice in small bowl. Garnish, if desired. Refrigerate until ready to use.
*Makes ¾ cup*

# Hot Chocolate

3 ounces semisweet chocolate, finely chopped
¼ to ½ cup sugar
4 cups milk, divided
1 teaspoon vanilla
    Whipped cream or marshmallows (optional)

Combine chocolate, sugar and ¼ cup milk in medium saucepan over medium-low heat. Cook, stirring constantly, until chocolate melts. Add remaining 3¾ cups milk; heat until hot, stirring occasionally. *Do not boil.* Remove from heat; stir in vanilla.

Beat with wire whisk until frothy. Pour into mugs and top with whipped cream or marshmallows, if desired. Serve immediately. *Makes 4 servings*

**Hot Cocoa:** Substitute ¼ cup unsweetened cocoa powder for semisweet chocolate and use ½ cup sugar; heat as directed.

**Hot Mocha:** Add 4 teaspoons instant coffee to milk mixture; heat as directed.

# Whipped Feta With Herbs

1 cup (6 ounces) crumbled ATHENOS® Feta Natural Cheese
2 tablespoons sour cream
½ teaspoon lemon juice
¼ teaspoon *each* dried oregano and basil leaves, crushed *or* 2 teaspoons each chopped fresh oregano and basil
    Black pepper

• Blend all ingredients in blender or food processor container until smooth. Refrigerate 1 hour. Season with pepper. Serve with pita bread wedges or crackers.
*Makes about ½ cup*

**Prep Time:** 15 minutes plus refrigerating

*Batter-Fried Shark Bites*

# Holiday Pâté

1 (8-ounce) package JONES®
    Braunschweiger
1 (3-ounce) package cream cheese
1 tablespoon finely chopped onion
1 tablespoon Worcestershire sauce
1 to 2 tablespoons dry sherry
⅓ to ½ teaspoon ground nutmeg
    Dash hot pepper sauce

Blend all ingredients and serve with
crackers or bread.    *Makes about 1¼ cups*

# Picante Party Snack

1 package (8 ounces) cream cheese
1 jar (12 ounces) peach preserves
⅔ cup PACE® Picante Sauce or PACE®
    Thick & Chunky Salsa
2 to 3 teaspoons coarse-grained mustard,
    as desired

Place cream cheese on rimmed serving
dish; let stand at room temperature at least
20 minutes. Combine remaining
ingredients; pour over cream cheese. Serve
with crackers.    *Makes 6 to 8 servings*

**Picante Party Snack**

# Cranberry Sangria

1 orange
1 lime
1 bottle (750 ml) Beaujolais or dry red
    wine
1 cup cranberry juice cocktail
1 cup orange juice
½ cup cranberry-flavored liqueur
    (optional)

Cut orange and lime into thin slices with
utility knife. Combine orange slices, lime
slices, wine, cranberry juice, orange juice
and liqueur in large glass pitcher.
Refrigerate 2 to 8 hours before serving.
Pour into glasses; add orange and/or lime
slices from the punch to each glass.
   *Makes about 7 cups*

# Lobster Medallions in Citrus Cream

2 spiny lobster tails, 4 to 6 ounces each
1 cup sour cream
¼ cup orange juice
2 teaspoons ground coriander
1 tablespoon finely grated orange peel

Using kitchen shears, cut thinner
undershell away from lobster tails. Drop
tails into boiling water; cover and simmer 8
minutes or until lobster meat is no longer
translucent in center. Drain and refrigerate.

Combine remaining ingredients, mixing
just until blended. Refrigerate.

Remove lobster meat from shells and cut
crosswise into ¼-inch-thick medallions; set
aside.

Spoon sour cream mixture onto four salad
plates. Arrange lobster medallions over top.
   *Makes 4 appetizer servings*

*Favorite recipe from **Florida Department of Agriculture and
Consumer Services***

*Swiss 'n' Cheddar Cheeseball*

## Swiss 'n' Cheddar Cheeseball

  1 package (8 ounces) cream cheese,
     softened
½ cup DANNON® Plain Nonfat or
     Lowfat Yogurt
  2 cups (8 ounces) shredded Swiss cheese
  2 cups (8 ounces) shredded Cheddar
     cheese
½ cup finely chopped onion
  1 jar (2 ounces) diced pimiento,
     undrained
  2 tablespoons sweet pickle relish
10 slices bacon, crisp-cooked, drained,
     crumbled and divided
½ cup finely chopped pecans, divided
     Salt and pepper (optional)
¼ cup snipped fresh parsley
  1 tablespoon poppy seeds
     Assorted crackers

In large bowl, beat cream cheese and yogurt until fluffy. Beat in Swiss cheese, Cheddar cheese, onion, undrained pimiento, pickle relish, half the bacon and ¼ cup pecans. If desired, season with salt and pepper. Cover; chill until firm. Shape into 1 large or 2 small balls on waxed paper; set aside.

In small bowl, combine remaining bacon, remaining ¼ cup pecans, parsley and poppy seeds; turn out onto clean sheet of waxed paper. Roll ball in bacon mixture to coat. Cover in plastic wrap; chill. Serve with crackers.    *Makes 24 servings*

## Baked Stuffed Shrimp

  1 pound raw jumbo shrimp (about
     10 to 16), peeled, leaving tails on
  4 ounces fresh mushrooms, chopped
     (about 1 cup)
⅓ cup chopped onion
  1 clove garlic, finely chopped
  1 teaspoon WYLER'S® or STEERO®
     Chicken-Flavor Instant Bouillon
¼ cup margarine or butter
1½ cups fresh bread crumbs (3 slices)
  1 tablespoon chopped pimiento
     Melted margarine or butter

Preheat oven to 400°F. In large skillet, cook and stir mushrooms, onion, garlic and bouillon in ¼ *cup* margarine until tender. Remove from heat; add crumbs and pimiento. Cut lengthwise slit along underside of each shrimp; do not cut through. Remove vein; brush both sides of shrimp with melted margarine. Place shrimp, cut side up, in greased shallow baking dish. Mound equal portion of mushroom mixture on top of each shrimp. Bake 10 to 12 minutes or until hot and shrimp are opaque. Garnish as desired. Refrigerate leftovers.

*Makes 6 to 8 servings*

*Top to bottom: Cheese Twists and Deviled Mixed Nuts*

yolks and water, mixing until dough forms. Shape into a ball; flatten and wrap in plastic wrap. Refrigerate 2 hours or until firm.

Roll out dough on lightly floured surface into 12-inch square (about ⅛ inch thick). Brush surface lightly with egg white and sprinkle with remaining 1 tablespoon cheese and sesame seeds, if desired. Cut dough in half. Cut each half crosswise into ¼-inch strips. Twist 2 strips together. Repeat with remaining strips. Place 1 inch apart on prepared baking sheets.

Bake 6 to 8 minutes until light golden brown. Remove from baking sheets and cool completely on wire racks. Store in airtight container.     *Makes about 48 twists*

**Variation:** Prepare dough and cut as directed. Place ¾ of strips on baking sheets. Form rings with remaining strips; seal edges. Place on baking sheets. Bake and cool as directed. To serve, arrange 3 to 4 strips into small stacks. Insert stacks into rings.

## Cheese Twists

  1 cup all-purpose flour
½ teaspoon baking soda
½ teaspoon dry mustard
½ teaspoon salt
⅛ teaspoon ground red pepper
¾ cup grated Parmesan cheese, divided
½ cup butter or margarine, softened
  3 egg yolks
  2 teaspoons water
  1 egg white, slightly beaten
  1 tablespoon sesame seeds (optional)

Preheat oven to 400°F. Grease two baking sheets. Combine flour, baking soda, mustard, salt and red pepper in large bowl. Reserve 1 tablespoon cheese; stir remaining cheese into flour mixture. Cut in butter with pastry blender or 2 knives until mixture resembles fine crumbs. Add egg

## Deviled Mixed Nuts

  3 tablespoons vegetable oil
  2 cups assorted unsalted nuts, such as
      peanuts, almonds, Brazil nuts or
      walnuts
  2 tablespoons sugar
  1 teaspoon paprika
½ teaspoon ground chili powder
½ teaspoon curry powder
½ teaspoon ground cumin
½ teaspoon ground coriander
½ teaspoon ground black pepper
¼ teaspoon salt

Heat oil in large skillet over medium heat; cook and stir nuts in hot oil 2 to 3 minutes or until browned. Combine remaining ingredients in small bowl; sprinkle over nuts. Stir to coat evenly. Heat 1 to 2 minutes more. Drain nuts on wire rack lined with paper towels. Serve warm.
*Makes 6 to 8 servings (2 cups nuts)*

# Italian Soda

Ice
3 to 4 tablespoons flavored syrup
2 tablespoons half-and-half (optional)
¾ cup chilled club soda

Fill 12-ounce glass with ice. Add syrup and half-and-half. Pour in club soda and stir. Serve immediately.            *Makes 1 serving*

# Reuben Rolls

⅓ cup HELLMANN'S® or BEST FOODS® Real or Light Mayonnaise or Low Fat Cholesterol Free Mayonnaise Dressing
1 tablespoon Dijon mustard
½ teaspoon caraway seeds
1 cup (4 ounces) cooked corned beef, finely chopped
1 cup (4 ounces) shredded Swiss cheese
1 cup sauerkraut, rinsed, drained and patted dry with paper towels
1 package (10 ounces) refrigerated pizza crust dough

Preheat oven to 420°F. In medium bowl, combine mayonnaise, mustard and caraway seeds. Add corned beef, cheese and sauerkraut; toss to blend well. Unroll dough onto large ungreased cookie sheet. Gently stretch to 14 × 12-inch rectangle. Cut dough lengthwise in half. Spoon half of the filling onto each piece, spreading to within 1 inch from edges. From long side, roll each jelly-roll style; pinch to seal edges. Arrange rolls, seam side down, 3 inches apart. Bake 10 minutes or until golden brown. Let stand 5 minutes. Cut into 1-inch slices.            *Makes about 30 appetizers*

# Seafood Pizza Primavera

2 (8-ounce) packages refrigerated crescent rolls
1 (8-ounce) container BORDEN® or MEADOW GOLD® Sour Cream
½ cup BENNETT'S® Chili, Cocktail or Hot Seafood Sauce
¼ pound peeled, cooked small shrimp *or* 1 (4¼-ounce) can ORLEANS® Shrimp, drained and soaked as label directs
¼ pound imitation crab blend flaked *or* 1 (6-ounce) can HARRIS® or ORLEANS® Crab Meat, drained
1 cup chopped broccoli
½ cup sliced green onions
½ cup chopped green bell pepper
½ cup chopped red bell pepper

Preheat oven to 400°F. Unroll crescent roll dough; press on bottom of 15 × 10-inch baking pan, pressing perforations together. Bake 10 minutes or until golden. Cool. Combine sour cream and sauce; spread over crust. Top with remaining ingredients. Chill. Cut into squares to serve. Refrigerate leftovers.            *Makes one 15 × 10-inch pizza*

*Seafood Pizza Primavera*

## Tortelloni Wreath with Pesto Dip

1 (9-ounce) package DI GIORNO®
   Mushroom Tortelloni
1 (9-ounce) package DI GIORNO® Hot
   Red Pepper Tortelloni
1 (8-ounce) container PHILADELPHIA
   BRAND® Soft Cream Cheese
1 (7-ounce) package DI GIORNO® Pesto
   Sauce
1 teaspoon lemon juice
   Green and red bell pepper chunks
   Pitted ripe olives

• Add both packages of pasta to 4 quarts boiling water. Boil gently, uncovered, 6 minutes, stirring frequently. Drain; rinse with cold water.

• Mix cream cheese, pesto sauce and lemon juice. Place in small bowl.

• Place bowl in middle of round serving platter. Arrange pasta, peppers and olives around bowl for dipping.
*Makes 24 servings*

**Prep Time:** 10 minutes
**Cook Time:** 6 minutes

## Pineapple-Champagne Punch

1 quart pineapple sherbet
1 quart unsweetened pineapple juice,
   chilled
1 bottle (750 ml) dry champagne, chilled
2 fresh or canned pineapple slices, each
   cut into 6 wedges
   Mint sprigs

Process sherbet and pineapple juice in blender until smooth and frothy. Pour into punch bowl. Stir in champagne. Float pineapple wedges in punch in groups of 3 or 4 to form flowers; garnish with mint sprigs. Serve immediately.
*Makes 20 (4-ounce) servings*

## Black Olive Tapenade

1 can (6 ounces) pitted ripe olives,
   drained
¼ cup chopped red bell pepper
3 tablespoons olive oil
1 tablespoon lemon juice
1½ teaspoons dried oregano leaves
½ teaspoon minced garlic
½ cup (3 ounces) crumbled ATHENOS®
   Feta Natural Cheese

• Place all ingredients except cheese in blender or food processor container fitted with steel blade; cover. Process until smooth. Stir in cheese.

• Refrigerate several hours or overnight.

• Serve with crackers or French bread chunks. Sprinkle with additional feta cheese, if desired. *Makes 1½ cups*

**Prep Time:** 15 minutes plus refrigerating

*Tortelloni Wreath with Pesto Dip*

# Spinach-Cheese Appetizers

¼ cup olive oil
½ cup chopped onion
2 eggs
16 ounces (1 pound) feta cheese, drained
    and crumbled
3 (10-ounce) packages frozen chopped
    spinach, thawed
½ cup minced fresh parsley
1 teaspoon dried oregano leaves *or*
    2 tablespoons fresh oregano,
    chopped
    Freshly grated nutmeg to taste
    Salt and black pepper to taste
1 package (16 ounces) frozen phyllo
    dough, thawed to room temperature
2 cups margarine, melted

Preheat oven to 375°F. Heat oil in small
skillet over medium-high heat. Add onion;
cook and stir until translucent.

Beat eggs in large bowl; stir in onion, feta
cheese, spinach, parsley and oregano.
Season with nutmeg, salt and pepper.

Remove phyllo from package; unroll and
place on large sheet of waxed paper. Fold
phyllo crosswise into thirds. Use scissors to
cut along folds into thirds. Cover phyllo
with large sheet of plastic wrap and damp
clean kitchen towel. Lay 1 strip of phyllo at
a time on a flat surface and brush with
melted margarine. Fold strip in half
lengthwise; brush with margarine again.
Place rounded teaspoonful of spinach
filling on 1 end of strip; fold over one
corner to make triangle. Continue folding
end to end, as you would fold a flag,
keeping edges straight. Brush top with
margarine. Repeat process until all filling is
used.

Place triangles in a single layer, seam side
down, on baking pan. Bake 20 minutes or
until lightly browned. Serve warm.

*Makes 5 dozen appetizers*

# Sparkling Apple Punch

2 bottles (750 ml each) sparkling apple
    cider, chilled
1½ quarts papaya or apricot nectar, chilled
    Ice
1 to 2 papayas, peeled and chopped
    Orange slices, quartered

Combine apple cider, papaya nectar and ice
in punch bowl. Add papaya and orange
slices. Serve immediately.

*Makes about 4 quarts*

# Lamb Meatballs with Tomato Mint Dip

1½ cups fine bulgur
2 pounds ground American lamb
2 medium onions, minced
1 cup minced fresh parsley
1 tablespoon salt
½ teaspoon black pepper
½ teaspoon ground allspice
½ teaspoon ground cinnamon
½ teaspoon ground nutmeg
¼ to ½ teaspoon ground red pepper
1 piece fresh ginger, about 2 × 1 inch,
    peeled and minced
1 cup ice water
    Tomato Mint Dip (page 21)

In medium bowl, pour enough cold water
over bulgur to cover; let soak about 10
minutes. Drain and place in fine-meshed
strainer; squeeze out water.

In large bowl, knead together lamb, onions,
parsley and spices. Add bulgur; knead
well. Add about 1 cup ice water to keep
mixture smooth.

Use about 1 teaspoon meat mixture to make
bite-sized meatballs. Place on ungreased

jelly-roll pan. Bake in preheated 375°F oven 20 minutes.

Place meatballs in bowl; keep warm. Serve hot or at room temperature with toothpicks to dip into Tomato Mint Dip.

*Makes 10 dozen meatballs*

## Tomato Mint Dip

**2 cans (15 ounces each) tomato sauce
   with tomato bits**
**1½ teaspoons ground allspice**
**1 teaspoon dried mint**

In small saucepan, heat all ingredients about 5 minutes to blend flavors. Serve warm.

*Favorite recipe from **American Lamb Council***

# Oysters Romano

**1 dozen oysters
   Salt**
**2 slices bacon, cut into 1-inch pieces**
**½ cup Italian-seasoned dry bread crumbs**
**2 tablespoons butter or margarine,
   melted**
**½ teaspoon garlic salt**
**6 tablespoons grated Romano, Parmesan
   or provolone cheese**
**Fresh chives for garnish**

Scrub oysters thoroughly with stiff brush under cold running water. Soak in mixture of ⅓ cup salt to 1 gallon water 20 minutes. Drain water; repeat 2 more times. Place oysters on tray and refrigerate 1 hour. To shuck oysters, take pointed oyster knife in one hand and thick towel or glove in the other. With towel, grip shell in palm of

*Oysters Romano*

hand. Keeping oyster level with knife, insert tip of knife between shell next to hinge; twist to pry shell until you hear a snap. (Use knife as leverage; do not force.) Twist to open shell, keeping oyster level at all times to save liquor.* Cut the muscle from the shell and discard top shell. Cut the muscle from the lower shell, being careful not to spill liquor; do not remove oyster from shell.

Preheat oven to 375°F. Place shells with oysters on baking sheet. Top each oyster with 1 piece bacon. Bake 10 minutes or until bacon is crisp.

Meanwhile, combine bread crumbs, butter and garlic salt in small bowl. Spoon mixture over oysters; top with cheese. Bake 5 to 10 minutes or until cheese melts. Serve immediately. Garnish, if desired.

*Makes 4 appetizer servings*

*Liquor is the term used to describe the natural juices of an oyster.

*Raspberry Wine Punch*

## Raspberry Wine Punch

1 package (10 ounces) frozen red
   raspberries in syrup, thawed
1 bottle (750 ml) white Zinfandel or
   blush wine
¼ cup raspberry-flavored liqueur
   Empty ½ gallon milk or juice carton
3 to 4 cups distilled water, divided
   Sprigs of pine and tinsel
   Fresh cranberries

Process raspberries with syrup in food
processor or blender until smooth; press
through strainer, discarding seeds.
Combine wine, raspberry purée and
liqueur in pitcher; refrigerate until serving
time.

Rinse out wine bottle and remove label.
Fully open top of carton. Place wine bottle
in center of carton. Tape bottle securely to
carton so bottle will not move when adding
water. Pour 2 cups distilled water into
carton. Carefully push pine sprigs, tinsel
and cranberries into water between bottle
and carton to form decorative design. Add
remaining water to almost fill carton.

Freeze until firm, 8 hours or overnight.
Just before serving, peel carton from ice
block. Using funnel, pour punch back into
wine bottle. Wrap bottom of ice block with
white cotton napkin or towel to hold while
serving. *Makes 8 servings*

**Note:** Punch may also be served in punch
bowl if desired.

## Seasoned Fish Dip

2 cups cooked flaked fish
1 cup large curd cottage cheese
¾ cup sour cream
2 tablespoons chicken stock base
1 tablespoon chopped pimiento, drained
1 tablespoon chopped fresh parsley
   Additional chopped fresh parsley for
     garnish
   Assorted chips, crackers or raw
     vegetables

Combine all ingredients except garnish and
chips. Refrigerate 1 hour. Garnish with
parsley. Serve with chips, crackers or
vegetables. *Makes about 3 cups dip*

*Favorite recipe from **Florida Department of Agriculture and
Consumer Services***

## Blue Crab Stuffed Tomatoes

½ pound blue crabmeat
10 plum tomatoes
½ cup finely chopped celery
⅓ cup plain low fat yogurt
2 tablespoons minced green onions
2 tablespoons finely chopped red bell pepper
½ teaspoon lemon juice
¼ teaspoon salt
⅛ teaspoon black pepper

Remove any remaining shell or cartilage from crabmeat. Cut tomatoes in half. Carefully scoop out centers of tomatoes; discard pulp. Invert onto paper towels. Combine crabmeat, celery, yogurt, onions, red pepper, lemon juice, salt and pepper; mix well. Fill tomato halves with crab mixture. Refrigerate 2 hours.

*Makes 20 appetizers*

*Favorite recipe from* **Florida Department of Agriculture and Consumer Services**

*Blue Crab Stuffed Tomatoes*

## Sausage Cheese Puffs

1 pound BOB EVANS FARMS® Original Recipe Roll Sausage
2½ cups (10 ounces) shredded sharp Cheddar cheese
2 cups biscuit mix
½ cup water
1 teaspoon baking powder

Preheat oven to 350°F. Combine ingredients in large bowl until blended. Shape into 1-inch balls. Place on baking sheets. Bake about 25 minutes or until golden brown. Serve hot. Refrigerate leftovers.

*Makes about 60 appetizers*

## Smoked Turkey Sandwiches

⅓ cup light processed cream cheese
1 tablespoon sweet and hot mustard
1½ teaspoons fresh dill, chopped *or* ½ teaspoon dried dill weed
4 slices pumpernickel bread, crusts removed
2 packages (6 ounces each) smoked turkey breast slices, cut in half
Fresh dill for garnish

1. In small bowl, combine cream cheese, mustard and dill. Spread mixture evenly over bread slices. Cut each bread slice into thirds lengthwise. Cut each third in half crosswise.

2. Roll each turkey slice half into a cornucopia shape. Dip larger edge of cornucopia in dill to garnish edge of turkey. Arrange turkey cornucopia rolls on bread sections.

*Makes 24 servings*

*Favorite recipe from* **National Turkey Federation**

# Sausage Pinwheels

2 cups biscuit mix
½ cup milk
¼ cup butter or margarine, melted
1 pound BOB EVANS FARMS® Original
    Recipe Roll Sausage
    Fresh basil sprig and carrot triangles
    (optional)

Combine biscuit mix, milk and butter in large bowl. Refrigerate 30 minutes. Divide dough into two portions. Roll out one portion on floured surface to ⅛-inch-thick rectangle, about 10 × 7 inches. Spread with half the sausage. Roll lengthwise into long roll. Repeat with remaining dough and sausage. Place rolls in freezer until hard enough to cut easily. Preheat oven to 400°F. Cut rolls into thin slices. Place on baking sheets. Bake 15 minutes or until golden brown. Garnish with basil and carrot, if desired. Refrigerate leftovers.

*Makes about 48 appetizers*

# Spicy Turkey Ham Spread

1 pound turkey ham, cut into chunks
¼ cup onion, chopped
¼ cup Dijon mustard
4 teaspoons Worcestershire sauce
¼ teaspoon ground red pepper

1. In food processor bowl fitted with metal blade, process turkey ham, onion, mustard, Worcestershire sauce and ground red pepper until smooth.

2. To serve, spoon mixture into red or green bell pepper halves, accompanied with melba toast rounds, if desired.

*Makes 2 cups*

*Favorite recipe from* **National Turkey Federation**

# Shrimp Butter

½ pound medium shrimp, peeled and
    deveined, reserving shells
1 cup water
½ teaspoon onion powder
½ teaspoon garlic salt
1 package (8 ounces) cream cheese,
    softened
4 tablespoons butter, softened
2 tablespoons mayonnaise
2 tablespoons cocktail sauce
1 tablespoon lemon juice
1 tablespoon chopped fresh parsley
    Assorted crackers or raw vegetables
    Green onion, star fruit, kiwifruit and
    radish slices for garnish

Place reserved shrimp shells, water, onion powder and garlic salt in medium saucepan. Bring to a simmer over medium heat; simmer 5 minutes. Remove shells and discard. Add shrimp; simmer 1 minute or until shrimp turn pink and opaque. Remove shrimp and place on cutting board; let cool. Continue cooking shrimp liquid to reduce until it just barely covers bottom of pan.

Blend cream cheese, butter, mayonnaise, cocktail sauce and lemon juice in large bowl until smooth. Stir in 1 tablespoon reduced cooking liquid. Discard remaining liquid.

Chop shrimp finely. Fold shrimp and parsley into cheese mixture. Pack Shrimp Butter into decorative serving crock or plastic mold lined with plastic wrap. Cover and refrigerate overnight. Serve Shrimp Butter in decorative crock or invert mold onto serving platter and remove plastic wrap. Serve with assorted crackers. Garnish, if desired.

*Makes 2½ to 3 cups*

*Shrimp Butter*

## Crunchy Mexican Turkey Tidbits

1 pound ground turkey
¼ cup *each* finely chopped onion and
    dry bread crumbs
1 egg, beaten
2 cloves garlic, minced
1 teaspoon chili powder
½ teaspoon ground cumin
4 ounces tortilla chips, finely crushed
    Nonstick cooking spray
¾ cup nonfat sour cream
½ cup salsa

1. In medium bowl, combine turkey, onion, bread crumbs, egg, garlic, chili powder and cumin; shape into approximately 36 (¾-inch) balls.

2. Place crushed chips on plate. Roll each meatball in chips, coating thoroughly. On 15 × 10-inch baking pan lightly coated with cooking spray, arrange meatballs. Bake at 350°F 20 minutes or until meat is no longer pink in center.

3. In small bowl, combine sour cream and salsa. Serve as dip for meatballs.

*Makes about 36 meatballs*

*Favorite recipe from* **National Turkey Federation**

## Antipasto with Marinated Mushrooms

Marinated Mushrooms (page 27)
4 teaspoons red wine vinegar
½ teaspoon dried basil leaves
½ teaspoon dried oregano leaves
    Generous dash freshly ground black
    pepper
¼ cup olive oil
4 ounces mozzarella cheese, cut into
    ½-inch cubes
4 ounces prosciutto or cooked ham,
    thinly sliced
4 ounces provolone cheese, cut into
    2-inch sticks
1 jar (10 ounces) pepperoncini peppers,
    drained
8 ounces hard salami, thinly sliced
2 jars (6 ounces each) marinated
    artichoke hearts, drained
1 can (6 ounces) pitted ripe olives,
    drained
    Lettuce leaves (optional)
    Fresh basil leaves and chives for
    garnish

*Crunchy Mexican Turkey Tidbits*

Prepare Marinated Mushrooms; set aside. Combine vinegar, basil, oregano and black pepper in small bowl. Add oil in slow steady stream, whisking until thoroughly blended. Add mozzarella cubes; stir to coat. Cover and marinate in refrigerator at least 2 hours. Wrap ½ the prosciutto slices around provolone sticks; roll up remaining slices separately.

Drain mozzarella cubes; reserve marinade. Arrange mozzarella cubes, prosciutto-wrapped provolone sticks, prosciutto rolls, Marinated Mushrooms, pepperoncini, salami, artichoke hearts and olives on large platter lined with lettuce, if desired. Drizzle reserved marinade over pepperoncini, artichoke hearts and olives. Garnish, if desired. *Makes 6 to 8 servings*

## Marinated Mushrooms

 3 tablespoons lemon juice
 2 tablespoons chopped fresh parsley
 ½ teaspoon salt
 ¼ teaspoon dried tarragon leaves
    Generous dash freshly ground black pepper
 ½ cup olive oil
 1 clove garlic
 ½ pound fresh medium mushrooms

For marinade, combine lemon juice, parsley, salt, tarragon and pepper in medium bowl. Add oil in slow steady stream, whisking until thoroughly blended. Lightly crush garlic; add to marinade. Slice stems from mushrooms; reserve stems for another use. Add mushrooms to marinade; mix well. Cover and marinate in refrigerator 4 hours or overnight, stirring occasionally.

To serve, remove and discard garlic. Serve mushrooms on antipasto tray or as relish. Or, add mushrooms to tossed green salad, using marinade as dressing.

*Makes about 2 cups*

# New York Chocolate Egg Cream

 1 square (1 ounce) semisweet chocolate (optional)
 ¼ cup chocolate syrup
 1 cup chilled club soda or carbonated mineral water
    Ice

Shave chocolate with vegetable peeler (makes about ½ cup); refrigerate.*

Pour syrup into 12-ounce glass. Stir in club soda until foamy. Add ice. Garnish with 1 teaspoon chocolate shavings. Serve immediately. *Makes 1 serving*

*Cover and refrigerate remaining chocolate shavings for another use.

# Creamy Florentine Dip

 2 cups dairy sour cream
 1¾ cups mayonnaise
 2½ tablespoons lemon juice
 1¼ teaspoons LAWRY'S® Seasoned Salt
 ½ teaspoon LAWRY'S® Garlic Powder with Parsley
 ½ teaspoon dried oregano leaves
 ½ teaspoon dried basil leaves
 ½ teaspoon dry mustard
 ½ teaspoon LAWRY'S® Seasoned Pepper
 1 package (10 ounces) frozen chopped spinach, thawed and well drained

In large bowl, combine all ingredients except spinach. Squeeze excess moisture from spinach; add and mix thoroughly. Chill several hours to blend flavors.

*Makes about 4 cups*

**Presentation:** Serve with assorted crisp, raw vegetables as dippers.

*Shrimp Crescents*

# Shrimp Crescents

1 can (14 ounces) artichoke hearts,
  drained and chopped
1 can (4 ounces) diced green chilies,
  drained
1 cup (4 ounces) grated Parmesan cheese
¼ cup mayonnaise
¼ teaspoon ground red pepper
¼ teaspoon garlic powder
2 cans (8 ounces each) refrigerated
  crescent rolls
32 peeled and deveined cooked shrimp

In medium bowl, combine all ingredients
except crescent rolls and shrimp. Mix well;
set aside.

Unroll crescent rolls and cut each triangle
in half lengthwise, forming 32 triangles.
Stretch dough and flatten.

Spoon rounded tablespoon of artichoke
mixture onto each triangle; place 1 shrimp
on top. Roll up, starting at wide end, and

place on well-greased baking sheet. (At this
point, crescents may be refrigerated until
ready to bake and serve.)

Bake at 375°F 12 to 15 minutes or until
golden brown. Serve warm.

*Makes 32 appetizers*

*Favorite recipe from* **Florida Department of Agriculture and
Consumer Services**

# Orange Maple Sausage Balls

1 pound BOB EVANS FARMS® Original
  Recipe Roll Sausage
1 small onion, finely chopped
1 small red or yellow bell pepper, finely
  chopped
1 egg
2 tablespoons uncooked cream of wheat
½ cup maple syrup or maple-flavored
  syrup
3 to 5 tablespoons frozen orange juice
  concentrate to taste, slightly thawed

Mix sausage, onion, pepper, egg and cream
of wheat thoroughly in large bowl. Shape
into ¾-inch balls. Cook in large skillet over
medium-high heat until browned and no
longer pink in centers, turning at least once.
Drain off any drippings. Add syrup and
orange juice to sausage. Cook and stir over
medium heat 2 to 3 minutes or until thick
bubbly syrup forms. Serve hot. Refrigerate
leftovers. *Makes about 24 appetizers*

**Serving Suggestions:** Serve on party picks
with sautéed mushrooms and water
chestnuts. These meatballs would also
make an excellent breakfast item; serve
with small pancakes.

# Warm Herb Cheese Spread

3 (8-ounce) packages cream cheese, softened
¼ cup BORDEN® or MEADOW GOLD® Milk
¼ cup REALEMON® Lemon Juice from Concentrate
½ teaspoon *each* dried basil, marjoram, oregano and thyme leaves
¼ teaspoon garlic powder
½ pound cooked shrimp, chopped (1½ cups), optional

Preheat oven to 350°. In large mixer bowl, beat cheese *just* until smooth. Gradually beat in milk then ReaLemon® brand and seasonings. Add shrimp if desired. Spoon into 9-inch quiche dish or pie plate. Cover; bake 15 minutes or until hot. Garnish as desired. Serve warm with crackers, breadsticks and assorted fresh vegetables. Refrigerate leftovers.

*Makes about 4 cups*

**Microwave Directions:** Prepare cheese mixture as above; spoon into 8- or 9-inch glass pie plate. Cook on 50% power (medium) 5 to 6 minutes or until hot. Stir before serving. Proceed as above.

*Warm Herb Cheese Spread*

# Strawberry-Peach Cooler

1 cup sliced strawberries
1 cup chopped peaches
2 tablespoons sugar
1 bottle (750 ml) white wine, chilled
1 bottle (750 ml) sparkling water, chilled
  Mint sprigs
  Ice

Combine strawberries and peaches in small bowl. Sprinkle with sugar; stir gently. Let stand at room temperature 30 minutes. Pour fruit into punch bowl. Gradually stir in wine and sparkling water. Add mint sprigs and ice. *Makes about 2 quarts*

**Nonalcoholic Cooler:** Use only 1 tablespoon sugar. Substitute 1 quart apple juice for wine.

# Rosemary Chicken Wings

2 tablespoons olive oil
2 tablespoons butter
2 tablespoons finely chopped shallots
2 teaspoons dried rosemary leaves, crushed
½ cup NEWMAN'S OWN® Lemonade
1 teaspoon black pepper
1 teaspoon salt
10 to 12 chicken wings

Preheat oven to 425°F.

In small saucepan, heat oil and butter over medium heat. Add shallots and rosemary and cook 2 to 3 minutes. Add lemonade, pepper and salt, and simmer over low heat 6 to 8 minutes or until slightly reduced and syrupy. Cool slightly.

Meanwhile, cut chicken wings into thirds, discarding wing-tip joint. Place wings in shallow pan and coat well with sauce. Bake in oven until skin is golden brown, about 30 minutes. *Makes 20 to 24 pieces*

## Best-Ever Black Bean & Bacon Dip

6 slices bacon, diced
2 cloves garlic, minced
1 can (16 ounces) black beans, rinsed, drained and mashed
1½ cups (6 ounces) shredded Cheddar or Monterey Jack cheese, divided
⅔ cup PACE® Picante Sauce
⅓ cup sliced green onions with tops
1 teaspoon ground cumin
Chopped cilantro and diced red bell pepper for garnish

Place bacon in 4-cup glass measuring cup or 1½-quart microwavable dish. Cover with paper towel. Microwave at HIGH 5 to 6 minutes or until bacon is crisp, stirring after 2 minutes. Remove bacon to paper towels; pour off all but 1 tablespoon drippings. Toss garlic in drippings. Cover with vented plastic wrap and microwave at HIGH 2 minutes. Stir in beans, 1 cup cheese, picante sauce, onions and cumin; mix well. Cover with vented plastic wrap and microwave at HIGH 3 minutes. Stir until cheese is melted. Stir in bacon; transfer to serving bowl. Sprinkle with remaining ½ cup cheese, cilantro and bell pepper. Serve warm with vegetable dippers or tortilla chips.

*Makes 6 to 8 servings*

## Alouette® French Pastry Puffs

1 (10-ounce) package frozen puff pastry sheets
1 (6.5-ounce) container of your favorite savory flavor ALOUETTE® gourmet spreadable cheese
½ cup chopped fresh spinach
3 tablespoons finely chopped onion
Freshly ground black pepper
1 egg, beaten with 1 teaspoon water

Thaw pastry according to package directions.

In medium bowl, combine Alouette®, spinach, onion and pepper to taste.

Preheat oven to 400°F. Roll each sheet of pastry to 15-inch square; cut into 3-inch squares. Brush lightly with egg. Place 1 teaspoon Alouette® mixture in center of each square. Fold to form triangle; crimp edges with fork to seal. Place on ungreased baking sheets. Brush with egg. Bake 10 to 12 minutes or until puffed and golden. Serve warm.

*Makes 50 puffs*

## Champagne Punch

1 orange
1 lemon
¼ cup cranberry-flavored liqueur or cognac
¼ cup orange-flavored liqueur or triple sec
1 bottle (750 ml) pink or regular champagne *or* sparkling white wine, well chilled
Fresh cranberries (optional)
Citrus strips for garnish

Remove colored peel, not white pith, from orange and lemon in long thin strips. Refrigerate orange and lemon for another use. Combine peels, cranberry-flavored and orange-flavored liqueurs in glass pitcher. Cover and refrigerate 2 to 6 hours.

Just before serving, tilt pitcher to one side and slowly pour in champagne. Leave peels in pitcher for added flavor.

Place a cranberry in the bottom of each champagne glass. Pour punch into glasses. Garnish with citrus strips tied into knots, if desired. *Makes 4 cups, 6 to 8 servings*

**Nonalcoholic Cranberry Punch:** Pour 3 cups well-chilled club soda into ⅔ cup (6 ounces) cranberry cocktail concentrate, thawed. *Makes 3½ cups, 6 servings*

*Champagne Punch*

*Top to bottom: Creamy Cucumber-Yogurt Dip and Spicy Cocktail Sauce*

Cover; refrigerate 1 hour. Spoon dip into glass bowl or gift container; sprinkle reserved chives over top. Cover and store up to 2 days in refrigerator. Stir before serving with vegetables.

*Makes about 2 cups dip*

## Spicy Cocktail Sauce

1 cup ketchup
2 cloves garlic, finely chopped
1 tablespoon fresh lemon juice
1 teaspoon prepared horseradish
¾ teaspoon chili powder
½ teaspoon salt
¼ teaspoon hot pepper sauce *or*
  ⅛ teaspoon ground red pepper

Combine all ingredients in medium bowl; blend well. Spoon into glass bowl and serve with cooked seafood *or* pour into clean glass jar and seal tightly. Store up to 1 year in refrigerator.

*Makes 1⅓ cups sauce, enough for
1 pound of seafood*

## Creamy Cucumber-Yogurt Dip

1 cucumber, peeled, seeded and finely
  chopped
  Salt
¼ cup chopped fresh chives, divided
1 package (8 ounces) cream cheese,
  softened
¼ cup plain yogurt
1 tablespoon fresh lemon juice
1½ teaspoons dried mint leaves
  Freshly ground black pepper
  Assorted cut-up vegetables

Lightly salt cucumber in small bowl; toss. Refrigerate 1 hour. Drain cucumber; dry on paper towels. Set aside.

Reserve 1 tablespoon chives for garnish. Place remaining 3 tablespoons chives, cream cheese, yogurt, lemon juice, mint and pepper in food processor or blender; process until smooth. Stir into cucumber.

## Holiday Meat and Vegetable Kabobs

1 cup fresh pearl onions
⅓ cup olive oil
2 tablespoons balsamic vinegar
1 tablespoon TABASCO® pepper sauce
1 tablespoon dried basil leaves
2 large cloves garlic, crushed
1 teaspoon salt
1 pound boneless skinless chicken
  breasts
1 pound boneless beef sirloin
2 large red peppers, cored, seeded and
  cut into ¾-inch pieces
1 large green pepper, cored, seeded and
  cut into ¾-inch pieces
1 large zucchini, cut into ¾-inch pieces

Soak 3 dozen 4-inch-long wooden skewers in water overnight. In 1-quart saucepan over high heat, bring onions and enough water to cover to a boil. Reduce heat to low. Cover and simmer 3 minutes or until onions are tender. Drain. When cool enough to handle, peel away outer layer of skin from onions.

In medium bowl, combine oil, balsamic vinegar, TABASCO sauce, basil, garlic and salt. Pour half the mixture into another bowl. Cut chicken and beef into ¾-inch pieces and place in 1 bowl with TABASCO sauce mixture, tossing well to coat. In remaining bowl of TABASCO sauce mixture toss pearl onions, red and green peppers and zucchini. Let stand at least 30 minutes, tossing occasionally.

Preheat the broiler. Skewer 1 piece of chicken or beef and 1 piece each of red pepper, green pepper, onion and zucchini onto each wooden pick. Broil 4 to 6 minutes, turning occasionally.

*Makes 3 dozen appetizers*

# Party Polenta Stars

3 cups water
2 tablespoons butter or margarine, divided
¾ teaspoon salt
1 cup yellow cornmeal
½ cup grated Parmesan cheese
1 teaspoon TABASCO® pepper sauce
1 tablespoon olive oil
Spicy Tomato Salsa (recipe follows)

Grease large jelly-roll pan; set aside. In 2-quart saucepan over high heat, bring water, 1 tablespoon butter and salt to a boil. Reduce heat to low; slowly add cornmeal in steady stream, stirring constantly. Continue to cook, stirring constantly until mixture thickens, about 5 to 10 minutes. Remove from heat; stir in cheese and TABASCO sauce.

Spread cornmeal mixture in prepared jelly-roll pan to ½-inch thickness. Refrigerate, uncovered, for 30 minutes.

With 2½-inch star-shaped cookie cutter, cut cooled polenta mixture into stars. In 12-inch skillet over medium-high heat, heat oil and remaining 1 tablespoon butter. Add polenta stars; cook 2 minutes on each side until lightly browned, turning carefully. Repeat with remaining stars, adding oil and butter if necessary. Serve with Spicy Tomato Salsa. Garnish as desired.  *Makes 18 stars*

## Spicy Tomato Salsa

8 ounces ripe tomatoes, finely diced (about 1 cup)
3 tablespoons minced green onions
1 tablespoon minced cilantro
1½ teaspoons lemon juice
½ clove garlic, minced
½ teaspoon TABASCO® pepper sauce
¼ teaspoon ground cumin
⅛ teaspoon salt

Mix all ingredients in small bowl. Cover and refrigerate 1 to 2 hours to blend flavors.

*Makes about 1 cup*

*Top to bottom: Party Polenta Stars, Little Christmas Pizzas (page 34) and Holiday Meat and Vegetable Kabobs (page 32)*

# Little Christmas Pizzas

⅓ cup olive oil
1 tablespoon TABASCO® pepper sauce
2 large cloves garlic, crushed
1 teaspoon dried rosemary, crushed
1 (16-ounce) package hot roll mix with yeast packet
1¼ cups hot water

## Toppings

1 large tomato, diced
¼ cup crumbled goat cheese
2 tablespoons chopped fresh parsley
½ cup shredded mozzarella cheese
½ cup pitted green olives
⅓ cup roasted red pepper strips
½ cup chopped artichoke hearts
½ cup cherry tomatoes, sliced into wedges
⅓ cup sliced green onions

In small bowl, combine olive oil, TABASCO sauce, garlic and rosemary. In large bowl, combine hot roll mix, packet of yeast, hot water and 2 tablespoons of oil mixture; stir until the dough pulls away from the side of the bowl. Turn dough onto lightly floured surface; shape dough into a ball. Knead until smooth, adding additional flour as necessary to prevent sticking.

Preheat oven to 425°F. Cut dough into quarters; cut each quarter into 10 equal pieces. Roll each piece into a ball. On large cookie sheet, press each ball into 2-inch round. Brush each with remaining oil mixture. Arrange approximately 2 teaspoons of toppings (see below) on each dough round. Bake 12 minutes or until dough is lightly browned and puffed.

*Makes 40 pizzas*

## Toppings:

**French:** Combine tomato, goat cheese and fresh parsley.

**Italian:** Combine mozzarella, pitted green olives and roasted red pepper strips.

**Spanish:** Combine artichoke hearts, cherry tomatoes and sliced green onions.

# Cucumber Dill Dip

1 package (8 ounces) light cream cheese, softened
1 cup HELLMANN'S® or BEST FOODS® Real or Light Mayonnaise or Low Fat Cholesterol Free Mayonnaise Dressing
2 medium cucumbers, peeled, seeded and chopped
2 tablespoons sliced green onions
1 tablespoon lemon juice
2 teaspoons snipped fresh dill *or* ½ teaspoon dried dill weed
½ teaspoon hot pepper sauce

In medium bowl, beat cream cheese until smooth. Stir in mayonnaise, cucumbers, green onions, lemon juice, dill and hot pepper sauce. Cover; chill. Serve with fresh vegetables, crackers or chips. Garnish as desired.

*Makes about 2½ cups*

# Spinach Dip

1 package (10 ounces) frozen chopped spinach, thawed and drained
1½ cups sour cream
1 cup HELLMANN'S® or BEST FOODS® Real or Light Mayonnaise or Low Fat Cholesterol Free Mayonnaise Dressing
1 package (1.4 ounces) KNORR® Vegetable Soup and Recipe Mix
1 can (8 ounces) water chestnuts, drained and chopped (optional)
3 green onions, chopped

In medium bowl, combine spinach, sour cream, mayonnaise, soup mix, water chestnuts and green onions. Cover; chill. Serve with fresh vegetables, crackers or chips. Garnish as desired.

*Makes about 3 cups*

*Left to right: French Onion Dip, Cucumber Dill Dip (page 34) and Spinach Dip (page 34)*

# French Onion Dip

**2 cups sour cream**
**½ cup HELLMANN'S® or BEST FOODS®**
    **Real or Light Mayonnaise or Low**
    **Fat Cholesterol Free Mayonnaise**
    **Dressing**
**1 package (1.9 ounces) KNORR® French**
    **Onion Soup and Recipe Mix**

In medium bowl, combine sour cream, mayonnaise and soup mix. Cover; chill. Serve with fresh vegetables or potato chips. Garnish as desired.

*Makes about 2½ cups*

# Citrus Punch

    **Frozen Fruit Ice (recipe follows)**
**2 cups orange juice**
**2 cups grapefruit juice**
**¾ cup lime juice**
**½ cup light corn syrup**
**1 bottle (750 ml) ginger ale, white grape**
    **juice, Asti Spumante or sparkling**
    **wine**
    **Fresh mint sprigs for garnish**

Prepare Frozen Fruit Ice.

Combine juices and corn syrup in 2-quart pitcher. Stir until corn syrup dissolves. (Stir in additional corn syrup to taste, if desired.) Refrigerate 2 hours or until cold. Stir in ginger ale just before serving.

Divide Frozen Fruit Ice between 8 (12-ounce) glasses or 10 wide-rimmed wine glasses. Fill glasses with punch. Garnish, if desired. Serve immediately.

# Frozen Fruit Ice

**4 oranges, sectioned**
**1 to 2 limes, cut into ⅛-inch slices**
**1 lemon, cut into ⅛-inch slices**
**1 pint strawberries, stemmed and**
    **halved**
**1 cup raspberries**

Spread oranges, limes, lemon, strawberries and raspberries on baking sheet. Freeze 4 hours or until firm.

*Makes 8 to 10 servings (about 5 cups)*

# Cajun Spiced Walnuts

2 egg whites, lightly beaten
1 tablespoon garlic salt
2 teaspoons ground red pepper
2 teaspoons mixed dried herbs
2 teaspoons paprika
4 cups walnut halves and pieces

Coat large, shallow baking pan with nonstick cooking spray. Mix egg whites with spices. Stir in walnuts and coat thoroughly. Spread in prepared pan. Bake at 350°F 15 to 18 minutes or until dry and crisp. Cool completely before serving.

*Makes 4 cups*

**Microwave Directions:** Prepare ingredients as directed above. Spread prepared walnuts in microwavable dish. Microwave at HIGH in 4 or 5 batches for 2 to 3 minutes each or until dry and crisp. Cool completely before serving.

**Note:** Best if made at least one day ahead. Store in sealed container.

*Favorite recipe from **Walnut Marketing Board***

*Clockwise from left: Indian-Spiced Walnuts (page 37), Cajun Spiced Walnuts and Christmas Spirits (page 151)*

# Mini Turkey Empanadas

1 pound ground turkey
1 cup chopped onion
½ cup chopped green bell pepper
1 clove garlic, minced
1 can (16 ounces) tomatoes, drained and crushed
1 tablespoon dried parsley
1 teaspoon *each* dried cilantro and cumin seed
½ teaspoon *each* dried oregano and crushed red pepper
⅛ teaspoon black pepper
2 packages (15 ounces each) refrigerated pie crusts
Nonstick cooking spray

1. In large nonstick skillet over medium-high heat, cook and stir turkey, onion, green pepper and garlic 5 to 6 minutes or until turkey is no longer pink and vegetables are tender. Stir in tomatoes, parsley, cilantro, cumin, oregano, crushed red pepper and black pepper. Reduce heat to medium and cook 10 to 15 minutes, stirring constantly, or until liquid is evaporated. Remove skillet from heat and cool.

2. Using 3-inch-round biscuit cutter, cut 12 rounds from each pie crust, combining remaining crust to make 48 rounds.

3. Spoon heaping teaspoon of filling in center of each round. Fold each pastry in half and pinch edges together to seal. Place empanadas on two 15 × 10-inch cookie sheets lightly coated with cooking spray. Bake at 400°F 15 to 20 minutes or until empanadas are golden brown.

*Makes 48 empanadas*

*Favorite recipe from **National Turkey Federation***

# Viennese Coffee

1 cup heavy cream, divided
1 teaspoon powdered sugar
1 bar (3 ounces) bittersweet or
    semisweet chocolate
3 cups strong freshly brewed hot coffee
¼ cup crème de cacao or Irish cream
    (optional)

Chill bowl, beaters and cream before whipping. Place ⅔ cup cream and sugar into chilled bowl. Beat with electric mixer at high speed until soft peaks form.

Cover and refrigerate up to 8 hours. If mixture has separated slightly after refrigeration, whisk lightly with a wire whisk before using.

To make chocolate shavings for garnish, place waxed paper under chocolate. Holding chocolate in one hand, make short, quick strokes across chocolate with vegetable peeler; set aside. Break remaining chocolate into pieces.

Place remaining ⅓ cup cream in heavy small saucepan. Bring to a simmer over medium-low heat. Add chocolate pieces; cover and remove from heat. Let stand 5 minutes or until chocolate is melted; stir until smooth.

Add hot coffee to chocolate mixture. Heat on low heat just until bubbles form around the edge of pan and coffee is heated through, stirring frequently. Remove from heat; stir in crème de cacao, if desired.

Pour into 4 warmed mugs. Top with whipped cream. Garnish with chocolate shavings.

*Makes about 4 (3½-cup) servings*

*Viennese Coffee*

# Indian-Spiced Walnuts

2 egg whites, lightly beaten
1 tablespoon ground cumin
1½ teaspoons curry powder
1½ teaspoons salt
½ teaspoon sugar
4 cups walnut halves and pieces

Coat large, shallow baking pan with nonstick cooking spray. Mix egg whites with spices and sugar. Stir in walnuts and coat thoroughly. Spread in prepared pan. Bake at 350°F 15 to 18 minutes or until dry and crisp. Cool completely before serving.

*Makes 4 cups*

**Microwave Directions:** Prepare ingredients as directed. Spread prepared walnuts in microwavable dish. Microwave at HIGH in 4 or 5 batches for 2 to 3 minutes each or until dry and crisp. Cool completely before serving.

*Favorite recipe from **Walnut Marketing Board***

# SALADS, SOUPS & SIDES

## Winter Pear and Stilton Salad

⅓ cup extra virgin olive oil

1½ tablespoons sherry wine vinegar or white wine vinegar

4 teaspoons honey

1 tablespoon Dijon mustard

¼ teaspoon salt

3 ounces assorted gourmet mixed salad greens, such as oakleaf, frisee, watercress, radicchio, arugula or escarole

1½ ounces Boston or Bibb lettuce leaves

2 ripe Bosc, Bartlett or Anjou pears Lemon juice

1½ cups (6 ounces) Stilton or Gorgonzola cheese, crumbled Freshly ground black pepper

Place oil, vinegar, honey, mustard and salt in small bowl. Whisk together until combined. Cover and refrigerate up to 2 days.

Wash greens in several changes of cold water. Drain well and, if necessary, pat with paper towels to remove excess moisture. Or, spin in salad spinner to remove moisture. Discard any wilted or bruised leaves. Cut or tear off woody stems.

Tear enough assorted gourmet mixed greens into bite-sized pieces to measure

5 packed cups. Tear enough Boston lettuce into bite-sized pieces to measure 2 packed cups.

Cut pears into quarters; remove stem and core. Cut each quarter into ½-inch pieces. To help prevent discoloration, brush pear pieces with lemon juice, if desired.

Combine all salad greens in large bowl. Add pears, cheese and dressing. Toss lightly to coat; sprinkle with pepper.

*Makes 6 to 8 servings*

## Sweet and Sour Carrots

1½ pounds whole baby carrots, pared and trimmed

1 cup slivered green bell pepper

⅓ cup honey

¼ cup lemon juice

½ teaspoon LAWRY'S® Seasoned Salt

¼ teaspoon LAWRY'S® Lemon Pepper Seasoning

¼ teaspoon ground cinnamon

⅛ teaspoon ground cardamon

In large saucepan with steamer insert, steam carrots over boiling water until crisp-tender; drain. Add remaining ingredients; cook over low heat, stirring occasionally, until carrots are glazed.

*Makes 6 servings*

*Winter Pear and Stilton Salad*

*Brussels Sprouts in Mustard Sauce*

## Brussels Sprouts in Mustard Sauce

1½ pounds fresh Brussels sprouts
 1 tablespoon butter or margarine
 ⅓ cup chopped shallots or onion
 ⅓ cup half-and-half
1½ tablespoons tarragon Dijon mustard or
   Dusseldorf mustard
 ¼ teaspoon salt
 ⅛ teaspoon freshly ground black pepper
   or ground nutmeg
1½ tablespoons grated Parmesan cheese
   (optional)

Cut stem from each Brussels sprout and pull off outer bruised leaves. For faster, more even cooking, cross-hatch core by cutting an "X" deep into the stem end of each Brussels sprout. Cut large Brussels sprouts lengthwise into halves. Use large enough saucepan to allow Brussels sprouts to fit in a single layer. Bring 2 quarts salted water to a boil in saucepan. Add Brussels sprouts; return to a boil. Boil, uncovered, 7 to 10 minutes or until almost tender when pierced with fork. Drain in colander. Rinse under cold water; drain thoroughly.

Melt butter in same saucepan over medium heat until foamy. Add shallots; cook 3 minutes, stirring occasionally. Add half-and-half, mustard, salt and pepper. Simmer 1 minute until thickened. Add Brussels sprouts; heat about 1 minute or until heated through, tossing gently with sauce. Just before serving, sprinkle with cheese, if desired.     *Makes 4 cups, 6 to 8 servings*

•

## Festive Green Beans

 1 tablespoon olive oil
 1 tablespoon butter or margarine
 3 medium leeks, well rinsed and sliced
 2 large red bell peppers, seeded and cut
   into thin strips
 2 pounds green beans, trimmed
 1 large clove garlic, minced
1½ teaspoons salt
 1 teaspoon TABASCO® pepper sauce
 1 teaspoon grated lemon peel
 ¼ cup sliced natural almonds, toasted

In 12-inch skillet over medium heat, heat oil and butter. Add leeks; cook 5 minutes, stirring occasionally. Add red pepper strips; cook 5 minutes longer or until vegetables are tender.

Meanwhile, steam green beans 5 minutes or until crisp-tender. Drain. Add green beans, garlic, salt, TABASCO sauce and grated lemon peel to skillet; toss to mix well. Sprinkle with almonds.

*Makes 8 servings*

## Creamed Spinach à la Lawry's®

4 bacon slices, finely chopped
1 cup finely chopped onion
¼ cup all-purpose flour
2 teaspoons LAWRY'S® Seasoned Salt
½ teaspoon LAWRY'S® Seasoned Pepper
½ teaspoon LAWRY'S® Garlic Powder
    with Parsley
1½ to 2 cups milk
2 packages (10 ounces each) frozen
    spinach, cooked and drained

In medium skillet, cook bacon until almost crisp. Add onion to bacon and cook until onion is tender, about 10 minutes. Remove from heat. Add flour, Seasoned Salt, Seasoned Pepper and Garlic Powder with Parsley; blend thoroughly. Gradually add milk, starting with 1½ cups, and stir over low heat until thickened. Add spinach and mix thoroughly. If too thick, add additional milk. *Makes 8 servings*

**Presentation:** Serve with prime rib of beef.

## Butternut Bisque

1 teaspoon margarine or butter
1 large onion, coarsely chopped
2 cans (about 14 ounces each) reduced-
    sodium or regular chicken broth,
    divided
1 medium butternut squash, peeled,
    seeded and cut into ½-inch pieces
    (about 1½ pounds)
½ teaspoon ground nutmeg or freshly
    grated nutmeg
⅛ teaspoon ground white pepper
    Plain nonfat yogurt and chives for
    garnish

Melt margarine in large saucepan over medium heat until foamy. Add onion. Cook and stir 3 minutes. Add 1 can broth and squash. Bring to a boil over high heat. Reduce heat to low. Cover and simmer 20 minutes until squash is very tender.

Process squash mixture, in 2 batches, in food processor until smooth. Return soup to saucepan; add remaining can of broth, nutmeg and pepper. Simmer, uncovered, 5 minutes, stirring occasionally.* Ladle into soup bowls. Place yogurt in pastry bag fitted with round decorating tip. Pipe onto soup in decorative design. Garnish with chives, if desired.

*Makes about 5 cups, 6 servings*

*Soup may be covered and refrigerated up to 2 days before serving. Reheat in large saucepan over medium heat until hot, stirring occasionally.

**Cream of Butternut Soup:** Add ½ cup heavy cream or half-and-half with broth. Proceed as directed.

*Butternut Bisque*

## Raspberry Vinegar

1 bottle (12 ounces) white wine vinegar
(1½ cups)
½ cup sugar
1 cup fresh raspberries or sliced
strawberries, crushed

Combine vinegar and sugar in
nonaluminum 2-quart saucepan. Heat until
very hot, stirring occasionally. *Do not boil.*
(If vinegar boils, it will become cloudy.)

Pour into glass bowl; stir in raspberries.
Cover with plastic wrap. Let stand in cool
place about 1 week until desired amount of
flavor develops. Strain through fine mesh
sieve or cheesecloth twice. Store up to 6
months in jar or bottle with tight-fitting lid
in refrigerator.

*Makes about 2 cups vinegar*

## 3-Green Salad with Cranberry Vinaigrette

1 cup bottled oil and vinegar dressing
½ cup ground cranberries
1 clove garlic, crushed
1 teaspoon dried tarragon leaves
1 head red leaf lettuce
1 head romaine lettuce
1 pound fresh spinach
Shredded red cabbage for garnish
Bean sprouts for garnish

Combine dressing, cranberries, garlic and
tarragon in jar with tight-fitting lid. Let
stand at least 2 hours to allow flavors to
blend.

Wash greens, removing tough stems or ribs;
tear into bite-sized pieces. Just before
serving toss with dressing. Garnish, if
desired.          *Makes 6 servings*

*Favorite recipe from* **Perdue® Farms**

## Holiday Harvest Rice

2 tablespoons margarine
1½ cups MAHATMA®, CAROLINA®,
RIVER® or WATER MAID® rice
½ teaspoon salt
2 cups unsweetened apple juice
1 cup cranberry juice
2 tablespoons fresh lemon juice
1 tablespoon chopped raisins
2 teaspoons light brown sugar
½ teaspoon cinnamon
2 small tart apples, peeled, cored and
chopped
½ cup chopped green onions

In large saucepan over medium heat, melt
margarine. Stir in rice and salt, stirring to
coat rice. Add juices, raisins, sugar and
cinnamon. Bring to a boil. Cover and
simmer 20 minutes. Stir in apples and green
onions. Cook until heated through.

*Makes 6 to 8 servings*

*Holiday Harvest Rice*

## Jones® Fancy Holiday Stuffing

2 (12-ounce) packages JONES®
    All-Natural Roll Sausage
¾ cup (6 ounces) unsalted butter
3 medium onions, coarsely chopped
2 cups chopped celery, including tops
¾ loaf day-old plain white bread with
    crusts, torn into small pieces
2 eggs, lightly beaten
1 (10-ounce) package frozen chopped
    spinach, thawed and squeezed dry
1 (8-ounce) can whole water chestnuts,
    coarsely chopped *or* 1 apple, peeled
    and chopped
½ cup chopped fresh parsley
1½ tablespoons poultry seasoning *or*
    mixture of dried tarragon, thyme
    and sage, proportioned to taste
2 teaspoons salt or to taste
1½ teaspoons freshly ground black
    pepper

Crumble sausage into large skillet. Cook
over medium-high heat 5 to 8 minutes or
until no longer pink in center. Transfer
sausage and drippings, if desired, to large
bowl.

Melt butter in same skillet over medium
heat. Add onions; cook and stir until soft.
Add celery and continue cooking briefly, so
that celery retains its bright green color.
Add to sausage. Add remaining ingredients
to sausage, mixing thoroughly but gently.

Just before roasting, stuff loosely into body
and neck cavities of bird. Place any
remaining stuffing in greased, shallow
casserole dish; bake during last 30 minutes
of roasting.

*Makes enough stuffing for 12- to
16-pound turkey*

*Fresh Vegetable Casserole*

## Fresh Vegetable Casserole

8 small new potatoes
8 baby carrots
1 small cauliflower, broken into florets
4 stalks asparagus, cut into 1-inch pieces
3 tablespoons butter or margarine
3 tablespoons all-purpose flour
2 cups milk
    Salt
    Black pepper
¾ cup (3 ounces) shredded Cheddar
    cheese
    Chopped fresh cilantro

Cook vegetables until crisp-tender. Arrange
vegetables in buttered 2-quart casserole. To
make sauce, melt butter in medium
saucepan over medium heat. Stir in flour
until smooth. Gradually stir in milk. Cook
until thickened, stirring constantly. Season
to taste with salt and pepper. Add cheese,
stirring until cheese is melted. Pour sauce
over vegetables and sprinkle with cilantro.
Bake in preheated 350°F oven 15 minutes or
until heated through.

*Makes 4 to 6 servings*

# Jones® Sausage and Wild Rice

1 cup wild rice
1 package JONES® All-Natural Sausage Links
1 medium onion, chopped
1 rib celery, sliced
1 can cream of mushroom soup
1 (4-ounce) can sliced mushrooms, drained
½ cup dry white wine

Prepare wild rice according to package directions, omitting salt; do not overcook. Prepare sausage links according to package directions; do not overcook. Drain well, leaving 1 tablespoon of fat in pan. Cool sausages slightly and cut in bite-sized pieces.

In same pan, sauté onion and celery. Add soup, cooked rice, sausage slices, mushrooms and wine, stirring carefully to mix. Place in well-buttered casserole and bake at 350°F 30 minutes. Garnish as desired. *Makes 6 servings*

# Cheesy Mashed Potatoes and Turnips

2 pounds all-purpose potatoes, peeled
1 pound turnips, peeled
¼ cup milk
½ cup (2 ounces) shredded Cheddar cheese
¼ cup butter or margarine
1 teaspoon TABASCO® pepper sauce
½ teaspoon salt

Combine potatoes, turnips and enough water to cover in 5-quart saucepan. Bring to a boil over high heat. Reduce heat to low; cover and simmer 25 to 30 minutes or until vegetables are tender. Drain. Return

vegetables to saucepan; heat over high heat for a few seconds to eliminate any excess moisture, shaking saucepan to prevent sticking.

Bring milk to a simmer over medium heat in small saucepan. Mash vegetables in large bowl. Stir warmed milk, Cheddar cheese, butter, TABASCO sauce and salt into vegetable mixture. *Makes 8 servings*

**Note:** Recipe may be made up to 2 days in advance and reheated in microwave oven or double boiler set over simmering water.

# Carrot Cream Soup

¼ cup margarine
¼ cup chopped onion
½ teaspoon LAWRY'S® Garlic Powder with Parsley
¼ teaspoon LAWRY'S® Seasoned Salt
2 cups chopped carrots
½ cup all-purpose flour
4½ cups chicken broth
¼ cup whipping cream
Chopped fresh parsley for garnish

In large saucepan, melt margarine and sauté onion, Garlic Powder with Parsley and Seasoned Salt. Add carrots and cook 5 minutes. Stir in flour; blend well. Stirring constantly, add chicken broth; blend well. Bring to a boil. Reduce heat; cover and simmer 30 minutes, stirring occasionally. In blender or food processor, purée carrot mixture and return to pan. Stir in cream; heat through. *Makes 4 servings*

**Presentation:** Serve warm soup topped with parsley. Warm French bread or crackers is a welcome accompaniment.

*Jones® Sausage and Wild Rice*

*Easy Glazed Yams*

# Easy Glazed Yams

2 (17- or 23-ounce) cans yams or sweet
 potatoes, drained
¾ cup BAMA® Pineapple or Peach
 Preserves
½ to 1 cup CAMPFIRE® Miniature
 Marshmallows
¼ cup chopped nuts
1 tablespoon margarine or butter,
 melted

Preheat oven to 350°F. Arrange yams in
ungreased 1½-quart shallow baking dish.
Spoon preserves evenly over yams; top
with marshmallows, nuts and margarine.
Bake 25 minutes or until hot. Refrigerate
leftovers. *Makes 4 to 6 servings*

# Shrimp-Macadamia Stuffing

 1 pound shrimp, peeled and deveined
½ cup chopped celery
¼ cup chopped onion
½ cup butter
 2 cups herb-seasoned stuffing mix
 1 cup water
½ cup chopped macadamia nuts
 1 egg, beaten

Cut large shrimp in half.

Cook and stir celery and onion in butter
until tender; add shrimp and cook 1
minute. Remove from heat.

Add remaining ingredients to shrimp
mixture; mix thoroughly. Place mixture into
lightly greased 2-quart baking dish. Bake at
350°F 15 to 20 minutes or until heated
through. *Makes 6 servings*

**Note:** Makes approximately 4 cups stuffing,
enough for 4 Rock Cornish game hens.

*Favorite recipe from* **Florida Department of Agriculture and
Consumer Services**

# Holiday Split Peas Vinaigrette

4 cups green or yellow split peas,
 washed
2 quarts water
4 pounds finely chopped onions,
 steamed or sautéed (12 medium)
3 pounds cooked smoked sausage,
 sliced

**Dressing**

2 cups olive oil
1½ cups chopped fresh parsley
¾ cup vinegar
⅓ cup German hot or coarse-grained
 mustard
 Sugar to taste
 Salt and white pepper to taste
4 pounds coarsely chopped tomatoes
 or red bell peppers, sautéed
 (12 medium)

1. Combine peas and water in stockpot or
Dutch oven. Bring to a boil; reduce heat
and simmer 20 minutes or until peas are
tender.

2. Remove from heat; drain. Stir in onions and sausage. Keep warm.

3. To prepare dressing, blend together oil, parsley, vinegar, mustard, sugar, salt and pepper.

4. Pour dressing over split pea mixture; blend.

5. Gently blend in tomatoes. Serve warm or cold. *Makes 24 (1½-cup) servings*

*Favorite recipe from* **USA Dry Pea & Lentil Industry**

# Couscous with Vegetables in Savory Broth

**2 tablespoons butter or margarine**
**1 large onion, sliced**
**½ cup dry white wine or water**
**⅓ cup sliced carrots**
**1 medium zucchini, sliced**
**1 small red or green bell pepper, sliced**
**1 envelope LIPTON® Recipe Secrets®**
   **Savory Herb with Garlic Soup Mix**
**2 cups water**
**1⅓ cups (8 ounces) couscous, cooked***

*Substitute hot cooked penne or ziti pasta for the couscous.

In 12-inch skillet, melt butter over medium heat and cook onion, stirring occasionally, 5 minutes or until golden. Add wine and boil over high heat 1 minute. Stir in carrots, zucchini, red pepper and savory herb with garlic soup mix blended with water. Bring to a boil over high heat. Reduce heat to low and simmer uncovered, stirring occasionally, 15 minutes. To serve, spoon over hot couscous.

*Makes about 5 side-dish or*
*2 main-dish servings*

**Menu Suggestion:** Serve with a mixed green salad and sliced fresh fruit drizzled with honey for dessert.

# Turkey Pan Gravy

**6 tablespoons turkey fat**
**6 tablespoons all-purpose flour**
**4 cups turkey or chicken broth, milk or**
   **water**
   **LAWRY'S® Seasoned Salt**
   **LAWRY'S® Seasoned Pepper**

Pour drippings from turkey into bowl, leaving any brown bits in roasting pan. Let fat rise to top; skim off all fat. Measure amount of fat needed for gravy; return to roasting pan. The liquid under the fat can be used as part of the liquid for gravy. Place roasting pan over low heat; blend in flour and cook, stirring constantly, until bubbly. Add cooled liquid, all at once. Cook, stirring constantly with wire whisk, until thickened. Continue cooking about 5 minutes, stirring constantly. Season to taste with Seasoned Salt and Seasoned Pepper.

*Makes about 4 cups*

*Couscous with Vegetables in Savory Broth*

# Cranberry-Raisin Stuffing

12 slices cinnamon-raisin bread
½ cup (1 stick) butter or margarine
2 medium onions, chopped
1 teaspoon dried rubbed sage
1 bag (12 ounces) fresh or partially
　　thawed frozen cranberries, washed,
　　picked through, coarsely chopped
¼ cup sugar
¼ to ½ cup chicken broth*

*If cooking stuffing outside of turkey, use ½ cup chicken broth and bake, covered, at 350°F 45 minutes or until heated through.

Toast bread. Stack several pieces of toast and cut into ½-inch cubes. Repeat until all toast is cubed. Place in large bowl; set aside. Melt butter in large skillet; add onions. Cook and stir about 10 minutes or until tender. Add sage; cook 1 minute more.

Toss cranberries with sugar in medium bowl. Add onion mixture and sugared cranberries to bread cubes; mix well. Pour ¼ cup chicken broth over bread cube mixture; mix until evenly moistened. Stuff body and neck cavity of turkey and cook according to instructions given with turkey.
*Makes 7½ cups stuffing*

*Cranberry-Raisin Stuffing*

# Creamed Horseradish

½ pint whipping cream
1 ounce fresh horseradish root, peeled
　　and finely grated *or* 1 tablespoon
　　prepared horseradish
1 teaspoon LAWRY'S® Seasoned Salt
2 to 3 drops hot pepper sauce to taste

In medium bowl, whip cream until soft peaks form. Gradually add horseradish, Seasoned Salt and hot pepper sauce. Continue whipping until very stiff. Refrigerate until served. *Makes 2 cups*

**Presentation:** Serve with prime rib of beef.

# Sweet Potato Soufflé

3 eggs, separated
¾ cup sugar
1¼ cups mashed sweet potatoes, fresh or
　　canned
1 cup chopped walnuts, divided
　　Sugar
　　Whipped cream (optional)

Preheat oven to 350°F.

Beat egg yolks in large bowl until frothy. Gradually add sugar; beat until lemon colored. Add sweet potatoes and ½ the walnuts; beat until blended.

Beat egg whites in separate bowl until stiff peaks form; fold into sweet potato mixture. Turn into buttered and lightly sugared soufflé dish. Sprinkle remaining walnuts on top. Dust with sugar. Bake 15 minutes. Serve immediately with whipped cream, if desired. *Makes 6 servings*

*Favorite recipe from **Walnut Marketing Board***

## Sausage 'n' Apples

1 pound BOB EVANS FARMS® Original
   Recipe Roll Sausage
2 tablespoons chopped onion
1 clove garlic, minced *or* ⅛ teaspoon
   garlic powder
8 medium Granny Smith apples
1 cup apple juice
¼ cup packed brown sugar

Preheat oven to 350°F. Crumble sausage
into large skillet. Add onion and garlic.
Cook over medium-high heat until sausage
is browned, stirring occasionally. Drain off
any drippings. Core apples and stuff with
sausage mixture. Place in 13 × 9-inch
baking dish. Pour juice over apples;
sprinkle tops with brown sugar. Bake 40
minutes or until apples are soft. Serve
warm. Refrigerate leftovers.

*Makes 8 side-dish servings*

## Classic Spinach Salad

½ pound fresh spinach leaves
   (about 10 cups)
1 cup sliced mushrooms
1 medium tomato, cut into wedges
⅓ cup seasoned croutons
¼ cup chopped red onion
4 slices bacon, crisp-cooked and
   crumbled
½ cup WISH-BONE® Lite Dijon
   Vinaigrette Dressing
1 hard-cooked egg, sliced

In large salad bowl, combine spinach,
mushrooms, tomato, croutons, red onion
and bacon. Add lite Dijon vinaigrette
dressing and toss gently. Garnish with egg.

*Makes about 6 side-dish servings*

## Glazed Stir-Fry Holiday Vegetables

3 tablespoons fresh lemon juice
2 tablespoons sugar
1 tablespoon low sodium soy sauce
2 teaspoons cornstarch
½ teaspoon grated lemon peel
½ cup water
4 teaspoons vegetable oil
3 cups fresh broccoli florets
1 medium red bell pepper, cut into
   1-inch pieces
1 cup peeled, julienne-cut jicama
Lemon peel

Combine lemon juice, sugar, soy sauce,
cornstarch and lemon peel in small bowl.
Stir in ½ cup water; set aside. Heat oil in
large nonstick skillet. Add broccoli and bell
pepper; stir-fry over high heat 2 minutes.
Add jicama and continue cooking 1 to 2
minutes or until vegetables are crisp-tender.
Pour lemon juice mixture over vegetables
and continue cooking just until glaze
thickens. Toss vegetables to coat thoroughly
with glaze. Garnish with lemon peel.

*Makes 6 (½-cup) servings*

*Favorite recipe from **The Sugar Association, Inc.***

*Classic Spinach Salad*

# French Onion Soup

3 medium onions, thinly sliced and
    separated into rings
2 tablespoons butter
1 package (1 ounce) LAWRY'S® Au Jus
    Gravy Mix
3 cups water
4 thin slices sourdough French bread
    Unsalted butter, softened
4 slices Swiss or Gruyère cheese

In large skillet, sauté onions in butter until
golden. In large bowl, combine Au Jus
Gravy Mix and water; add to onions. Bring
to a boil. Reduce heat to low; cover and
simmer 15 minutes, stirring occasionally.
Broil bread on one side until lightly toasted.
Turn bread slices over; spread with butter.
Top with cheese; broil until cheese melts.

*Makes 4 servings*

**Presentation:** To serve, pour soup into
tureen or individual bowls. Top each
serving with toast.

**Hint:** If using individual ovenproof bowls,
pour soup into bowls; top with a slice of
untoasted bread. Top with cheese. Place
under broiler just until cheese is melted.

# Raisin Bread Stuffing with Orange Walnuts

6 cups cubed raisin bread
1 cup chopped onion
1 cup sliced celery
2 tablespoons butter or margarine
⅔ cup walnut pieces
1 orange
1 teaspoon basil
⅛ teaspoon allspice
⅛ teaspoon black pepper
    Salt

Preheat oven to 300°F. Spread bread cubes
on baking sheet and bake 20 minutes until
dry.

Meanwhile, in 3-quart saucepan cook and
stir onion and celery in butter over
medium-high heat 5 minutes. Add walnuts.
Cook and stir 2 minutes; set aside. Grate
enough orange peel to equal 2 teaspoons.
Squeeze orange into measuring cup. Add
enough water to juice to equal ¾ cup; stir in
orange peel, basil, allspice and pepper. Stir
juice mixture into saucepan. Add bread
cubes. Toss over low heat to blend flavors
and heat through. Season with salt. Serve
with pork or poultry, or use to stuff chicken
or duck before roasting.

*Makes 6 servings*

*Favorite recipe from **Walnut Marketing Board***

# Ensalada de Noche Buena (Christmas Eve Salad)

1 head iceberg lettuce, shredded
3 oranges, peeled and sectioned
2 firm bananas, sliced crosswise ¼ inch
    thick
1 large apple, unpeeled, cored and
    chopped
1 cup pineapple chunks
1 cup sliced canned beets
½ cup coarsely chopped toasted peanuts
    (not dry roasted)
    Seeds of 1 pomegranate *or* ¼ cup
    canned whole cranberry sauce
    Vinaigrette Dressing (page 55)

On large platter, arrange lettuce and top
with fruit and beets. Sprinkle with nuts and
pomegranate seeds. Serve with Vinaigrette
Dressing. *Makes 10 servings*

*Favorite recipe from **Lawry's® Foods, Inc.***

*French Onion Soup*

*Cherry Waldorf Gelatin Salad*

# Cherry Waldorf Gelatin Salad

2 cups boiling water
1 (8-serving size) package cherry flavor gelatin
1 cup cold water
¼ cup REALEMON® Lemon Juice from Concentrate
1½ cups chopped apples
1 cup chopped celery
½ cup chopped walnuts or pecans
Lettuce leaves

In large bowl, pour boiling water over gelatin; stir until dissolved. Add cold water and ReaLemon® brand; chill until partially set. Fold in apples, celery and nuts. Pour into lightly oiled 6-cup mold or 9-inch square baking pan. Cover; chill until set, 4 to 6 hours or overnight. Serve on lettuce leaves. Garnish as desired. Refrigerate leftovers. *Makes 8 to 10 servings*

# Herbed Vinegar

1 bottle (12 ounces) white wine vinegar (1½ cups)
½ cup fresh basil leaves

Pour vinegar into nonaluminum 2-quart saucepan. Heat until very hot, stirring occasionally. *Do not boil.* (If vinegar boils, it will become cloudy.)

Pour into glass bowl; add basil. Cover with plastic wrap. Let stand in cool place about 1 week until desired amount of flavor develops. Strain before using. Store up to 6 months in jar or bottle with tight-fitting lid.
*Makes about 1½ cups vinegar*

**Variations:** Substitute 1 tablespoon of either fresh oregano, thyme, chervil or tarragon for the basil. Or, substitute cider vinegar for the wine vinegar.

# Roasted Tomato and Mozzarella Pasta Salad

3 cups (8 ounces) rotelle pasta, uncooked
3 cups Roasted Fresh Tomatoes (page 53)
1 cup coarsely chopped green bell pepper
¾ cup (3 ounces) mozzarella cheese, cut into ½-inch pieces
¼ cup chopped mild red onion
½ teaspoon salt
¼ teaspoon black pepper
⅓ cup prepared red wine vinaigrette salad dressing

Cook pasta according to package directions; rinse and drain. Place pasta in large bowl. Cut Roasted Fresh Tomatoes into chunks; add to pasta. Add bell pepper, mozzarella, onion, salt and black pepper to pasta. Pour salad dressing over top; toss to combine. Garnish with fresh basil leaves, if desired. *Makes 4 servings*

## Roasted Fresh Tomatoes

6 large (about 3 pounds) Florida
    tomatoes
2 tablespoons vegetable oil
½ teaspoon dried basil leaves
¼ teaspoon dried thyme leaves
¼ teaspoon salt
¼ teaspoon black pepper

Preheat oven to 425°F. Use tomatoes held at
room temperature until fully ripe. Core
tomatoes; cut into halves horizontally.
Gently squeeze halves to remove seeds.
Place cut side up on rack in broiler pan; set
aside. Combine oil, basil, thyme, salt and
pepper in small bowl; brush over cut sides
of tomatoes. Place tomatoes cut side down
on rack. Bake about 30 minutes or until
well browned. Remove skins, if desired.
Serve hot, warm or cold.

*Makes 4 to 6 servings*

*Favorite recipe from* **Florida Tomato Committee**

# Split Pea Soup

1 package (16 ounces) dried green or
    yellow split peas
1 pound smoked pork hocks *or* 4 ounces
    smoked sausage link, sliced and
    quartered *or* 1 meaty ham bone
7 cups water
1 medium onion, chopped
2 medium carrots, chopped
¾ teaspoon salt
½ teaspoon dried basil leaves
¼ teaspoon dried oregano leaves
¼ teaspoon black pepper
    Ham and carrot strips for garnish

*Split Pea Soup*

Rinse peas thoroughly in colander under
cold running water, picking out any debris
or blemished peas. Place peas, pork hocks
and water in 5-quart Dutch oven. Add
onion, carrots, salt, basil, oregano and
pepper to Dutch oven. Bring to a boil over
high heat. Reduce heat to medium-low;
simmer, uncovered, 1 hour 15 minutes or
until peas are tender, stirring occasionally.
Stir frequently near end of cooking to keep
soup from scorching.

Remove pork hocks; cool. Cut meat into
bite-sized pieces.

Carefully ladle 3 cups hot soup into food
processor or blender; cover and process
until mixture is smooth. Return puréed
soup and meat to Dutch oven. (If soup is
too thick, add a little water until desired
consistency is reached.) Heat through.
Ladle into bowls. Garnish, if desired.

*Makes 6 servings*

*Mixed Greens with Raspberry Vinaigrette*

## Mixed Greens with Raspberry Vinaigrette

⅓ cup vegetable oil
2½ tablespoons raspberry vinegar
 1 shallot, minced
½ teaspoon salt
½ teaspoon sugar
   Romaine lettuce leaves
   Spinach leaves
   Red leaf lettuce leaves
 1 cup red seedless grapes, halved
½ cup toasted walnut pieces

Place oil, vinegar, shallot, salt and sugar in small bowl or small jar with lid. Whisk together or cover and shake jar until mixed. Cover; refrigerate up to 1 week.

Wash greens in several changes of cold water. Drain well and, if necessary, pat with paper towels to remove excess moisture. Or, spin in salad spinner to remove moisture.

Discard any wilted or bruised leaves. Cut or tear off woody stems. Tear enough romaine lettuce into bite-sized pieces to measure 2 packed cups. Tear enough spinach into bite-sized pieces to measure 2 packed cups. Tear enough red leaf lettuce into bite-sized pieces to measure 2 packed cups.

Combine greens, grapes and cooled walnuts in large bowl. Just before serving, add dressing; toss well to coat.

*Makes 6 to 8 servings*

## Cranberry and Red Pepper Relish

 2 medium red bell peppers, roasted, peeled, seeded and cut into 1-inch pieces*
 1 cup fresh cranberries, rinsed and drained
 1 green onion, cut into 1-inch pieces
 3 tablespoons fresh cilantro leaves
 2 tablespoons fresh orange juice
   Zest of ½ lime
½ cup sugar
⅛ teaspoon salt

*To roast bell peppers, place peppers under broiler, turning frequently, until slightly scorched on all sides. Place peppers in paper bag; close bag and set aside 5 minutes. Remove blistered skins from peppers.

1. In food processor bowl fitted with metal blade, combine peppers, cranberries, onion, cilantro, orange juice and lime zest; process until coarsely chopped.

2. In medium bowl, combine cranberry mixture, sugar and salt. Cover and refrigerate at least 1 hour to allow flavors to blend. *Makes 1½ cups*

*Favorite recipe from **National Turkey Federation***

# Vinaigrette Dressing

¼ cup red wine vinegar
1 tablespoon water
1 tablespoon lemon juice
1 teaspoon sugar
½ teaspoon LAWRY'S® Seasoned Pepper
½ teaspoon dried basil
½ teaspoon LAWRY'S® Seasoned Salt
½ teaspoon LAWRY'S® Garlic Salt
¼ teaspoon paprika
¼ teaspoon dry mustard
¼ teaspoon dried tarragon
¼ teaspoon celery seed
⅔ cup vegetable oil

In container with tight-fitting lid, combine vinegar, water, lemon juice, sugar and seasonings; blend or shake well. Add oil; blend or shake again. For best flavor, refrigerate several hours before serving.

*Makes about 1 cup*

# Sweet Potato Gratin

3 pounds sweet potatoes (about 5 large)
½ cup butter or margarine, divided
¼ cup plus 2 tablespoons packed light
    brown sugar, divided
2 eggs
⅔ cup orange juice
2 teaspoons ground cinnamon, divided
½ teaspoon salt
¼ teaspoon ground nutmeg
⅓ cup all-purpose flour
¼ cup uncooked old-fashioned oats
⅓ cup chopped pecans or walnuts

Bake sweet potatoes until tender in preheated 350°F oven 1 hour. Or, pierce sweet potatoes several times with table fork and place on microwavable plate. Microwave at HIGH 16 to 18 minutes, rotating and turning over sweet potatoes after 9 minutes. Let stand 5 minutes. While sweet potatoes are hot, cut lengthwise into halves. Scrape hot pulp from skins into large bowl.

Preheat oven to 350°F.

Beat ¼ cup butter and 2 tablespoons sugar into sweet potatoes with electric mixer at medium speed until butter is melted. Beat in eggs, orange juice, 1½ teaspoons cinnamon, salt and nutmeg, scraping down side of bowl once. Beat until smooth. Pour mixture into 1½-quart baking dish or gratin dish; smooth top.

For topping, combine flour, oats, remaining ¼ cup sugar and remaining ½ teaspoon cinnamon in medium bowl. Cut in remaining ¼ cup butter until mixture forms coarse crumbs. Stir in pecans. Sprinkle topping evenly over sweet potatoes.

Bake 25 to 30 minutes or until sweet potatoes are heated through. For a crisper topping, broil 5 inches from heat 2 to 3 minutes or until golden brown.

*Makes 6 to 8 servings*

*Sweet Potato Gratin*

# Cranberry-Apple Chutney

1¼ cups granulated sugar
½ cup water
1 package (12 ounces) fresh or frozen
   cranberries (about 3½ cups)
2 medium Granny Smith apples, peeled,
   cored and chopped
1 medium onion, chopped
½ cup golden raisins
½ cup packed light brown sugar
¼ cup cider vinegar
1 teaspoon ground cinnamon
1 teaspoon ground ginger
⅛ teaspoon ground cloves
⅛ teaspoon ground allspice
½ cup toasted walnuts or pecans,
   chopped (optional)

Combine granulated sugar and water in heavy 2-quart saucepan. Cook over high heat until boiling. Boil gently 3 minutes. Add cranberries, apples, onion, raisins, brown sugar, vinegar, cinnamon, ginger, cloves and allspice. Bring to a boil over high heat. Reduce heat to medium. Simmer, uncovered, 20 to 25 minutes or until mixture is very thick, stirring occasionally. Cool; stir in walnuts, if desired. Cover and refrigerate up to 2 weeks before serving.

*Makes about 3½ to 4 cups*

# Warm Tomato-Potato Salad

3 medium fresh Florida tomatoes
1 pound small red skinned potatoes,
   quartered
3 slices bacon, cut into ½-inch pieces
¼ cup chopped onion
½ cup all-purpose flour
1½ teaspoons sugar
1 teaspoon salt
⅛ teaspoon black pepper
1 tablespoon cider vinegar
1 cup fresh or frozen sugar snap peas

Core tomatoes and coarsely chop. Place potatoes and enough water to cover in large saucepan. Bring to a boil and cook 10 to 15 minutes or until tender; drain.

Meanwhile, cook bacon in large skillet 3 to 5 minutes or until crisp, stirring occasionally. Remove bacon from skillet with slotted spoon; drain on paper towels. Remove all but 1 tablespoon drippings from skillet. Add onion; cook 5 to 7 minutes, stirring occasionally. Add flour, sugar, salt and pepper; stir until smooth. Add vinegar, ¼ cup water and sugar snap peas; cook and stir 1 to 2 minutes or until mixture comes to a boil and thickens slightly. Stir in potatoes and bacon. Transfer potato mixture to large serving plate; add tomatoes, tossing to coat.

*Makes 6 servings*

*Favorite recipe from **Florida Tomato Committee***

# Cinnamon Apple Sweet Potatoes

4 medium sweet potatoes
1½ cups finely chopped apples
½ cup orange juice
¼ cup sugar
1½ teaspoons cornstarch
½ teaspoon ground cinnamon
½ teaspoon grated orange peel

Wash sweet potatoes and pierce with fork. Place on paper towels and microwave at HIGH 10 to 13 minutes or until tender, turning halfway through cooking. Set aside. Combine remaining ingredients in large microwavable bowl. Cover and microwave at HIGH 3 minutes. Stir; uncover and microwave at HIGH 1½ to 2½ minutes or until sauce is thickened. Cut slit in center of sweet potatoes and spoon sauce over top.

*Makes 4 servings*

*Favorite recipe from **The Sugar Association, Inc.***

*Cranberry-Apple Chutney*

# Brown Rice and Mushroom Timbales

2 tablespoons butter or margarine
1 cup sliced carrots
2 cups sliced fresh mushrooms
¾ cup sliced green onions
2 cups cooked brown rice
⅔ cup chopped pecans
½ cup chopped fresh parsley
1⅓ cups low fat milk
1 cup (4 ounces) shredded sharp
    Cheddar cheese
3 eggs, beaten
1 teaspoon Worcestershire sauce
    Salt and black pepper to taste
    Nonstick cooking spray
    Cooked chicken (optional)

Melt butter in large skillet over medium-high heat until hot. Add carrots; cook and stir 3 minutes. Add mushrooms and onions; cook and stir 2 minutes more. Combine rice, pecans, parsley and vegetables in large bowl. Combine milk, cheese, eggs,

Worcestershire, salt and pepper in small bowl; stir into rice mixture. Divide mixture evenly into 6 ovenproof molds, custard cups or large muffin tins coated with cooking spray. Bake at 350°F 25 to 30 minutes or until set. Serve with chicken.
*Makes 6 servings*

**Variation:** Mixture may be baked in greased 3-quart baking dish and cut into squares.

*Favorite recipe from* **USA Rice Council**

# Tarragon Tanged Shrimp and Orange Salad

12 ounces cooked, shelled and deveined
    shrimp
2 cups cooked brown rice
2 cups romaine lettuce leaves, torn into
    bite-sized pieces
1½ cups orange sections
1 cup halved cherry tomatoes
½ cup sliced red onion
    Orange Tarragon Dressing (recipe
    follows)

Combine shrimp, rice, romaine, orange sections, cherry tomatoes and red onion in large serving bowl. Toss with Orange Tarragon Dressing just before serving.
*Makes 4 servings*

## Orange Tarragon Dressing

3 tablespoons frozen orange juice
    concentrate, thawed
2 tablespoons cider vinegar
1 tablespoon olive oil
1 teaspoon garlic powder
½ teaspoon salt
¾ teaspoon tarragon leaves, crushed
¼ teaspoon black pepper

Combine all ingredients in small bowl. Whisk until combined. *Makes ⅓ cup*

*Favorite recipe from* **American Spice Trade Association**

*Brown Rice and Mushrooms Timbales*

*Shrimp Bisque*

Cook and stir just until bubbly. Stir in fish stock and cook until bubbly. Cook 2 minutes, stirring constantly. Remove from heat.

Process soup in small batches in food processor or blender until smooth. Return soup to saucepan. Stir in half-and-half, wine, salt, lemon peel and red pepper. Heat through. Garnish, if desired.

*Makes 4 servings*

## Shrimp Bisque

 1 pound medium shrimp, peeled and
   deveined
 ¼ cup butter or margarine
 1 large clove garlic, minced
 2 large green onions, sliced
 ¼ cup all-purpose flour
 1 cup fish stock or canned chicken broth
 3 cups half-and-half
 2 tablespoons white wine (optional)
 ½ teaspoon salt
 ½ teaspoon grated lemon peel
   Dash ground red pepper
   Lemon peel twists and sliced green
     onion tops
   Whole shrimp for garnish

Coarsely chop shrimp into ½-inch pieces. Refrigerate until needed.

Melt butter in large saucepan over medium heat. Cook and stir shrimp, garlic and onions in butter until shrimp turn pink and opaque. Remove from heat. Blend in flour.

## Grandma's Old-Fashioned Sausage Stuffing

 1 pound BOB EVANS FARMS® Original
   Recipe or Sage Roll Sausage
 4 large apples, such as Red Delicious,
   McIntosh or Granny Smith
 8 cups dried or toasted fresh bread
   cubes or prepared seasoned bread
   cubes
 1 small onion, minced (optional)
 ½ cup milk
 ½ cup chopped celery
 2 teaspoons salt
   Chicken broth (optional)

Crumble sausage into medium skillet. Cook over medium heat until lightly browned, stirring occasionally. Place sausage and drippings in large bowl. Core, peel and chop apples into ½-inch pieces. Add apples and all remaining ingredients except chicken broth to sausage mixture; blend thoroughly. Bake loosely stuffed in bird or place stuffing in greased 13 × 9-inch baking dish. Add turkey drippings and/or broth to adjust moistness and bake 30 to 45 minutes in 350°F oven. Leftover stuffing should be removed from bird and stored separately in refrigerator. Reheat thoroughly before serving.

*Makes 10 side-dish servings, enough
for 12- to 15-pound turkey*

*Pine Nut Rice Dressing*

## Pine Nut Rice Dressing

  1 bag SUCCESS® Rice
⅓ cup chopped onion
⅓ cup chopped celery
  1 tablespoon margarine
¼ cup pine nuts
  1 tablespoon chopped fresh parsley
¾ teaspoon poultry seasoning
½ teaspoon black pepper
¼ teaspoon salt
¼ cup chopped green onions
¼ cup chicken stock

Prepare rice according to package directions. Meanwhile, cook and stir onion and celery in margarine. Add pine nuts, parsley, poultry seasoning, pepper and salt. Fold in cooked rice. Add green onions and chicken stock.  *Makes 4 servings*

## Five Bean Salad

¾ cup thinly sliced purple onion
  1 clove garlic, minced
  2 tablespoons water
  1 can (15 ounces) garbanzo beans, rinsed and drained
1½ cups green beans, cut into thirds
  1 can (8 ounces) Great Northern beans, rinsed and drained
  1 can (8 ounces) black beans, rinsed and drained
  1 can (8 ounces) kidney beans, rinsed and drained
⅓ cup cider vinegar
1½ tablespoons sugar
  1 teaspoon olive oil
¼ teaspoon dry mustard
  3 carrots, sliced
½ cup chopped red bell pepper

Combine onion, garlic and water in large microwavable casserole. Microwave at HIGH 1 to 2 minutes. Stir in all remaining ingredients except carrots and pepper. Microwave at HIGH 3 to 5 minutes or until green beans are crisp-tender. Stir in carrots and pepper. Serve immediately. Recipe may be made in advance; refrigerate and serve cold.  *Makes 8 to 10 servings*

*Favorite recipe from* **The Sugar Association, Inc.**

## Double Cheddar Salad

  4 cups lightly packed romaine lettuce leaves, thinly sliced
  2 cups sliced mushrooms
  1 cup cherry tomatoes, quartered
  1 cup sliced red bell pepper
  1 cup sliced yellow bell pepper
⅔ cup sharp Cheddar cheese, cut into ½-inch cubes
⅓ cup sliced red onion
   Creamy Cheddar Dressing (page 61)

Arrange lettuce, mushrooms, tomatoes, bell peppers, Cheddar cheese and onion in large bowl. Just before serving toss with Creamy Cheddar Dressing. *Makes 4 servings*

## Creamy Cheddar Dressing

½ cup (2 ounces) shredded white or
    yellow Cheddar cheese
¼ cup low fat plain yogurt
¼ cup reduced calorie mayonnaise
2 tablespoons milk
1½ teaspoons Dijon mustard
½ teaspoon salt
¼ teaspoon hot pepper sauce

Combine all ingredients in small bowl; stir until blended. *Makes ¾ cup*

*Favorite recipe from* **National Dairy Board**

*Sweet Potato and Ham Soup*

# Fresh Spinach Salad with Vinaigrette Dressing

½ pound spinach leaves, torn into pieces
2 hard-cooked eggs, peeled and chopped
6 bacon slices, cooked and crumbled
2 cups sliced fresh mushrooms
¾ cup Vinaigrette Dressing (page 55)

In large salad bowl, gently toss together all ingredients, except dressing; chill. Toss with dressing just before serving.
*Makes 6 servings*

**Presentation:** Chill salad plates and forks, too, if desired.

*Favorite recipe from* **Lawry's® Foods, Inc.**

# Sweet Potato and Ham Soup

1 tablespoon butter or margarine
1 small leek, sliced
1 clove garlic, minced
½ pound ham, cut into ½-inch cubes
2 medium sweet potatoes, peeled and
    cut into ¾-inch cubes
4 cups low sodium chicken broth
½ teaspoon dried thyme leaves
2 ounces fresh spinach, rinsed, stemmed
    and coarsely chopped

Melt butter in large saucepan over medium heat. Add leek and garlic. Cook and stir until leek is tender. Add ham, sweet potatoes, chicken broth and thyme to saucepan. Bring to a boil over high heat. Reduce heat to medium-low; cook 10 minutes or until sweet potatoes are tender. Stir spinach into soup. Simmer, uncovered, 2 minutes or until spinach is wilted. Serve immediately. *Makes 6 servings*

## Layered Vegetable Bake

2 slices day-old white bread, crumbled
2 tablespoons chopped fresh parsley (optional)
2 tablespoons butter or margarine, melted
1 large all-purpose potato (about ½ pound), thinly sliced
1 large yellow or red bell pepper, sliced
1 envelope LIPTON® Recipe Secrets® Savory Herb with Garlic or Golden Onion Soup Mix
1 large tomato, sliced

Preheat oven to 375°F.

Spray 1½-quart round casserole or baking dish with no stick cooking spray. In small bowl, combine bread crumbs, parsley and butter; set aside.

In prepared baking dish, arrange potato slices; top with yellow pepper. Sprinkle with savory herb with garlic soup mix. Arrange tomato slices over pepper, overlapping slightly. Sprinkle with bread crumb mixture. Cover with aluminum foil and bake 45 minutes. Remove foil and continue baking 15 minutes or until vegetables are tender.

*Makes about 6 servings*

**Menu Suggestion:** Serve with your favorite pork, beef or lamb roast and parslied rice.

## Gourmet Grits

½ pound BOB EVANS FARMS® Italian Roll Sausage
3 cups water
1 cup uncooked white grits
½ (10-ounce) package frozen chopped spinach, thawed and squeezed dry
¼ cup grated Parmesan cheese
¼ cup chopped sun-dried tomatoes
¼ cup olive oil
1 clove garlic, chopped

Crumble sausage into medium skillet. Cook over medium heat until browned, stirring occasionally. Drain off any drippings; set aside. Bring water to a rapid boil in large saucepan. While stirring, add grits in steady stream until mixture thickens into smooth paste. Reduce heat to low; simmer 5 to 7 minutes, stirring frequently to prevent sticking. Stir in sausage, then spinach, cheese and tomatoes. Pour into greased 9 × 5-inch loaf pan. Refrigerate until cool and firm.

Unmold. Slice into ½-inch-thick slices. Heat oil in large skillet over medium-high heat until hot. Add garlic; cook and stir 30 seconds or until soft. Add grit slices, 4 to 5 at a time, and cook until golden brown on both sides. Repeat until all slices are cooked. Serve hot. Refrigerate leftovers.

*Makes 4 to 6 side-dish servings*

**Serving Suggestions:** Melt thin slice of mozzarella cheese on top of each browned slice. This also makes a wonderful side dish for chicken topped with warmed seasoned tomato or spaghetti sauce.

*Layered Vegetable Bake*

## Pappa al Pomodoro alla Papa Newman (Bread and Tomato Soup)

¾ cup olive oil, divided
3 large cloves garlic, crushed
1 teaspoon dried sage
12 ounces day-old Italian or French bread, thinly sliced, crusts removed, divided (about 30 slices)
1 jar NEWMAN'S OWN® Bombolina Sauce (about 3 cups)
4 cups chicken broth
½ teaspoon crushed red pepper
½ teaspoon freshly ground black pepper
Freshly grated Parmesan cheese

1. In large skillet, heat ¼ cup oil over medium heat. Add garlic and sage and cook, stirring frequently, 1 to 2 minutes. Remove garlic from oil. Add ⅓ of the bread slices and cook, turning once, until golden brown on both sides, 2 to 3 minutes per side. Remove from heat; repeat with remaining ½ cup oil and bread.

2. In large heavy saucepan, heat Bombolina Sauce and chicken broth over medium-high heat to a boil. Reduce heat to low. Add crushed red pepper, black pepper and bread; simmer, covered, 30 minutes. Remove from heat and let stand 30 minutes. Ladle into soup bowls. Drizzle with additional olive oil and sprinkle with Parmesan cheese.     *Makes 6 to 8 servings*

## Yorkshire Pudding

2 eggs
1 cup all-purpose flour
½ teaspoon salt
¾ cup milk
¼ cup water
1 package (1.0 ounce) LAWRY'S® Seasoning Blend for Au Jus Gravy
1½ cups water
½ cup port wine
Dash LAWRY'S® Seasoned Pepper
Salad oil

In medium bowl, using electric beater, beat eggs until frothy. Reduce speed and gradually add flour and salt; beat until smooth. Slowly add milk and ¼ cup water; beat until blended. Increase speed to high and continue beating 10 minutes. Let stand 1 hour.

In medium saucepan, prepare Seasoning Blend for Au Jus Gravy with 1½ cups water, wine and Seasoned Pepper according to package directions. Set aside.

Preheat oven to 400°F. Coat 5-inch omelette pan with oil and place in oven. When pan is very hot, remove and pour off excess oil. In pan, place 1 tablespoon Au Jus Gravy and ½ cup batter. Bake 20 to 30 minutes until puffed and brown. Remove and wrap in foil. Repeat until all batter has been used.
*Makes 8 servings*

**Presentation:** Cut each pudding into quarters and serve with prime rib or roast beef. Serve remaining Au Jus Gravy over meat.

**Hint:** Pudding may be made ahead and reheated individually wrapped in foil.

*Oven-Roasted Vegetables*

## Oven-Roasted Vegetables

**1 envelope LIPTON® Recipe Secrets®
   Savory Herb with Garlic Soup Mix***
**1½ pounds assorted fresh vegetables****
**2 tablespoons olive or vegetable oil**

*Also terrific with Lipton® Recipe Secrets® Golden Herb with Lemon, Italian Herb with Tomato, Onion or Golden Onion Soup Mix.

**Use any combination of the following, sliced: zucchini, yellow squash, red or green bell peppers, carrots, celery and mushrooms.

Preheat oven to 450°F.

In large plastic bag or bowl, add all ingredients. Close bag and shake, or toss in bowl, until vegetables are evenly coated. Empty vegetables into 13 × 9-inch baking or roasting pan; discard bag. Bake, stirring once, 20 minutes or until vegetables are tender.          *Makes 4 (½-cup) servings*

## Jones® Sausage Stuffing

**1 (12-ounce) package JONES®
   All-Natural Roll Sausage**
**2 medium onions, chopped**
**2 ribs celery, diced or chopped**
**1 (16-ounce) package stuffing mix
   (less for small bird)**
**2 cups chicken broth, apple juice or hot
   water**

Crumble sausage into large skillet. Add onions and celery; cook over medium-high heat until sausage is no longer pink in center. Add stuffing mix and enough chicken broth to desired consistency. *Do not pour off drippings.* Blend thoroughly and stuff bird loosely.

*Makes enough stuffing for 14- to
16-pound bird*

# BREADS & COFFEE CAKES

## Apple Ring Coffee Cake

3 cups all-purpose flour
1 teaspoon baking soda
1 teaspoon salt
1 teaspoon ground cinnamon
1 cup walnuts, chopped
2 medium tart apples
1½ cups granulated sugar
1 cup vegetable oil
2 teaspoons vanilla
2 eggs
    Powdered sugar for garnish

Preheat oven to 325°F. Grease 10-inch tube pan; set aside.

Sift flour, baking soda, salt and cinnamon into large bowl. Stir in walnuts; set aside.

Peel apples with vegetable peeler or paring knife. Cut apples lengthwise into halves, then into quarters. Chop apples.

Combine granulated sugar, oil, vanilla and eggs in medium bowl. Stir in apples. Stir into flour mixture just until moistened.

Spoon batter into prepared pan, spreading evenly. Bake 1 hour or until wooden skewer inserted in center comes out clean.

Cool cake in pan on wire rack 10 minutes. Loosen edges with metal spatula if necessary. Remove from pan; cool completely on wire rack. Transfer to serving plate. Place powdered sugar in fine-meshed sieve; sprinkle over cake and serve immediately. Store leftover cake in airtight container.          *Makes 12 servings*

*Apple Ring Coffee Cake*

*Maple Nut Twist*

# Maple Nut Twist

1 recipe Sweet Yeast Dough (page 69)
2 tablespoons butter or margarine, melted
2 tablespoons honey
½ cup chopped pecans
¼ cup granulated sugar
2½ teaspoons maple flavoring, divided
½ teaspoon ground cinnamon
1 cup sifted powdered sugar
5 teaspoons milk

Prepare Sweet Yeast Dough; let rise as directed.

Combine butter and honey in custard cup; set aside.

Combine pecans, granulated sugar, 2 teaspoons maple flavoring and cinnamon in small bowl. Toss to coat pecans; set aside.

Grease 2 baking sheets; set aside. Cut dough into quarters. Roll out one piece of dough into 9-inch circle on lightly floured surface with lightly floured rolling pin. (Keep remaining dough covered with towel.) Place on prepared baking sheet. Brush half of butter mixture over dough. Sprinkle half of pecan mixture over butter.

Roll another piece of dough into 9-inch circle. Place dough over pecan filling, stretching dough as necessary to cover. Pinch edges to seal.

Place 1-inch biscuit cutter in center of circle as cutting guide. *(Do not cut into dough.)* Cut dough into 12 wedges with scissors or sharp knife, from edge of circle to edge of biscuit cutter, cutting through all layers.

Pick up wide edge of 1 wedge, twist several times and lay back down on baking sheet. Repeat twisting procedure with remaining 11 wedges. Remove biscuit cutter. Repeat with remaining 2 pieces of dough, butter mixture and pecan mixture.

Cover coffee cakes with towels; let rise in warm place about 1 hour or until almost doubled in bulk.

Preheat oven to 350°F. Bake on separate racks in oven 20 to 25 minutes or until coffee cakes are golden brown and sound hollow when tapped. (Rotate baking sheets top to bottom halfway through baking.) Immediately remove from baking sheets; cool on wire racks about 30 minutes.

Combine powdered sugar, milk and remaining ½ teaspoon maple flavoring in small bowl until smooth. Drizzle over warm twists.

*Makes 24 servings (2 coffee cakes)*

# Sweet Yeast Dough

4 to 4¼ cups all-purpose flour, divided
½ cup sugar
2 packages active dry yeast
1 teaspoon salt
¾ cup milk
4 tablespoons butter or margarine
2 eggs
1 teaspoon vanilla

Combine 1 cup flour, sugar, yeast and salt in large bowl; set aside.

Combine milk and butter in 1-quart saucepan. Heat over low heat until mixture is 120°F to 130°F. (Butter does not need to completely melt.) Gradually beat milk mixture into flour mixture with electric mixer at low speed. Increase speed to medium; beat 2 minutes, scraping down side of bowl once. Reduce speed to low. Beat in eggs, vanilla and 1 cup flour. Increase speed to medium; beat 2 minutes, scraping down side of bowl once. Stir in enough additional flour, about 2 cups, with wooden spoon to make soft dough.

Turn out dough onto lightly floured surface; flatten slightly. Knead dough about 5 minutes or until smooth and elastic, adding remaining ¼ cup flour to prevent sticking if necessary. Shape dough into a ball; place in large greased bowl. Turn dough over so that top is greased. Cover with towel; let rise in warm place 1 hour 30 minutes to 2 hours or until doubled in bulk. Punch down dough. Knead dough on lightly floured surface 1 minute. Cover with towel; let rest 10 minutes.

**Refrigerator Sweet Yeast Dough:** Prepare Sweet Yeast Dough as directed, except cover with greased plastic wrap; refrigerate 3 to 24 hours. Punch down dough. Knead dough on lightly floured surface 1 to 2 minutes. Cover with towel; let dough rest 20 minutes before shaping and second rising. (Second rising may take up to 1 hour 30 minutes.)

# Chocolate Popovers

¾ cup plus 2 tablespoons all-purpose flour
¼ cup granulated sugar
2 tablespoons unsweetened cocoa powder
¼ teaspoon salt
4 eggs
1 cup milk
2 tablespoons butter or margarine, melted
½ teaspoon vanilla
Powdered sugar

Position rack in lower third of oven. Preheat oven to 375°F. Grease 6-cup popover pan or 6 (6-ounce) custard cups. Set custard cups in jelly-roll pan for easier handling.

Sift flour, granulated sugar, cocoa and salt into medium bowl; set aside.

Beat eggs in large bowl with electric mixer at low speed 1 minute. Beat in milk, butter and vanilla. Beat in flour mixture until smooth. Pour batter into prepared pan. Bake 50 minutes. Immediately remove popovers to wire rack. Generously sprinkle powdered sugar over popovers. Serve immediately. *Makes 6 popovers*

*Chocolate Popovers*

# Sweet Potato Biscuits

2½ cups all-purpose flour
¼ cup packed brown sugar
1 tablespoon baking powder
¾ teaspoon salt
¾ teaspoon ground cinnamon
¼ teaspoon ground ginger
¼ teaspoon ground allspice
½ cup vegetable shortening
½ cup chopped pecans
¾ cup mashed canned sweet potatoes
½ cup milk

Preheat oven to 450°F. Combine flour, sugar, baking powder, salt, cinnamon, ginger and allspice in medium bowl. Cut in shortening with pastry blender or 2 knives until mixture resembles coarse crumbs. Stir in pecans.

Combine sweet potatoes and milk in separate medium bowl with wire whisk until smooth. Make well in center of dry ingredients. Add sweet potato mixture; stir until mixture forms soft dough that clings together and forms a ball.

*Sweet Potato Biscuits*

Turn out dough onto well-floured surface. Knead dough gently 10 to 12 times. Roll or pat dough to ½-inch thickness. Cut out dough with floured 2½-inch biscuit cutter. Place biscuits 2 inches apart on *ungreased* large baking sheet. Bake 12 to 14 minutes or until tops and bottoms are golden brown. Serve warm.        *Makes about 12 biscuits*

# Caribbean Christmas Ring

3 tablespoons shortening
2½ cups finely chopped walnuts, divided
1 cup all-purpose flour
½ cup whole wheat flour
1 teaspoon baking powder
1 teaspoon baking soda
1⅓ cups sugar
¾ cup butter, softened
3 eggs
1 cup sour cream or plain nonfat yogurt
1 ripe banana, mashed
2 tablespoons orange liqueur

**Orange Sugar Glaze**

1 cup powdered sugar, sifted
2 tablespoons orange juice

Thoroughly grease 10- to 12-cup microwavable Bundt pan with shortening; sprinkle with ½ cup chopped walnuts to coat evenly. Sift flours, baking powder and baking soda. In separate bowl, cream sugar and butter until fluffy; beat in eggs, one at a time. Stir sour cream, banana and liqueur into egg mixture. Fold in flour mixture; stir in remaining 2 cups walnuts. Spoon into prepared pan and place on top of inverted microwavable bowl in microwave, bringing cake up to center of oven. Microwave at MEDIUM (50% power) 10 minutes. Microwave at HIGH 5 to 7 minutes until wooden pick inserted in center comes out clean, turning twice. Let cake stand 15 minutes. Turn out onto serving plate. Let cool.

Mix powdered sugar and orange juice until smooth. Pour glaze evenly over cake and serve.        *Makes 20 to 24 servings*

*Favorite recipe from* **Walnut Marketing Board**

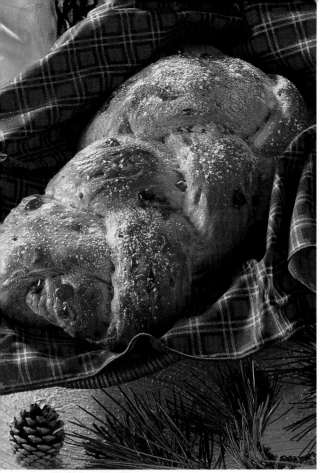

*Holiday Stollen*

# Holiday Stollen

1½ cups (3 sticks) unsalted butter,
    softened
4 egg yolks
½ cup granulated sugar
1 teaspoon salt
    Grated peel from 1 lemon
    Grated peel from 1 orange
1 teaspoon vanilla
2½ cups hot milk (120°F to 130°F)
8 to 8½ cups all-purpose flour, divided
2 packages active dry yeast
½ cup each golden raisins, candied
    orange peel, candied lemon peel,
    chopped candied red cherries,
    chopped candied green cherries,
    chopped almonds
1 egg, beaten
    Powdered sugar

In large mixer bowl, beat butter, egg yolks, granulated sugar, salt, lemon peel, orange peel and vanilla until light and fluffy. Slowly add milk; mix thoroughly. Add 2 cups flour and yeast; mix well. When mixture is smooth, add remaining flour, ½ cup at a time, until dough forms a ball that can be lifted out of bowl. Lightly flour work surface; knead dough until smooth and elastic, about 10 minutes. Mix raisins, candied orange and lemon peels, cherries and almonds in medium bowl; knead fruit mixture into dough.

Place dough in large greased bowl; cover with plastic wrap and let rise in warm place until doubled in bulk, about 1 hour.

Grease 2 large baking sheets. Turn dough out onto floured work surface. Divide dough in half. Place one half back into bowl; cover and set aside. Cut remaining half into thirds. Roll each third into 12-inch rope. Place on prepared baking sheet. Braid ropes together. Repeat procedure with remaining dough.

Brush beaten egg on braids. Let braids stand at room temperature until doubled in bulk, about 1 hour.

Preheat oven to 350°F. Bake braids until golden brown and sound hollow when tapped, about 45 minutes. Remove to wire rack to cool. Sprinkle with powdered sugar before serving.        *Makes 2 loaves*

# Teddy Bear Gift Bread

Teddy bear baking pan
1½ cups all-purpose flour
¾ cup granulated sugar
½ cup whole wheat flour
½ cup brown sugar
3 teaspoons baking powder
1 teaspoon pumpkin pie spice
½ teaspoon salt
½ teaspoon cinnamon
¼ teaspoon ginger
¼ teaspoon baking soda
1 egg, beaten
1 cup low fat milk
1½ teaspoons vegetable oil
Candy to decorate

Preheat oven to 350°F. Generously grease baking pan.

In food processor or large bowl, combine all dry ingredients. Add egg, milk and oil. Mix just until blended. Add to prepared pan. Bake 20 to 25 minutes or until knife inserted in center comes out clean. Cool completely in pan. Remove from pan onto flat surface.

Use candy to decorate. Try jelly beans for the eyes, a nonpareil for the nose, red shoestring licorice for the mouth, black shoestring licorice for a bowtie and jelly beans for buttons.            *Makes 1 bread*

**Microwave Directions:** Generously grease microwavable teddy bear baking pan. Combine ingredients as directed. Microwave 1 minute at MEDIUM (50% power). Turn. Microwave 2 minutes and 30 seconds at HIGH, turning halfway through cooking. Microwave 3 minutes more at MEDIUM or until knife inserted in center comes out clean. Cool completely in pan. Remove from pan onto flat surface.

*Favorite recipe from* **The Sugar Association, Inc.**

# Cinnamon-Date Scones

¼ cup sugar, divided
¼ teaspoon ground cinnamon
2 cups all-purpose flour
2½ teaspoons baking powder
½ teaspoon salt
5 tablespoons cold butter or margarine
½ cup chopped pitted dates
2 eggs
⅓ cup half-and-half or milk

Preheat oven to 425°F. Combine 2 tablespoons sugar and cinnamon in small bowl; set aside.

Combine flour, baking powder, salt and remaining 2 tablespoons sugar in medium bowl. Cut in butter with pastry blender until mixture resembles coarse crumbs. Stir in dates.

Beat eggs in another small bowl with fork. Add half-and-half; beat until well combined. Measure 1 tablespoon mixture into small cup; set aside. Stir remaining egg mixture into flour mixture. Stir until mixture forms soft dough that clings together and forms a ball.

Turn out dough onto well-floured surface. Knead dough gently 10 to 12 times. Roll out dough into 9 × 6-inch rectangle with floured rolling pin. Cut rectangle into 6 (3-inch) squares with floured sharp knife. Cut each square diagonally in half, making 12 triangles. Place triangles 2 inches apart on *ungreased* baking sheets. Brush triangles with reserved egg mixture; sprinkle with reserved sugar mixture. Bake 10 to 12 minutes or until golden brown. Immediately remove from baking sheets; cool on wire racks 10 minutes. Serve warm.

*Makes 12 scones*

## Sour Cream Coffee Cake with Chocolate and Walnuts

¾ cup butter or margarine, softened
1½ cups packed light brown sugar
 3 eggs
 2 teaspoons vanilla
 3 cups all-purpose flour
 2 teaspoons baking powder
 2 teaspoons ground cinnamon
1½ teaspoons baking soda
 ½ teaspoon ground nutmeg
 ¼ teaspoon salt
1½ cups dairy sour cream
 ½ cup semisweet chocolate chips
 ½ cup chopped walnuts
    Powdered sugar

Preheat oven to 350°F. Grease and flour 12-cup Bundt pan or 10-inch tube pan. Beat butter in large bowl with electric mixer at medium speed until creamy. Add brown sugar; beat until light and fluffy. Beat in eggs and vanilla until well blended. Combine flour, baking powder, cinnamon, baking soda, nutmeg and salt in large bowl; add to butter mixture at low speed alternately with sour cream, beginning and ending with flour mixture until well blended. Stir in chocolate and walnuts. Spoon into prepared pan.

Bake 45 to 50 minutes until wooden pick inserted in center comes out clean. Cool in pan 15 minutes. Remove from pan to wire rack; cool completely. Store tightly covered at room temperature. Sprinkle with powdered sugar before serving.

*Makes one 10-inch coffee cake*

*Whole Wheat Herbed Bread Wreath*

## Whole Wheat Herbed Bread Wreath

 4 cups all-purpose flour, divided
 2 packages active dry yeast
 2 tablespoons sugar
 4 teaspoons dried rosemary leaves, crushed
 1 tablespoon salt
2½ cups water
 2 tablespoons olive oil
 3 cups whole wheat flour, divided
 1 egg, beaten

Combine 2½ cups all-purpose flour, yeast, sugar, rosemary and salt in large bowl. Heat water until very warm (120°F to 130°F). Gradually add to flour mixture with oil until blended. Beat with electric mixer at medium speed 2 minutes. Add 1 cup whole wheat flour. Beat at high speed 2 minutes, scraping side of bowl occasionally. By hand, stir in enough of remaining flours to make a soft, sticky dough. Place in greased bowl; turn to grease top of dough. Cover with towel. Let rise in warm, draft-free place about 1½ hours or until doubled in volume.

Punch down dough. Turn out onto well-floured surface. Knead about 10 minutes or until smooth and elastic. Divide into thirds. Roll each piece to form 24-inch rope. Place on large greased cookie sheet. Braid ropes beginning at center and working toward ends. Seal edges. Shape into circle around greased 10-ounce *ovenproof* round bowl. Seal ends well. Cover with towel. Let rise in warm, draft-free place about 30 minutes or until doubled in volume.

Preheat oven to 450°F. Carefully brush wreath with egg. Bake 25 to 30 minutes until wreath sounds hollow when tapped and top is golden brown. Cool on cookie sheet 10 minutes. Carefully remove from cookie sheet and bowl; cool completely on wire rack. Store tightly wrapped in plastic wrap at room temperature.

*Makes one 12-inch wreath*

**Cranberry Oat Bread**

# Cranberry Oat Bread

¾ cup honey
⅓ cup vegetable oil
2 eggs
½ cup milk
2½ cups all-purpose flour
1 cup quick-cooking rolled oats
1 teaspoon baking soda
1 teaspoon baking powder
½ teaspoon salt
½ teaspoon ground cinnamon
2 cups fresh or frozen cranberries
1 cup chopped nuts

Combine honey, oil, eggs and milk in large bowl; mix well. Combine flour, oats, baking soda, baking powder, salt and cinnamon in medium bowl; mix well. Stir into honey mixture. Fold in cranberries and nuts. Spoon into two 8½ × 4½ × 2½-inch greased and floured loaf pans.

Bake in preheated 350°F oven 40 to 45 minutes or until wooden toothpick inserted near center comes out clean. Cool in pans on wire racks 15 minutes. Remove from pans; cool completely on wire racks.

*Makes 2 loaves*

*Favorite recipe from* **National Honey Board**

# Nutty Coconut Coffeecake

## Topping

    2 tablespoons butter, melted
    ⅔ cup flaked coconut
    ⅓ cup packed dark brown sugar
    ⅓ cup coarsely chopped nuts
        (macadamia, walnuts, almonds or
        pecans)
    2 tablespoons undiluted CARNATION®
        Evaporated Milk

## Batter

    2 cups all-purpose flour
    ½ cup packed brown sugar
    ¼ cup granulated sugar
    2 teaspoons baking powder
    ½ teaspoon salt
    ¼ cup butter
    1 cup undiluted CARNATION®
        Evaporated Milk
    1 egg
    1 teaspoon vanilla extract

**For Topping: Pour** 2 tablespoons butter into greased 9-inch round cake pan. Combine coconut, dark brown sugar, nuts and 2 tablespoons evaporated milk in small bowl. Sprinkle over butter.

**For Batter: Combine** flour, brown sugar, granulated sugar, baking powder and salt in bowl. Cut in ¼ cup butter. Beat 1 cup evaporated milk, egg and vanilla together in small bowl; stir into flour mixture just until blended. Pour over nut mixture.

**Bake** in preheated 350°F oven 30 to 35 minutes or until wooden pick inserted in center comes out clean. Cool for 10 minutes on wire rack. Invert onto serving plate.

*Makes one 9-inch round cake*

# Apple Cinnamon Coffee Ring

## Sweet Dough

    1 package active dry yeast
    ¼ cup warm water (110° to 115°F)
    1 cup milk
    ⅓ cup granulated sugar
    ⅓ cup butter or margarine
    ½ teaspoon salt
    2 eggs
    4½ to 5 cups all-purpose flour

## Apple Cinnamon Filling

    3 tablespoons butter
    1 cup thinly sliced Golden Delicious
        apples
    ½ cup chopped pecans
    ½ cup firmly packed brown sugar
    1 teaspoon ground cinnamon
    1 teaspoon grated orange peel

## Glaze

    ¾ cup confectioners' sugar
    1 tablespoon orange juice

1. To make Sweet Dough, in small bowl, dissolve yeast in water; set aside until foamy. Meanwhile, heat milk in small saucepan; add granulated sugar, ⅓ cup butter and salt. Cool to warm (110°F). In large bowl, combine milk mixture, yeast mixture, eggs and flour, stirring until soft

*Nutty Coconut Coffeecake*

dough forms. Turn out onto lightly floured surface and knead dough 5 minutes or until elastic. Wash, dry and oil mixing bowl; place dough in bowl. Cover and let rise in warm place about 1 hour.

2. Meanwhile, prepare Apple Cinnamon Filling. In skillet, melt 3 tablespoons butter; add apples and sauté until soft. Remove from heat and add pecans, brown sugar, cinnamon and orange peel, mixing well. Set aside.

3. When dough has risen, roll out on lightly floured surface to an 11 × 9-inch rectangle. Brush with remaining melted butter and top with apple mixture, leaving ½-inch border at edges. Fold dough in thirds lengthwise to make an 11 × 3-inch roll. Cut into 12 equal pieces. Arrange pieces, cut side up, in greased 9-inch springform pan, forming a ring. Cover and let rise 40 minutes.

4. Heat oven to 325°F. Bake coffee ring 30 to 35 minutes or until golden. Cool on wire rack. In small bowl, combine confectioners' sugar and orange juice, mixing to make glaze. Drizzle glaze over coffee ring and serve.                    *Makes 12 servings*

*Favorite recipe from* **Washington Apple Commission**

# Cherry Eggnog Quick Bread

2½ cups all-purpose flour
 ¾ cup sugar
 1 tablespoon baking powder
 ½ teaspoon ground nutmeg
1¼ cups prepared dairy eggnog
 6 tablespoons butter or margarine, melted
 2 eggs, slightly beaten
 1 teaspoon vanilla
 ½ cup chopped pecans
 ½ cup chopped candied red cherries

*Cherry Eggnog Quick Bread*

Preheat oven to 350°F. Grease 9 × 5-inch loaf pan.*

Combine flour, sugar, baking powder and nutmeg in large bowl. Stir eggnog, butter, eggs and vanilla in medium bowl until well blended. Add eggnog mixture to flour mixture. Mix just until all ingredients are moistened. Stir in pecans and cherries. Spoon into prepared pan.

Bake 45 to 50 minutes until wooden pick inserted in center comes out clean. Cool in pan 15 minutes. Remove from pan and cool completely on wire rack. Store tightly wrapped in plastic wrap at room temperature.                    *Makes 1 loaf*

*Bread may also be baked in three 5½ × 3-inch greased mini-loaf pans. Prepare batter as directed. Bake at 350°F for 35 to 40 minutes until wooden pick inserted in center comes out clean. Proceed as directed.

# Chocolate Walnut Coffee Rings

6½ to 7 cups all-purpose flour, divided
 ½ cup granulated sugar
1½ teaspoons salt
1½ teaspoons ground cinnamon
 2 packages active dry yeast
 1 cup (2 sticks) butter or margarine
 1 cup milk
 ½ cup water
 2 whole eggs
 2 egg yolks
 2 cups (12-ounce package) NESTLÉ® Toll
   House® Semi-Sweet Chocolate
   Morsels
 1 cup walnuts, chopped
 ⅓ cup firmly packed brown sugar
   Vegetable oil

## Glaze

 1 cup confectioners' sugar
 5 to 6 teaspoons milk
 ½ teaspoon vanilla
   Dash of ground cinnamon

In large mixer bowl, combine 2 cups flour, granulated sugar, salt, 1½ teaspoons cinnamon and yeast; set aside. In small saucepan, combine butter, 1 cup milk and water. Cook over medium heat just until very warm (120°F to 130°F), stirring occasionally. Gradually add milk mixture to flour mixture, beating until well blended. Beat in whole eggs, egg yolks and 1 cup flour. Stir in 2½ cups flour or enough to make stiff dough. Cover with waxed paper and towel; let stand at room temperature 20 minutes.

In small bowl, combine semi-sweet chocolate morsels, walnuts and brown sugar; set aside. Grease two large cookie sheets.

Sprinkle work surface with ½ cup flour. Turn dough onto surface; sprinkle dough with ½ cup flour. Knead 2 to 3 minutes until dough is smooth and elastic, adding additional flour if necessary to prevent sticking. Cut dough in half.

On floured surface, roll one dough half into 16 × 10-inch rectangle. Sprinkle with half of walnut mixture to within ½ inch of edges. Roll up jelly-roll style beginning at long side. Moisten edge with water; pinch seam together to seal. Place seam side down on prepared cookie sheet; shape into circle, pinching ends together to seal. With scissors or knife, cut dough at 1½-inch intervals almost to center of ring; twist ends up to expose filling. Brush with oil. Cover with plastic wrap.

Repeat with remaining dough and filling. Refrigerate 2 to 24 hours.

Preheat oven to 375°F. Remove dough from refrigerator. Carefully remove plastic wrap; let stand at room temperature 10 minutes.

Bake 25 to 30 minutes until golden brown. Cool completely on wire racks.

For Glaze, in small bowl, stir confectioners' sugar, 5 teaspoons milk, vanilla and dash of cinnamon until smooth. (Add additional 1 teaspoon milk if necessary for desired consistency.) Drizzle Glaze over rings.

*Makes 2 coffee rings*

*Chocolate Walnut Coffee Rings*

# Cranberry Raisin Nut Bread

1½ cups all-purpose fiour
¾ cup packed light brown sugar
1½ teaspoons baking powder
½ teaspoon baking soda
½ teaspoon ground cinnamon
½ teaspoon ground nutmeg
1 cup halved fresh or frozen cranberries
½ cup golden raisins
½ cup coarsely chopped pecans
1 tablespoon grated orange peel
2 eggs
¾ cup milk
3 tablespoons butter or margarine,
    melted
1 teaspoon vanilla
    Cranberry-Orange Spread
        (page 81), optional

Preheat oven to 350°F. Grease 8½ × 4½-inch loaf pan.

Combine flour, brown sugar, baking powder, baking soda, cinnamon and nutmeg in large bowl. Stir in cranberries, raisins, pecans and orange peel. Mix eggs, milk, butter and vanilla in small bowl until combined; stir into flour mixture just until moistened. Spoon into prepared pan.

Bake 55 to 60 minutes until wooden pick inserted in center comes out clean. Cool in pan 15 minutes. Remove from pan and cool completely on wire rack. Store tightly wrapped in plastic wrap at room temperature. Serve slices with Cranberry-Orange Spread, if desired.     *Makes 1 loaf*

*Cranberry Raisin Nut Bread*

## Cranberry-Orange Spread

1 container (12 ounces) cranberry-orange
    sauce
1 package (8 ounces) cream cheese,
    softened
1 package (3 ounces) cream cheese,
    softened
¾ cup chopped pecans

Combine cranberry-orange sauce and
cream cheese in small bowl. Stir with spoon
until blended. Stir in pecans. Store
refrigerated.    *Makes about 3 cups spread*

# Cinnamon Twists

*Cinnamon Twists*

### Rolls

1 package DUNCAN HINES® Bakery
    Style Cinnamon Swirl Muffin Mix,
    divided
2 cups all-purpose flour
1 package (¼ ounce) quick-rise yeast
1 egg, slightly beaten
1 cup hot water (120°F to 130°F)
2 tablespoons butter or margarine,
    melted
1 egg white, slightly beaten
1 teaspoon water

### Topping

1½ cups confectioners' sugar
2½ tablespoons milk

1. Grease 2 large baking sheets.

2. **For rolls,** combine Muffin Mix, flour and
yeast in large bowl; set aside.

3. Combine contents of swirl packet from
Mix, egg, hot water and melted butter in
medium bowl. Stir until thoroughly
blended. Pour into flour mixture; stir until

thoroughly blended. Invert onto well-
floured surface; let rest for 10 minutes.
Knead for 10 minutes or until smooth,
adding flour as necessary. Divide dough in
half. Cut and shape 24 small ropes from
each half. Braid 3 ropes to form small twist
and place on greased baking sheet.
Combine egg white and 1 teaspoon water
in small bowl. Brush each twist with egg
white mixture and sprinkle with contents of
topping packet from Mix. Allow twists to
rise 1 hour or until doubled in size.

4. Preheat oven to 375°F.

5. Bake at 375°F for 17 to 20 minutes or
until deep golden brown. Remove to
cooling racks.

6. **For topping,** combine confectioners'
sugar and milk in small bowl. Stir until
smooth. Drizzle over warm rolls. Serve
warm or cool completely.    *Makes 16 rolls*

# Apple Butter Spice Muffins

½ cup sugar
1 teaspoon ground cinnamon
¼ teaspoon ground nutmeg
⅛ teaspoon ground allspice
½ cup pecans or walnuts, chopped
2 cups all-purpose flour
2 teaspoons baking powder
¼ teaspoon salt
1 cup milk
¼ cup vegetable oil
1 egg
¼ cup apple butter

Preheat oven to 400°F. Grease or paper-line 12 (2½-inch) muffin cups.

Combine sugar, cinnamon, nutmeg and allspice in large bowl. Toss 2 tablespoons sugar mixture with pecans in small bowl; set aside. Add flour, baking powder and salt to remaining sugar mixture.

Combine milk, oil and egg in medium bowl. Stir into flour mixture just until moistened.

Spoon 1 tablespoon batter into each prepared muffin cup. Spoon 1 teaspoon apple butter into each cup. Spoon remaining batter evenly over apple butter. Sprinkle reserved pecan mixture over each muffin. Bake 20 to 25 minutes or until golden brown and wooden toothpick inserted in center comes out clean. Immediately remove from pan; cool on wire rack 10 minutes. Serve warm or cold.

*Makes 12 muffins*

# Spicy Cheese Bread

2 envelopes active dry yeast
1 teaspoon sugar
½ cup warm water (110°F)
8½ cups all-purpose flour, divided
3 cups (12 ounces) shredded Jarlsberg or Swiss cheese
2 tablespoons fresh chopped rosemary *or* 2 teaspoons dried rosemary
1 tablespoon salt
1 tablespoon TABASCO® pepper sauce
2 cups milk
4 large eggs

In small bowl stir yeast, sugar and warm water. Let stand 5 minutes until foamy.

Meanwhile, in large bowl, combine 8 cups flour, cheese, rosemary, salt and TABASCO sauce. In small saucepan over low heat, heat the milk until warm (120°F to 130°F). Stir into flour mixture. In medium bowl, lightly beat eggs; set aside 1 tablespoon beaten egg (to brush on dough later). Add eggs to flour mixture along with foamy yeast mixture; stir until mixture makes soft dough.

On lightly floured surface, knead dough 5 minutes or until smooth and elastic, kneading in remaining ½ cup flour. Shape dough into a ball and place in large greased bowl, turning dough over to grease the top. Cover with towel and let rise in warm place until doubled, about 1½ hours.

Grease two large cookie sheets. Punch down dough and divide in half. Cut each half in three strips and braid. Place each braid on cookie sheet. Cover and let rise in warm place until almost doubled, 30 minutes to 1 hour.

Preheat oven to 375°F. Brush braids with reserved egg. Bake about 45 minutes or until braids sound hollow when lightly tapped. Remove to wire racks to cool.

*Makes 2 braids*

*Apple Butter Spice Muffins*

# ENTRÉES

## Baked Country Cured Ham

1 country cured ham (10 to 14 pounds)
  Whole cloves
6 cups hot water
1 cup vinegar
1 cup apple cider
1 tablespoon Worcestershire sauce
2 bay leaves
1 cup molasses

Remove rind or skin from ham without removing the delicate layer of fat. Gently wash ham under running water. Pat dry and score fat into diamond shapes. Place a whole clove in each diamond. Insert meat thermometer into meaty part of ham, being careful not to touch fat or bone. Place ham, fat side up, in large roasting pan with cover. Use heavy duty aluminum foil to make a cover, if necessary. In large bowl, combine water, vinegar, cider and Worcestershire sauce; pour over ham. Place bay leaves in liquid. Bake at 325°F 20 minutes per pound or to an internal temperature of 160°F. Baste often during cooking time with molasses. Bake uncovered last 30 minutes. Garnish with fruit, if desired. Cool before slicing.

*Makes 20 to 25 servings*

*Favorite recipe from **National Pork Producers Council***

## Herbed Roast

1 (3-pound) beef top round roast
⅓ cup Dijon mustard
1½ teaspoons dried thyme leaves, crushed
1 teaspoon dried rosemary leaves, crushed
1 teaspoon LAWRY'S® Seasoned Pepper
1 teaspoon LAWRY'S® Garlic Powder with Parsley
½ teaspoon LAWRY'S® Seasoned Salt

Brush all sides of roast with mustard. In small bowl, combine remaining ingredients and sprinkle on top and sides of roast, pressing into meat. Place roast, fat side up, on rack in roasting pan. Roast in 325°F oven 50 minutes to 1 hour. Remove roast from oven. Let stand, covered, 15 minutes.

*Makes 6 to 8 servings*

**Presentation:** Slice thin and serve with roasted potato wedges and steamed vegetables.

*Herbed Roast*

*Chicken Pesto Mozzarella*

# Chicken Pesto Mozzarella

6 to 8 ounces uncooked linguine or
   corkscrew pasta
4 boneless skinless chicken breast
   halves
   Salt and black pepper (optional)
1 tablespoon olive oil
1 can (14½ ounces) DEL MONTE® Pasta
   Style Chunky Tomatoes
½ medium onion, chopped
⅓ cup sliced pitted ripe olives
4 teaspoons pesto sauce*
¼ cup (1 ounce) shredded skim milk
   mozzarella cheese
   Hot cooked pasta (optional)

*Available frozen or refrigerated at the
supermarket.

Cook pasta according to package
directions; drain. Meanwhile, season
chicken with salt and pepper, if desired. In
large skillet, brown chicken in oil over
medium-high heat. Add tomatoes, onion
and olives; bring to a boil. Reduce heat to
medium; cover and cook 8 minutes.
Remove cover; cook over medium-high
heat about 8 minutes or until chicken is no
longer pink in center. Spread 1 teaspoon
pesto over each chicken breast; top with
cheese. Cook, covered, until cheese melts.
Serve over pasta, if desired.

*Makes 4 servings*

**Prep Time:** 10 minutes
**Cook Time:** 25 minutes

# Pork Roast with Corn Bread & Oyster Stuffing

1 (5- to 7-pound) pork loin roast*
2 tablespoons butter or margarine
½ cup chopped onion
½ cup chopped celery
2 cloves garlic, minced
½ teaspoon fennel seeds, crushed
1 teaspoon TABASCO® pepper sauce
½ teaspoon salt
2 cups packaged corn bread stuffing mix
1 can (8 ounces) oysters, undrained,
   chopped

*Have butcher crack backbone of pork loin
roast.

Preheat oven to 325°F. Make a deep slit in
back of each chop on pork loin. In large
saucepan, melt butter; add onion, celery,
garlic and fennel seeds. Cook 5 minutes or
until vegetables are tender; stir in
TABASCO sauce and salt. Add stuffing
mix, oysters and oyster liquid; toss to mix
well.

Stuff corn bread mixture into slits in pork.
(Any leftover stuffing may be baked in
covered baking dish during last 30 minutes
of roasting.) Place meat in shallow roasting
pan. Cook 30 to 35 minutes per pound or
until meat thermometer inserted into meat
registers 170°F. Remove to heated serving
platter. Allow meat to stand 15 minutes
before serving.    *Makes 10 to 12 servings*

## Fruited Lamb Stew

1 pound boneless lamb
2 tablespoons all-purpose flour
½ teaspoon salt
   Dash ground red pepper
2 tablespoons vegetable oil
1 small leek, sliced
3 cups chicken broth
½ teaspoon grated fresh ginger
8 ounces peeled baby carrots
¾ cup cut-up mixed dried fruit (½ of
   8-ounce package)
½ cup frozen peas
   Black pepper
1⅓ cups hot cooked couscous
   Fresh chervil for garnish

Preheat oven to 350°F. Cut lamb into ¾-inch cubes.

In medium bowl, combine flour, salt and red pepper. Toss meat with flour mixture.

Heat oil in 5-quart ovenproof Dutch oven over medium-high heat. Add lamb; brown, stirring frequently. Add leek, chicken broth and ginger to Dutch oven. Bring to a boil over high heat. Cover; cook in oven 45 minutes.

Remove from oven; stir in carrots. Cover and cook in oven 30 minutes more or until meat and carrots are almost tender.

Stir fruit and peas into stew. Cover and cook 10 minutes. If necessary, skim off fat with large spoon. Season with black pepper to taste. Serve stew in bowls; top with couscous. Garnish, if desired.

*Makes 4 servings*

## Pâté-Stuffed Chicken Breasts with Sour Cream

1 (8-ounce) package JONES® Chub
   Braunschweiger
8 boneless skinless chicken breast
   halves
3 cups sour cream
1 can cream of celery soup
½ teaspoon curry powder
½ teaspoon paprika

Cut Braunschweiger chub in half crosswise and then cut each half in fourths lengthwise into 8 equal strips. Cut pocket in each chicken breast and insert 1 strip of Braunschweiger in each pocket. Place stuffed breasts in 13 × 9-inch baking pan.

Blend together sour cream, soup, curry powder and paprika; pour over meat. Cover tightly and bake at 275°F 2 hours. Uncover and continue baking 30 minutes. Serve with mashed potatoes or rice.

*Makes 8 servings*

*Fruited Lamb Stew*

*Clockwise from top left: Veal Fricassee, Cheesy Chicken Tetrazzini (page 89) and Country Captain Jarlsberg (page 89)*

# Veal Fricassee

3 pounds lean boneless veal, cut into
   1½-inch cubes
2 tablespoons oil
2 cups water
2 teaspoons paprika
1 teaspoon salt
¼ teaspoon black pepper
½ pound mushrooms, quartered
2 cups thickly sliced celery
½ cup half-and-half
3 tablespoons all-purpose flour
1 cup (4 ounces) shredded gjetost cheese
¼ cup chopped fresh parsley
   Hot cooked rice

In large saucepan or Dutch oven, brown veal in oil. Add water, paprika, salt and pepper. Cover and simmer 1 hour. Add vegetables and simmer 15 minutes, stirring occasionally.

Blend together half-and-half and flour. Stir into sauce. Cook and stir until thickened and smooth. Gradually stir in cheese. Add parsley. Serve over rice.

*Makes 6 to 8 servings*

*Favorite recipe from **Norseland, Inc.***

# Cheesy Chicken Tetrazzini

2 whole boneless skinless chicken breasts, cut into 1-inch pieces (about 1½ pounds)
2 tablespoons butter or margarine
1½ cups sliced mushrooms
1 small red bell pepper, cut into julienne strips
½ cup sliced green onions
¼ cup all-purpose flour
1¾ cups chicken broth
1 cup half-and-half
2 tablespoons dry sherry
½ teaspoon salt
¼ teaspoon black pepper
¼ teaspoon dried thyme leaves, crushed
1 package (8 ounces) tri-color rotelle pasta cooked until just tender and drained
¼ cup freshly grated Parmesan cheese
2 tablespoons chopped fresh parsley
1 cup (4 ounces) shredded nökkelost or Jarlsberg cheese

In large skillet, brown chicken in butter. Add mushrooms and brown. Add red pepper and green onions; cook 1 to 2 minutes, stirring occasionally. Stir in flour and cook 1 to 2 minutes until blended. Gradually blend in chicken broth, half-and-half and sherry. Cook, stirring, until thickened and smooth. Season with salt, black pepper and thyme. Toss with pasta, Parmesan cheese and parsley. Spoon into 1½-quart baking dish. Bake at 350°F 30 minutes. Top with cheese. Bake until cheese is melted. *Makes 6 servings*

*Favorite recipe from* **Norseland, Inc.**

# Country Captain Jarlsberg

3½ pounds chicken pieces
1 tablespoon butter or margarine
1 teaspoon salt
¼ teaspoon black pepper
1 small green bell pepper, cut into strips
1 small red bell pepper, cut into strips
2 tablespoons vegetable oil
1½ cups chicken broth, divided
1 large tomato, seeded and chopped
1 medium clove garlic, minced
1 teaspoon curry powder
¼ teaspoon ground cumin
1 tablespoon cornstarch
¼ cup toasted slivered almonds
¼ cup currants
1½ cups (6 ounces) shredded Jarlsberg cheese

Arrange chicken in shallow baking dish. Dot with butter. Season with salt and black pepper. Bake at 350°F 45 minutes or until tender.

Meanwhile, in large saucepan, cook and stir bell peppers in oil until just tender. Add 1¼ cups chicken broth, tomato, garlic, curry powder and cumin. Simmer 10 minutes, stirring occasionally.

Stir together cornstarch and remaining ¼ cup chicken broth. Gradually stir into sauce and cook, stirring, until mixture is thickened and smooth. Add almonds and currants. Pour over chicken. Top with cheese. Bake an additional 10 minutes. *Makes 6 servings*

*Favorite recipe from* **Norseland, Inc.**

# Prime Ribs of Beef à la Lawry's

1 (8-pound) prime rib roast
LAWRY'S® Seasoned Salt
Rock salt

Score fat on meat and rub generously with Seasoned Salt. Cover the bottom of roasting pan with rock salt 1 inch thick. Place roast directly on rock salt and roast, uncovered, in 500°F oven 8 minutes per pound for rare.

*Makes 8 servings*

**Presentation:** Garnish with watercress and spiced crab apples. Carve at tableside.

# Company Crab

1 pound blue crabmeat, fresh, frozen or
    pasteurized
1 can (15 ounces) artichoke hearts,
    drained
1 can (4 ounces) sliced mushrooms,
    drained
2 tablespoons butter or margarine
2½ tablespoons all-purpose flour
½ teaspoon salt
⅛ teaspoon ground red pepper
1 cup half-and-half
2 tablespoons dry sherry
2 tablespoons crushed corn flakes
1 tablespoon grated Parmesan cheese
    Paprika

Thaw crabmeat if frozen. Remove any pieces of shell or cartilage. Cut artichoke hearts in half. Place artichokes in well-greased, shallow 1½-quart casserole. Add crabmeat and mushrooms; cover and set aside.

Melt butter over medium heat in small saucepan. Stir in flour, salt and ground red pepper. Gradually stir in half-and-half.

Continue cooking until sauce thickens, stirring constantly. Stir in sherry. Pour sauce over crabmeat. Combine corn flakes and cheese in small bowl; sprinkle over casserole. Sprinkle with paprika. Bake in preheated 450°F oven 12 to 15 minutes or until bubbly.

*Makes 6 servings*

*Favorite recipe from* **Florida Department of Agriculture and Consumer Services**

# Chicken Sauté with Olive Sauce

1 tablespoon olive oil
4 boneless skinless chicken breast
    halves (about 1½ pounds)
¼ cup orange juice
2 tablespoons white wine vinegar
2 tablespoons sliced green olives
2 tablespoons chopped pimiento
2 tablespoons chopped fresh parsley
2 tablespoons sliced almonds
1 clove garlic, minced
1 tablespoon sliced pitted ripe olives
1 large green bell pepper, sliced into
    rings
1 Roma tomato, sliced
3 cups hot cooked rice

Heat oil in large skillet over medium-high heat until hot. Add chicken; cook 6 to 8 minutes on each side or until no longer pink in center. Remove chicken; keep warm. Reduce heat to medium; add orange juice, vinegar, green olives, pimiento, parsley, almonds, garlic and black olives to skillet. Cook and stir 2 to 3 minutes. To serve, arrange pepper and tomato over hot rice on serving platter. Top with chicken. Spoon sauce mixture over top.

*Makes 4 servings*

*Favorite recipe from* **National Broiler Council**

*Chicken Sauté with Olive Sauce*

## Hot & Spicy Arroz con Pollo

2 tablespoons vegetable oil
1 onion, chopped
1 can (16 ounces) whole tomatoes, undrained
1 can (13¾ ounces) chicken broth
1¼ cups long-grain rice
1 teaspoon salt
    Pinch saffron threads (optional)
1 jar (4 ounces) chopped pimientos, drained
½ cup sliced ripe pitted olives
1 package (10 ounces) frozen peas, thawed
1 package (12 ounces) PERDUE DONE IT!® hot & spicy chicken wings
    Water

In large deep skillet or Dutch oven over medium-high heat, heat oil. Add onion; cook and stir 3 to 5 minutes or until tender. Stir in tomatoes with liquid, broth, rice, salt and saffron; bring to a boil. Reduce heat to low; cover and simmer 10 minutes. Stir in pimientos, olives and peas; gently stir in chicken wings. Cover and cook 10 to 15 minutes or until all liquid is absorbed, rice is tender and chicken wings are heated through. Add ¼ to ½ cup water if mixture becomes too dry. Serve immediately.

*Makes 4 servings*

**Note:** For a larger crowd, recipe may be doubled using Perdue Done It!® hot & spicy chicken wings party pak (20 ounces). Double other ingredients and use a large Dutch oven.

*Shepherd's Pie*

## Shepherd's Pie

2 cups diced cooked leg of American lamb
2 cups prepared brown gravy
2 large potatoes, cubed and cooked
1 cup cooked peas
1 cup cooked carrot slices
3 green onions, sliced
1 clove garlic, minced
1 teaspoon black pepper
2 sheets prepared pie dough*

*Or, use mashed potatoes on top in place of second crust.

In large bowl, combine lamb, brown gravy, potatoes, peas, carrots, green onions, garlic and black pepper.

Place 1 sheet pie dough in pie plate; fill with lamb mixture. Cover with second sheet of pie dough. Crimp edges; cut slits in top to allow steam to escape.

Bake 30 minutes at 350°F or until pie crust is golden brown.     *Makes 4 to 6 servings*

*Favorite recipe from **American Lamb Council, Inc.***

# Sausage "Brunch" Casserole

6 slices white bread
2 (12-ounce) packages JONES®
    All-Natural Roll Sausage *or*
    1½ pounds JONES® ham, diced
1 can (8 ounces) chopped mushrooms
1 pound (16 ounces) Cheddar cheese,
    grated
6 eggs
2 cups light cream or milk

Tear bread into bite-sized pieces and place in 13 × 9-inch casserole dish. Crumble sausage; cook and drain. Spread over bread. Add mushrooms and top with Cheddar cheese.

Beat eggs; add light cream. Mix well and pour over casserole. Bake uncovered at 350°F 30 to 45 minutes.

*Makes 6 to 8 servings*

# Peach-Glazed Virginia Ham

### Glazed Ham

1 (8-pound) smoked Virginia ham
    (shank end)
½ cup peach preserves
1 tablespoon coarse-grained mustard
¾ teaspoon TABASCO® pepper sauce
⅛ teaspoon ground cloves

### Peach-Corn Piccalilli

3 large ripe peaches
1 tablespoon vegetable oil
1 medium red bell pepper, cored and
    diced
¼ cup sliced green onions
1 (17-ounce) can corn, drained
2 tablespoons brown sugar
2 tablespoons cider vinegar
1 teaspoon TABASCO® pepper sauce
¼ teaspoon salt

Preheat oven to 325°F. Remove skin from ham; trim off any excess fat. Score fat ¼ inch deep in 1-inch diamonds. Place ham, fat side up, in roasting pan. Insert meat thermometer into thickest part of ham, not touching the bone. Bake 1½ hours or until thermometer reaches 135°F.

Meanwhile, to make glaze, stir peach preserves, mustard, TABASCO sauce and cloves in small bowl. Remove ham from oven, maintaining temperature; brush with peach glaze. Bake 20 minutes longer or until thermometer reaches 140°F.

Meanwhile, to make Peach-Corn Piccalilli, cut peaches in half and remove pits. Chop two peach halves; set aside. Heat oil over medium heat in 2-quart saucepan. Add red pepper and green onions. Cook and stir 3 minutes. Add corn, brown sugar, vinegar, TABASCO sauce and salt. Heat to boiling and stir in chopped peaches. Reduce heat to low; cover and simmer 5 minutes until peaches are just tender.

To serve, arrange ham on a large platter. Fill remaining peach halves with Peach-Corn Piccalilli and arrange around ham on platter.

*Makes 10 to 12 servings*

*Peach-Glazed Virginia Ham*

# Quick Turkey Tortelloni

1 (10-ounce) package DI GIORNO® Alfredo or Four Cheese Sauce

1 (10-ounce) package frozen chopped broccoli, thawed, drained *or* 2 cups broccoli flowerets, cooked crisp-tender

½ pound cooked turkey, cut into strips (about 1½ cups)

1 (2½-ounce) jar sliced mushrooms, drained (optional)

1 (9-ounce) package DI GIORNO® Mushroom or Mozzarella Garlic Tortelloni, cooked, drained

Toasted sliced almonds (optional)

• Mix sauce, broccoli, turkey and mushrooms in saucepan; heat thoroughly.

• Serve over pasta. Top with almonds.

*Makes 3 to 4 servings*

**Prep Time:** 5 minutes
**Cook Time:** 10 minutes

*Quick Turkey Tortelloni*

# Pork Chops with Shallot Stuffing

6 tablespoons olive oil, divided

1½ cups minced shallots (about 1 pound)

1 rounded tablespoon dried oregano leaves *or* 4 tablespoons chopped fresh oregano

1 cup white wine or chicken broth

2 cups (8 ounces) shredded gjetost cheese

8 (¾- to 1-inch-thick) loin pork chops, with bone, pockets slit for bread stuffing (about 3½ to 4 pounds)

¼ cup all-purpose flour

In 2 tablespoons olive oil, cook shallots and oregano, stirring until softened. Add wine and cook 5 minutes or until liquid is reduced by half.

Remove from heat and stir in cheese. Stuff mixture into pockets of pork chops, dividing stuffing evenly. Secure with wooden picks, if desired. Dredge chops lightly in flour.

Heat 2 tablespoons oil in heavy skillet over medium-high heat. Add 4 chops and cook 4 minutes. Turn chops. Reduce heat to medium; cook 6 minutes or until done. Repeat with remaining 2 tablespoons oil and 4 chops.

Serve with noodles or brown rice, green beans and crusty rolls, if desired.

*Makes 8 servings*

*Favorite recipe from **Norseland, Inc.***

*Soleful Roulette*

# Apple Brandy Chicken

**3** whole boneless skinless chicken
   breasts, halved
**3** tablespoons butter
**⅓** cup Calvados or other apple brandy
**½** cup minced shallots
**6** tablespoons apple cider
**1** tablespoon minced fresh parsley
**⅛** teaspoon dried thyme leaves
   LAWRY'S® Seasoned Salt to taste
   LAWRY'S® Seasoned Pepper to taste
**6** tablespoons whipping cream

In large skillet, brown chicken in butter and
continue cooking, uncovered, over low heat
15 minutes. Add Calvados and ignite.
When flame subsides, add shallots, apple
cider, parsley, thyme, Seasoned Salt and
Seasoned Pepper. Bring to a boil. Reduce
heat; cover and simmer about 20 minutes or
until chicken is tender. Remove chicken to
serving platter and keep warm. Gradually
add cream to skillet; heat but do not boil.
Adjust seasoning and pour some of sauce
over chicken. Serve remaining sauce in
separate bowl.   *Makes 4 to 6 servings*

# Soleful Roulettes

**1** package (6¼ ounces) long-grain and
   wild rice mix
**1** package (3 ounces) cream cheese,
   softened
**2** tablespoons milk
**32** medium fresh spinach leaves
**4** sole fillets (about 1 pound)
   Salt and black pepper
**½** cup water
**¼** cup dry white wine

Cook rice mix according to package
directions. Place 2 cups cooked rice in large
bowl. Cover and refrigerate remaining rice
for another use. Combine cream cheese and
milk in medium bowl. Stir into rice; set
aside.

Wash spinach leaves in cold water. Repeat
several times with fresh cold water to
remove sand and grit. Place spinach in
heatproof bowl. Pour very hot water (not
boiling) over spinach to wilt leaves slightly.

Rinse sole and pat dry with paper towels.
Place fish on work surface. Sprinkle both
sides of each fillet with salt and pepper.
Cover each fillet with spinach leaves.
Divide rice mixture evenly and spread over
top of each spinach-lined fillet. To roll
fillets, begin with thin end of fillet; roll up
and secure with wooden toothpicks.

Combine water and wine in large, heavy
saucepan. Stand fillets upright on rolled
edges in saucepan; cover. Simmer over low
heat. *(Do not boil. This will cause fish to break
apart.)* Simmer 10 minutes or until fish
flakes easily when tested with fork.
*Makes 4 servings*

## Spicy-Sweet Brisket

4 to 5 pounds boneless beef brisket,
    well trimmed
1 pound fresh mushrooms, cleaned
3 carrots, cut into 2-inch pieces
3 onions, thinly sliced
1 rib celery, cut into 2-inch pieces
1 (26-ounce) jar NEWMAN'S OWN®
    Diavolo Sauce
½ cup water
½ cup packed brown sugar
1 tablespoon garlic powder
½ teaspoon black pepper

Preheat oven to 350°F. Brown meat in large
skillet. Remove to large Dutch oven. Add
vegetables to meat. In separate bowl, add
Diavolo Sauce, water and brown sugar; stir
and pour over meat. Sprinkle with garlic
powder and pepper.

Cover tightly with aluminum foil and bake
3 hours. Uncover and allow meat to brown
30 minutes.

Brisket should be made a day ahead of time
and refrigerated overnight to allow flavors
to blend. Thinly slice brisket across grain.

*Makes 12 servings*

## Dijon Chicken Elegant

4 whole boneless chicken breasts, split
⅓ cup GREY POUPON® Dijon or
    COUNTRY DIJON® Mustard
1 teaspoon dried dill weed *or*
    1 tablespoon chopped fresh dill
4 ounces Swiss cheese slices
2 frozen puff pastry sheets, thawed
1 egg white
1 tablespoon cold water

Preheat oven to 375°F. Place chicken, skin
side down, between 2 pieces of waxed
paper or plastic wrap; pound with flat side
of meat mallet or rolling pin to ½-inch
thickness. In small bowl, combine mustard
and dill; spread over chicken breasts. Top
each breast with cheese slice; trim to fit.
Roll up chicken lengthwise, jelly-roll style.

Roll out each pastry sheet into 12-inch
square; cut each into 4 (6-inch) squares. In
small dish, beat egg white and water; brush
edges of each square with egg mixture.
Place 1 chicken roll diagonally on each
square. Join 4 points of pastry over chicken;
seal seams. Place on ungreased baking
sheets. Brush with remaining egg mixture.
Bake 30 minutes or until chicken is no
longer pink in center. Serve immediately.

*Makes 8 servings*

## Jones® Ham Quiche

1 cup JONES® ham, cut into strips
⅓ cup red bell pepper, cut into strips
⅓ cup chopped asparagus
⅓ cup sliced leek
1 cup (4 ounces) shredded Swiss cheese
2 tablespoons all-purpose flour
2⅓ cups half-and-half or whipping cream
3 eggs, slightly beaten
1 (9-inch) pie crust

Combine ham, pepper, asparagus, leek,
cheese and flour; toss lightly. Gently mix
half-and-half and eggs. Gently fold ham
mixture into egg mixture.

Pour mixture into pastry-lined 9-inch
quiche dish or pie plate. Bake 10 minutes at
425°F; reduce heat to 325°F. Continue
baking 20 minutes or until done.

*Makes 6 to 8 servings*

*Jones® Ham Quiche*

*Prime Rib with Yorkshire Pudding and Horseradish Cream Sauce*

# Prime Rib with Yorkshire Pudding and Horseradish Cream Sauce

3 cloves garlic, minced
1 teaspoon freshly ground black pepper
  3-rib standing beef roast, trimmed*
    (about 6 to 7 pounds)
  Yorkshire Pudding (recipe follows)
  Horseradish Cream Sauce (page 99)

*Ask meat retailer to remove the chine bone for easier carving. Fat should be trimmed to ¼-inch thickness.

Preheat oven to 450°F. Combine garlic and pepper; rub over surfaces of roast. Place roast, bone side down (the bones take the place of a meat rack), in shallow roasting pan. Insert meat thermometer in thickest part of roast, not touching bone or fat. Roast 15 minutes.

*Reduce oven temperature to 325°F.* Roast 20 minutes per pound or until internal temperature is 120°F to 130°F for rare or 135°F to 145°F for medium.

Meanwhile, prepare Yorkshire Pudding and Horseradish Cream Sauce.

When roast has reached desired temperature, transfer to cutting board; tent with foil. Let stand in warm place 20 to 30 minutes to allow for easier carving. Temperature of roast will continue to rise about 10°F during stand time.

Reserve ¼ cup drippings from roasting pan. Immediately after roast has been removed from oven, increase oven temperature to 450°F.

While pudding is baking, carve roast. Serve with Yorkshire Pudding and Horseradish Cream Sauce.          *Makes 6 to 8 servings*

## Yorkshire Pudding

1 cup milk
2 eggs
½ teaspoon salt
1 cup all-purpose flour
¼ cup reserved drippings from roast or
    unsalted butter

Process milk, eggs and salt in food processor or blender 15 seconds. Add flour; process 2 minutes. Let batter stand in the blender at room temperature 30 minutes to 1 hour.

Place drippings in 9-inch square baking pan. Place in 450°F oven 5 minutes.

Process batter another 10 seconds; pour into hot drippings. *Do not stir.*

Immediately return pan to oven. Bake 20 minutes. *Reduce oven temperature to 350°F;* bake 10 minutes until pudding is golden brown and puffed. Cut into squares.

*Makes 6 to 8 servings*

## Horseradish Cream Sauce

1 cup heavy cream
⅓ cup prepared horseradish, undrained
2 teaspoons balsamic or red wine
vinegar
1 teaspoon dry mustard
¼ teaspoon sugar
⅛ teaspoon salt

Chill large bowl, beaters and cream before whipping. Pour cream into chilled bowl and beat with electric mixer at high speed until soft peaks form. *Do not overbeat.*

Combine horseradish, vinegar, mustard, sugar and salt in medium bowl.

Fold whipped cream into horseradish mixture until evenly incorporated. Cover and refrigerate at least 1 hour. Sauce may be made up to 8 hours before serving.

*Makes 1½ cups*

# Stuffed Chicken Breasts with Herbed Butter Sauce

8 boneless skinless chicken breast
halves (about 3 pounds)
½ teaspoon salt
¼ teaspoon black pepper
½ cup butter or margarine, softened
2 tablespoons chopped fresh parsley
½ teaspoon dried oregano leaves
½ teaspoon dried rosemary leaves,
crushed
½ teaspoon dried basil leaves
4 ounces Swiss cheese, cut into 8 strips
¼ cup all-purpose flour
1 egg, beaten
⅔ cup dry bread crumbs
½ cup dry white wine
1 teaspoon vegetable oil
½ cup red bell pepper strips
½ cup green bell pepper strips
4 cups cooked rice
1 tablespoon cornstarch
1 tablespoon cold water
Fresh oregano and rosemary sprigs for
garnish

Place chicken between plastic wrap; pound with meat mallet or rolling pin to ¼-inch thickness. Sprinkle chicken with salt and black pepper. Combine butter, parsley, oregano, rosemary and basil in small bowl. Place 1½ teaspoons herb butter on centers of chicken breast halves, reserving remaining herb butter. Place 1 cheese strip in center of each chicken breast half. Roll up chicken with cheese inside; tuck in ends. Roll in flour, then dip in egg. Coat with bread crumbs. Place in ungreased 13 × 9-inch baking dish; bake at 375°F 15 minutes. Stir wine into remaining herb butter in small saucepan; heat over low heat until butter melts. Pour over chicken; bake 20 minutes more. Heat oil in large skillet over medium heat until hot. Add bell peppers; cook and stir until crisp-tender. Add rice; toss lightly. Heat thoroughly. Serve chicken over rice. Pour pan drippings into small saucepan. Dissolve cornstarch in water. Add to drippings; heat until mixture boils and thickens, stirring constantly. Serve with chicken and rice. Garnish, if desired.

*Makes 8 servings*

*Favorite recipe from* **National Broiler Council**

*Stuffed Chicken Breast with Herbed Butter Sauce*

# Leg of Lamb with Apricot Stuffing

1 (6-ounce) package dried apricots, snipped
¼ cup apple juice
1½ cups chicken broth
¼ cup wild rice, rinsed and drained
½ cup long-grain rice
¼ cup chutney
¼ cup sliced green onions
2 teaspoons dried basil leaves
½ teaspoon lemon pepper
3 to 3½ pounds American leg of lamb, shank half, boned and butterflied
¼ teaspoon salt
¼ teaspoon black pepper

In small bowl, combine apricots and apple juice; cover and let stand 20 minutes, stirring occasionally. In saucepan, combine broth and wild rice. Bring to a boil. Reduce heat; cover and simmer 40 minutes. Add long-grain rice. Cover and simmer 15 minutes more. Remove from heat. Let stand, covered, 5 minutes. Stir in apricot mixture, chutney (cut up any large chutney pieces), green onions, basil and lemon pepper.

Trim any fat from lamb. With bone side up, pound meat with meat mallet to an even thickness. Sprinkle with salt and black pepper. Spread rice mixture over meat. Roll up, starting with narrow end; tie securely. Place roast on end, spiral side up, on rack in shallow roasting pan. Cover exposed rice mixture with foil. Roast at 325°F 1¾ hours for rare or to medium doneness (150° to 160°F). Remove from oven. Let stand about 10 minutes. Remove strings; cut into slices to serve. *Makes 12 servings*

*Favorite recipe from **American Lamb Council***

*Leg of Lamb with Apricot Stuffing*

## Turkey Loaf with Dried Tomatoes and Jarlsberg

2 cups dry white wine or chicken broth
12 pieces (about 1½ ounces) sun-dried
 tomatoes, chopped
1 (0.5-ounce) package dried mushrooms
1 tablespoon dried thyme leaves *or*
 3 tablespoons chopped fresh thyme
2½ pounds ground turkey
3 cups (12 ounces) shredded Jarlsberg
 Lite cheese, divided
1 cup flavored bread crumbs
½ cup toasted pine nuts or walnuts
 (optional)
2 egg whites

Bring wine, tomatoes, mushrooms and thyme to a boil; cover and simmer 10 minutes. Remove from heat and let stand 5 minutes. Allow to cool.

Preheat oven 350°F. Combine vegetable mixture, turkey, 2 to 2½ cups cheese, bread crumbs, pine nuts and egg whites. On baking sheet lined with foil and sprayed with nonstick cooking spray, form 12 × 5-inch loaf. (Recipe can be made ahead to this point and refrigerated. Bring to room temperature before baking.)

Bake 55 to 60 minutes. Sprinkle additional ½ cup cheese on top. Bake 8 to 10 minutes longer or until cheese is melted. Let stand 15 minutes before serving. Serve with baked potatoes and homemade red coleslaw or green salad.

*Makes 8 to 10 servings*

*Favorite recipe from* **Norseland, Inc.**

## Cornish Hens with Fruity Pilaf Stuffing

¼ cup Dijon mustard
2 tablespoons honey
¾ teaspoon curry powder, divided
1¼ cups water
1 can (5½ ounces) apricot nectar
2 tablespoons butter or margarine
½ cup chopped dried apricots
1 package LIPTON® Rice & Sauce–Pilaf
½ cup sliced green onions
¼ cup chopped walnuts
2 Cornish hens (1 to 1½ pounds each)

Preheat oven to 375°F. In small bowl, combine mustard, honey and ¼ teaspoon curry powder. Set aside.

In medium saucepan, bring water, nectar and butter to a boil. Add apricots; cook 1 minute. Stir in rice & pilaf sauce and remaining ½ teaspoon curry powder. Simmer, stirring occasionally, 10 minutes or until rice is tender. Stir in green onions and walnuts; let cool slightly. Stuff hens with rice mixture; secure cavities with skewers or wooden toothpicks. Tie legs together with wet kitchen string. Arrange hens on rack in roasting pan. Roast, basting occasionally with mustard mixture, 1 hour or until meat thermometer inserted in thickest part of thigh registers 185°F and legs move freely. Bake any remaining stuffing in covered casserole during last 20 minutes of cooking time.

*Makes 2 servings*

# Baked Stuffed Snapper

1 red snapper (1½ pounds)
2 cups hot cooked rice
1 can (4 ounces) sliced mushrooms, drained
½ cup diced water chestnuts
¼ cup thinly sliced green onions
¼ cup diced pimiento
2 tablespoons chopped fresh parsley
1 tablespoon grated lemon peel
½ teaspoon salt
⅛ teaspoon black pepper
   Nonstick cooking spray
1 tablespoon margarine, melted

Preheat oven to 400°F. Clean and butterfly fish. Combine rice, mushrooms, water chestnuts, onions, pimiento, parsley, lemon peel, salt and pepper; toss lightly. Fill cavity of fish with rice mixture; close with wooden toothpicks soaked in water. Place fish in 13 × 9-inch baking dish coated with cooking spray; brush fish with margarine. Wrap remaining rice in foil and bake in oven with fish. Bake 18 to 20 minutes or until fish flakes easily with fork.

*Makes 4 servings*

*Favorite recipe from* **USA Rice Council**

# Reuben Light Sausage Casserole

1 package JONES® All-Natural Light Breakfast Links
10 slices rye bread, cubed
1 small can sauerkraut, rinsed and drained
2 cups (8 ounces) low fat shredded cheese (such as mozzarella)
6 eggs, lightly beaten
3 cups skim milk
¼ teaspoon black pepper

Brown sausage over low heat, then drain and cool slightly. Cut crosswise into coin-sized pieces. Lightly butter 13 × 9-inch baking dish or spray with nonstick cooking spray. Arrange bread cubes in bottom of dish; sprinkle with sausage, sauerkraut and shredded cheese. Mix together eggs, milk and pepper until well blended. Pour over sausage mixture; cover and refrigerate overnight.

To bake, keep covered and place in preheated 350°F oven 45 minutes. Uncover and bake 10 minutes more, until puffed and bubbly. Serve hot. *Makes 10 servings*

# Head 'Em Off at the Pass White Chili

½ cup chopped onion
1 tablespoon olive oil
1½ cups cooked, chopped chicken *or* 2 (5-ounce) cans chicken
½ cup chicken broth
2 (15-ounce) cans cannellini beans, undrained
1 (11-ounce) jar NEWMAN'S OWN® Bandito Salsa, divided
1 teaspoon dried oregano leaves
½ teaspoon celery salt
1½ cups (6 ounces) shredded mozzarella cheese, divided

In 2-quart saucepan, cook and stir onion in olive oil until translucent. Stir in chicken, mixing thoroughly; add chicken broth. Stir in cannellini beans, ½ cup salsa, oregano and celery salt. Simmer over medium heat 10 minutes, gently stirring occasionally. Just before serving, stir in 1 cup mozzarella cheese. Divide among serving bowls and top each with a portion of remaining mozzarella and salsa. *Makes 4 servings*

*Baked Stuffed Snapper*

## Turkey Cordon Bleu with Wine Sauce

1 pound turkey breast cutlets (¼ inch thick)
4 slices (1 ounce each) lean ham
4 slices (1 ounce each) reduced fat Swiss cheese
2 tablespoons butter, divided
¼ cup dry white wine
2 tablespoons *plus* 1 cup 2% milk, divided
2 teaspoons cornstarch
½ teaspoon salt
  Chopped fresh dill or parsley (optional)

Top each cutlet with 1 slice of ham and cheese, trimming ham and cheese to fit turkey. Fold cutlets in half crosswise, pressing down firmly. In large nonstick skillet over medium-high heat, melt 1 tablespoon butter; add cutlets. Cook 3 to 4 minutes on each side or until no longer pink in center. Place cutlets on serving platter; cover to keep warm. Add wine to skillet; cook, scraping any browned bits from bottom of skillet, about 1 minute. Remove skillet from heat. In small bowl, combine 2 tablespoons milk and cornstarch until smooth; stir in remaining 1 cup milk. Add milk mixture and salt to skillet. Return skillet to heat; bring sauce to a boil. Reduce heat and simmer, stirring constantly, until sauce thickens. Stir in remaining 1 tablespoon butter. Cut each cutlet crosswise into slices, if desired. Pour sauce over cutlets. Serve hot. Garnish with dill, if desired. *Makes 4 servings*

*Favorite recipe from* **National Dairy Board**

*Turkey Cordon Bleu with Wine Sauce*

## Baked Ham with Sweet and Spicy Glaze

1 (8-pound) bone-in smoked half ham
  Sweet and Spicy Glaze (page 105)

Preheat oven to 325°F. Place ham, fat side up, on rack in roasting pan. Insert meat thermometer with bulb into thickest part of ham, not touching fat or bone. Roast ham in oven about 3 hours.

Prepare Sweet and Spicy Glaze. Remove ham from oven; *do not turn oven off.* Generously apply glaze to ham; return to oven 30 minutes longer or until meat thermometer registers internal temperature of 160°F. Remove ham from oven and reglaze. Let ham sit about 20 minutes before slicing. *Makes 8 to 10 servings*

## Sweet and Spicy Glaze

¾ cup packed brown sugar
⅓ cup cider vinegar
¼ cup golden raisins
1 can (8¾ ounces) sliced peaches in heavy syrup, drained, chopped, syrup reserved
1 tablespoon cornstarch
¼ cup orange juice
1 can (8¼ ounces) crushed pineapple in syrup, undrained
1 tablespoon grated orange peel
1 clove garlic, crushed
½ teaspoon crushed red pepper
½ teaspoon grated fresh ginger

Combine brown sugar, vinegar, raisins and peach syrup in medium saucepan. Bring to a boil over high heat; reduce heat to low and simmer 8 to 10 minutes. In small bowl, dissolve cornstarch in orange juice; add to brown sugar mixture. Add remaining ingredients; mix well. Cook over medium heat, stirring constantly, until mixture boils and thickens. Remove from heat.

*Makes about 2 cups*

**Baked Ham with Sweet and Spicy Glaze**

## Chicken Tandoori with Jarlsberg Lite

1 container (8 ounces) plain yogurt
1 tablespoon minced garlic (3 to 4 cloves)
2 teaspoons fresh thyme *or* 1 teaspoon dried thyme leaves
2 teaspoons paprika
2 teaspoons cumin
Pinch ground cloves (optional)
4 boneless skinless chicken breast halves, flattened to ¼-inch thickness (about 1½ pounds)
1 cup (4 ounces) shredded Jarlsberg Lite cheese
¼ cup seasoned bread crumbs

Combine yogurt, garlic, thyme, paprika, cumin and cloves in glass bowl. Add chicken, turning to coat evenly. Marinate in refrigerator 2 hours.

Remove chicken from marinade. Combine 4 tablespoons marinade with cheese and bread crumbs. Spread ¼ of the marinade mixture on each flattened chicken breast. Roll up from pointed end and secure with wooden picks.

Broil 10 to 12 inches from heat source, 12 to 15 minutes or until done, turning after 5 minutes.

Serve with brown rice and cucumbers in vinegar. Garnish with lemon slices and cilantro, if desired.      *Makes 4 servings*

*Favorite recipe from **Norseland, Inc.***

*Apricot Glazed Chicken*

Drain apricot halves, reserving syrup. Set aside 6 halves for garnish. Purée remaining apricots in food processor or blender with melted butter, seasoned salt, pepper and remaining 2 tablespoons honey. Brush over chicken. Pour wine and ¼ cup apricot syrup in bottom of pan. Cover chicken loosely with tented foil.

Roast at 350°F about 2 hours or until thermometer inserted in thigh registers 180°F and legs move freely. Baste occasionally with pan drippings to glaze. Remove foil during last 30 minutes of roasting. Serve chicken on platter garnished with clusters of grapes, apricot halves and fresh herbs, if desired.

*Makes 6 to 8 servings*

## Apricot Glazed Chicken

1 roasting chicken (4 to 5 pounds)
1 cup seedless red or green grapes
4 tablespoons honey, divided
1 can (16 ounces) apricot halves, divided
¼ cup butter or margarine, melted
2 teaspoons seasoned salt
¼ teaspoon black pepper
½ cup dry white wine or chicken broth
   Grape clusters and fresh herbs for
   garnish (optional)

Rinse chicken under cold water and pat dry with paper towels. Toss 1 cup grapes with 2 tablespoons honey in small bowl. Place grapes in body cavity. Tie legs close to body and fold wing tips back or secure with skewers or cotton string. Place chicken, breast side up, on rack in roasting pan.

## Lemon Fish Roll-Ups

1 cup cooked rice
1 (10-ounce) package frozen chopped
   broccoli, thawed and well drained
1 cup (4 ounces) shredded Cheddar
   cheese
⅓ cup margarine or butter, melted
⅓ cup REALEMON® Lemon Juice from
   Concentrate
½ teaspoon salt
¼ teaspoon pepper
8 fish fillets, fresh or frozen, thawed
   (about 2 pounds)
   Paprika

Preheat oven to 375°. In medium bowl, combine rice, broccoli and cheese. Combine margarine, ReaLemon® brand, salt and pepper; add ¼ cup margarine mixture to broccoli mixture. Place equal amounts of mixture on fillets; roll up. Place seam side down in shallow baking dish; pour remaining margarine mixture over roll-ups. Bake 20 minutes or until fish flakes with fork. Garnish with paprika. Refrigerate leftovers.

*Makes 8 servings*

## Shrimp in Angel Hair Pasta Casserole

1 tablespoon butter
2 eggs
1 cup half-and-half
1 cup plain yogurt
½ cup (2 ounces) shredded Swiss cheese
⅓ cup crumbled feta cheese
⅓ cup chopped fresh parsley
1 cup chopped fresh basil *or* 1 teaspoon dried basil leaves
1 teaspoon dried oregano leaves
1 package (9 ounces) uncooked fresh angel hair pasta
1 jar (16 ounces) mild, thick and chunky salsa
1 pound medium shrimp, peeled and deveined
½ cup (2 ounces) shredded Monterey Jack cheese
Snow peas for garnish
Plum tomatoes stuffed with cottage cheese for garnish

*Shrimp in Angel Hair Pasta Casserole*

Grease 12 × 8-inch pan with butter. Combine eggs, half-and-half, yogurt, Swiss cheese, feta cheese, parsley, basil and oregano in medium bowl; mix well. Spread ½ of the pasta on bottom of prepared pan. Cover with salsa. Add ½ of the shrimp. Cover with remaining pasta. Spread egg mixture over pasta and top with remaining shrimp. Sprinkle Monterey Jack cheese over top. Bake in preheated 350°F oven 30 minutes or until bubbly. Let stand 10 minutes. Garnish, if desired.

*Makes 6 servings*

*Favorite recipe from* **Southeast United Dairy Industry Association, Inc.**

## Creamy Ham and Noodle Dinner

¼ cup all-purpose flour
4 cups milk, divided
1½ teaspoons dill weed
1½ teaspoons Dijon mustard
2 tablespoons butter
1 cup diced carrots
1 teaspoon minced garlic
1 pound unsliced deli-style ham, cubed
1 package (16 ounces) wide egg noodles, cooked according to package directions
1 package (10 ounces) frozen peas, thawed

Combine flour and small amount of milk in small bowl; stir until smooth. Add remaining milk, dill and mustard; set aside. Melt butter in large saucepan over medium heat; add carrots and garlic. Cook, stirring occasionally, until carrots are crisp-tender. Stir in reserved milk mixture. Bring to a boil, stirring constantly, until mixture thickens; cook and stir 1 minute. Stir in ham, noodles and peas. Cook and stir until heated through. *Makes 8 servings*

*Favorite recipe from* **National Dairy Board**

## Roast Leg of Lamb

3 tablespoons coarse-grained mustard
2 cloves garlic, minced*
1½ teaspoons rosemary leaves, crushed
½ teaspoon freshly ground black pepper
1 leg of lamb, well-trimmed, boned,
   rolled and tied (about 4 pounds)
   Mint jelly (optional)

*For a more intense garlic flavor inside the meat, cut garlic into slivers. Cut small pockets at random intervals throughout roast with tip of sharp knife; insert garlic slivers.

Preheat oven to 400°F. Combine mustard, garlic, rosemary and pepper. Rub mustard mixture over surface of lamb. (At this point, lamb may be covered and refrigerated up to 24 hours before roasting.)

Place roast on meat rack in shallow foil-lined roasting pan. Insert meat thermometer into thickest part of roast.

Roast 15 minutes. *Reduce oven temperature to 325°F;* roast 20 minutes per pound until roast registers 150°F for medium.

Transfer roast to cutting board; tent with foil. Let stand 10 minutes before carving. Temperature of roast will continue to rise 5° to 10°F during stand time.

Cut strings with scissors; discard. Carve roast into thin slices. Serve with mint jelly, if desired.          *Makes 6 to 8 servings*

**Bone-in Roast Leg of Lamb:** Prepare as directed above, except roast a 5- to 6-pound bone-in leg of lamb 25 minutes per pound. After stand time, carve roast into thin slices with carving knife.

## Turkey Picadillo

2 tablespoons water
2 tablespoons instant minced onion
1 teaspoon instant minced garlic
1 pound ground turkey
1 teaspoon ground cumin
¾ teaspoon salt
½ teaspoon ground black pepper
¼ teaspoon ground red pepper
¼ teaspoon ground allspice
1 tablespoon olive oil
1 can (8 ounces) tomato sauce
¼ cup sliced pimiento-stuffed green
   olives
¼ cup golden or dark seedless raisins
12 large Boston or iceberg lettuce leaves
   Hot cooked rice

Combine water, onion and garlic in glass measure; let stand 10 minutes to soften. Combine turkey, cumin, salt, black pepper, red pepper and allspice in medium bowl. Heat oil until hot in large nonstick skillet. Add turkey mixture, onion mixture and remaining ingredients except lettuce; cook, stirring to break up turkey, 3 to 4 minutes or until most of the liquid has evaporated. To serve, place about ¼ cup turkey mixture in each lettuce leaf; roll up lettuce, folding sides to enclose filling. Serve with rice, if desired.

*Makes 4 servings*

*Favorite recipe from **American Spice Trade Association***

*Roast Leg of Lamb*

## Apricot-Stuffed Chicken

½ cup stuffing mix
¼ cup chopped green onions
2 tablespoons butter, melted
½ teaspoon ground ginger, divided
2 whole chicken breasts, boned
4 fresh California apricots, halved and
    pitted (about ½ pound)
½ cup apricot jam
1 tablespoon cider vinegar

In small bowl, combine stuffing mix, onions, butter and ¼ teaspoon ginger. Place chicken, skin side down, on tray or cutting board. Pound with flat side of meat mallet or rolling pin to flatten slightly.

Spoon half of the stuffing mixture in lengthwise strip along center of each chicken breast. Place 2 apricot halves on top of stuffing mixture. Roll up chicken lengthwise, jelly-roll style. Tie each chicken roll with string every 2 inches.

Prepare grill for direct cooking. Grill chicken, on covered grill, over medium-hot coals 15 minutes, turning once or twice.

*Apricot-Stuffed Chicken*

Combine apricot jam, vinegar and remaining ¼ teaspoon ginger in small bowl. Brush apricot mixture over chicken rolls; continue grilling 5 to 10 minutes or until chicken is no longer pink in center.

*Makes 4 servings*

*Favorite recipe from **California Apricot Advisory Board***

## Quick Shepherd's Pie

1 pound ground lean beef
½ cup seasoned dry bread crumbs
½ cup finely chopped onion
1 egg, lightly beaten
2 tablespoons water
1 tablespoon Worcestershire sauce
¼ teaspoon black pepper
2 cups hot prepared instant mashed
    potatoes
8 ounces sharp Cheddar cheese, cut into
    ¼-inch cubes
1 cup mixed frozen peas and carrots,
    cooked

Preheat oven to 400°F. Combine beef, bread crumbs, onion, egg, water, Worcestershire and pepper in large bowl; mix with hands until combined. Press meat mixture onto bottom and up side of 9-inch pie plate. Bake about 15 minutes or until meat is brown and firm. Remove from oven. Pour off excess fat; set aside. Reduce oven temperature to 350°F. Stir together potatoes, cheese and peas and carrots in large bowl. Spoon into reserved meat shell. Bake 10 to 15 minutes or until heated through and cheese begins to melt.

*Makes 4 to 6 servings*

*Favorite recipe from **National Dairy Board***

# Glazed Pork Tenderloin

2 whole well-trimmed pork tenderloins
  (about 1½ pounds)
½ cup currant jelly or canned jellied
  cranberry sauce
1 tablespoon bottled grated horseradish,
  drained
½ cup chicken broth
¼ cup Rhine or other sweet white wine
  Salt and black pepper to taste
  (optional)

Heat oven to 325°F. Place tenderloins on
meat rack in shallow roasting pan.

Combine jelly and horseradish in
microwavable dish or small saucepan. Heat
at HIGH 1 minute or over low heat on
rangetop until jelly is melted; stir well.

Brush half of mixture over tenderloins.

Roast 30 minutes; turn tenderloins over.
Brush with remaining jelly mixture.
Continue to roast 30 to 40 minutes,
depending on thickness of tenderloins or
until thermometer registers 165°F. Remove
thermometer and check temperature of
other tenderloin.

Transfer tenderloins to cutting board; tent
with foil. Let stand 10 minutes.

Remove meat rack from roasting pan. To
deglaze the pan, pour broth and wine into
pan. Place over burners and cook over
medium-high heat, stirring frequently
and scraping up any browned bits, 4 to 5
minutes or until sauce is reduced to ½ cup.

Strain sauce through a fine-mesh strainer;
season with salt and pepper.

Carve tenderloins into thin slices. Serve
with sauce.                    *Makes 6 servings*

*Glazed Pork Tenderloin*

# Coq au Vin

4 thin slices bacon, cut into ½-inch
  pieces
6 chicken thighs, skinned
¾ teaspoon dried thyme leaves, crushed
  Salt and black pepper (optional)
1 large onion, coarsely chopped
4 cloves garlic, minced
1 can (14½ ounces) DEL MONTE®
  Italian Style Stewed Tomatoes
½ pound small red potatoes, quartered
10 mushrooms, quartered
1½ cups dry red wine
  Chopped fresh parsley for garnish

In 4-quart heavy saucepan, cook bacon
until just beginning to brown. Sprinkle
chicken with thyme; season with salt and
pepper, if desired. Add chicken to pan;
brown over medium-high heat. Add onion
and garlic. Cook 2 minutes; drain. Add
tomatoes, potatoes, mushrooms and wine.
Cook, uncovered, over medium-high heat
about 25 minutes or until potatoes are
tender and sauce thickens, stirring
occasionally. Garnish, if desired.
                    *Makes 4 to 6 servings*

*Turkey Medallions with Cumberland Sauce*

# Country Ham Slices with Golden Sauce

1 can (20 ounces) DOLE® Pineapple
　Slices in Juice
½ cup packed brown sugar
⅓ cup prepared yellow mustard
2 teaspoons cornstarch
¼ teaspoon ground cloves
5 slices country ham (½ inch thick)
2 teaspoons margarine

•Drain pineapple; reserve juice. Combine reserved juice, brown sugar, mustard, cornstarch and cloves in medium saucepan; stir until blended. Cook, stirring constantly, until sauce boils and thickens. Add pineapple. Heat through.

•Cook and stir ham in margarine. Serve with sauce. *Makes 5 servings*

**Sauce Variations**

**Asian:** Add 3 tablespoons soy sauce and 1 teaspoon toasted sesame seeds.

**Indian:** Add 1 teaspoon curry powder.

**Southwestern:** Add 1 tablespoon chili powder.

# Turkey Medallions with Cumberland Sauce

2½ teaspoons margarine, divided
¼ cup currant jelly
1½ tablespoons port wine
2 teaspoons lemon juice
¾ teaspoon prepared mustard
　Dash of ground red pepper
1 teaspoon cornstarch
2 teaspoons cold water
1 turkey tenderloin (about ½ pound)
　Salt and black pepper
1 tablespoon olive oil
　Sour cream (optional)
　Fresh chives (optional)

1. In small saucepan over medium-high heat, melt 1 teaspoon margarine. Stir in jelly, wine, lemon juice, mustard and ground red pepper; heat until jelly is melted.

2. In small bowl, combine cornstarch and water. Stir into jelly mixture. Boil until mixture is thickened. Reduce heat; keep warm.

3. Cut tenderloin into ¾-inch-thick crosswise slices. Season with salt and black pepper.

4. In large skillet over medium-high heat, cook and stir medallions in oil and remaining 1½ teaspoons margarine about 2½ minutes per side or until no longer pink in center.

5. To serve, spoon a thin layer of sauce onto center of each plate. Arrange several turkey medallions over sauce. Garnish with sour cream and fresh chives, if desired.

*Makes 2 servings*

*Favorite recipe from **National Turkey Federation***

# Lemon-Ginger-Prune Veal Roll

1 cup chopped prunes
1 tablespoon finely shredded lemon
 peel
1 tablespoon grated fresh ginger
1 (4- to 4½-pound) boneless veal breast
½ teaspoon salt
2 teaspoons vegetable oil
⅔ cup Madeira
⅓ cup water
 Lemon wedges

In small bowl, combine prunes, lemon peel
and ginger. Unroll boneless veal breast;
trim fat. Sprinkle evenly with salt.
Distribute prune mixture evenly over
surface. Roll up veal breast; tie securely
with string. Heat oil in Dutch oven just
large enough to hold veal. Brown veal on
all sides. Drain excess fat, if necessary. Add
Madeira and water to pan; cover tightly.
Cook in 325°F oven until tender, 2 to 2½
hours. Transfer to warm platter; let stand.
Skim fat from pan juices. Place Dutch oven
over direct heat. Bring pan juices to a boil
and cook until reduced by half. Slice veal
roll; discard strings. Spoon sauce over each
serving. Garnish with lemon wedges.

*Makes 10 servings*

*Favorite recipe from* **National Live Stock & Meat Board**

*Lemon-Ginger-Prune Veal Roll*

# Golden Chicken Normandy Style

1 (2½- to 3-pound) chicken, cut up
 Salt and black pepper
¼ cup all-purpose flour
2 tablespoons butter or margarine
2 Golden Delicious apples (about
 12 ounces), cored and sliced
¾ cup half-and-half
⅓ cup dry white wine
1 tablespoon lemon juice
2 tablespoons chopped fresh parsley

Season chicken with salt and pepper; coat
in flour. In large skillet, melt butter. Brown
chicken on all sides; remove from skillet.
Add apples to skillet and brown lightly.
Arrange chicken and apples in shallow 2½-
quart baking dish. Bake at 350°F 20 minutes
or until chicken is tender. Reserve 2
tablespoons pan drippings in skillet.
Gradually add half-and-half to skillet; cook
and stir until thickened. Blend in wine and
lemon juice. Add salt and pepper to taste;
pour over chicken and apples. Sprinkle
with chopped parsley before serving.

*Makes 4 servings*

*Favorite recipe from* **Washington Apple Commission**

# Chesapeake Crab Strata

4 tablespoons butter or margarine
4 cups unseasoned croutons
2 cups (8 ounces) shredded Cheddar
    cheese
2 cups milk
8 eggs, beaten
½ teaspoon dry mustard
½ teaspoon seafood seasoning
    Salt and black pepper to taste
1 pound crabmeat, picked over to
    remove any shell
    Green and red bell pepper rings for
    garnish

Preheat oven to 325°F. Place butter in
11 × 7 × 1½-inch baking dish. Heat in oven
until melted, tilting to coat dish. Remove
dish from oven; spread croutons over
melted butter. Top with cheese; set aside.

Combine milk, eggs, dry mustard, seafood
seasoning, salt and black pepper in large
bowl; mix well. Pour egg mixture over
cheese in dish and sprinkle crabmeat on
top. Bake 50 minutes or until mixture is set.
Remove from oven and let stand about 10
minutes. Garnish, if desired.

*Makes 6 to 8 servings*

# Gourmet Chicken Bake

1 teaspoon seasoned salt
¼ teaspoon curry powder
¼ teaspoon dried savory leaves
¼ teaspoon white pepper
3 whole chicken breasts, cut into halves
1 cup buttermilk or sour milk*
2 packages (6 ounces each) seasoned
    long-grain and wild rice
5½ cups chicken broth, divided
1 pound fresh asparagus, trimmed
2 tablespoons slivered almonds, toasted
2 tablespoons chopped drained
    pimiento

*To sour milk, use 1 tablespoon lemon juice
or vinegar plus enough milk to equal 1 cup.
Stir; let stand 5 minutes before using.

Combine seasoned salt, curry powder,
savory and pepper in small bowl. Sprinkle
over chicken. Place chicken in large bowl;
pour buttermilk over chicken. Cover;
marinate in refrigerator overnight.

Preheat oven to 350°F. Drain chicken;
reserve buttermilk marinade. Arrange
chicken in single layer in 13 × 9-inch
baking pan. Pour buttermilk marinade over
chicken. Bake 1 hour or until chicken juices
run clear.

Cook rice according to package directions,
substituting 5 cups chicken broth for water.
Meanwhile, cut asparagus 3 inches from
tip, then cut remaining stalk into 1-inch
pieces. Place asparagus tips and stalk
pieces in remaining ½ cup broth in small
saucepan. Cover and cook over medium
heat 15 minutes or until tender. Set aside;
do not drain.

Remove chicken from baking pan. Remove
asparagus tips from saucepan; set aside.
Combine rice, asparagus stalk pieces and
broth from asparagus in baking pan.
Arrange chicken over rice mixture; place
asparagus tips around chicken. Sprinkle
with almonds and pimiento. Return to
oven; bake about 10 minutes or until heated
through.
*Makes 6 servings*

*Favorite recipe from **National Broiler Council***

*Gourmet Chicken Bake*

# French Toast Strata Pie

½ pound bulk country sausage
1 all-purpose apple, cored, pared and thinly sliced
5 eggs
2 cups BORDEN® or MEADOW GOLD® Milk
⅓ cup CARY'S®, MAPLE ORCHARDS® or MACDONALD'S™ Pure Maple Syrup
½ teaspoon ground nutmeg
½ (1-pound) loaf French or Italian bread, cut into ½-inch slices
Additional CARY'S®, MAPLE ORCHARDS® or MACDONALD'S™ Pure Maple Syrup

In large skillet, thoroughly cook sausage. Remove sausage from skillet; drain and crumble. Add apple slices to skillet; over medium heat, cook covered 3 minutes. In medium bowl, beat eggs; add milk, ⅓ cup pure maple syrup and nutmeg. Mix well. In buttered 10-inch pie plate, arrange about three-fourths of the bread slices. Top with sausage, apple and remaining bread slices. Pour milk mixture evenly over top. Cover; refrigerate overnight. Bake uncovered at 350° for 55 to 60 minutes or until set and golden. Serve immediately with additional pure maple syrup. Refrigerate leftovers.

*Makes one 10-inch pie*

*French Toast Strata Pie*

# Holiday Turkey with Herbed Corn Bread Dressing

1 pound bulk pork sausage
1½ cups chopped onions
1 cup chopped celery
6 cups coarsely crumbled corn bread (two 8-inch squares)
¼ cup dry sherry
⅓ cup light cream
1 teaspoon dried thyme leaves
1 teaspoon dried basil leaves
1 teaspoon dried oregano leaves
½ teaspoon LAWRY'S® Garlic Powder with Parsley
1 (14- to 16-pound) turkey, thawed
LAWRY'S® Seasoned Salt

In large skillet, brown sausage until crumbly; add onions and celery. Cook and stir 5 minutes. Blend in corn bread, sherry, cream, thyme, basil, oregano and Garlic Powder with Parsley. Rub cavities and outside of turkey with Seasoned Salt, using about ¼ teaspoon Seasoned Salt per pound of turkey. Pack dressing loosely into turkey cavities. Skewer openings closed. Insert meat thermometer in thickest part of breast away from bones. Place turkey, breast side up, on rack in roasting pan. Roast, uncovered, in 325°F oven 4 to 5 hours, basting frequently with melted butter or cover with foil and place on hot grill 16 to 18 minutes per pound. When internal temperature reaches 185°F, remove and let stand 20 minutes before carving. (Tent loosely with aluminum foil if turkey becomes too brown, being careful not to touch meat thermometer.)

*Makes 10 servings*

**Presentation:** Garnish with lemon leaves and whole fresh cranberries.

## Orange Roughy in Parchment Hearts

Parchment paper or foil
4 orange roughy fillets (about
    1½ pounds)
Butter
8 ounces fresh asparagus, steamed and
    diagonally cut into 2-inch pieces
1 yellow bell pepper, cut into
    16 julienne strips
1 red bell pepper, cut into 16 julienne
    strips
1 medium carrot, cut into julienne strips
¼ cup dry white wine
3 tablespoons Dijon mustard
2 tablespoons lemon juice
1 teaspoon dried marjoram leaves
¼ teaspoon black pepper

Preheat oven to 375°F. Cut parchment paper into 4 (12-inch) squares. Fold each square in half diagonally and cut into half heart shape.

Rinse orange roughy and pat dry with paper towels.

Lightly butter inside of each heart. Place 1 piece of fish on 1 side of each heart.

Divide asparagus over fish. Place 4 strips each yellow and red bell pepper over fish, then divide carrot strips over fish.

Combine wine, mustard, lemon juice, marjoram and black pepper in small bowl. Divide wine mixture over fish.

Fold parchment hearts in half. Beginning at top of heart, fold the edges together, 2 inches at a time. At tip of heart, fold paper up and over.

Place hearts on large baking sheet. Bake 20 to 25 minutes or until fish flakes easily when tested with fork. To serve, place hearts on plates and cut an "X" through top layer of parchment, folding points back to display contents.     *Makes 4 servings*

*Orange Roughy in Parchment Heart*

## Holiday Beef Rib Roast

1 (3- to 4-rib) beef rib roast, well
    trimmed (about 6 to 8 pounds)

Place roast, fat side up, on rack in roasting pan. Insert meat thermometer so bulb is centered in the thickest part, not touching fat or bone. Do not add water. Do not cover. Roast in 325°F oven to desired doneness, 23 to 25 minutes per pound for rare or 27 to 30 minutes per pound for medium. Remove roast when meat thermometer registers 135°F for rare or 155°F for medium. Allow roast to stand tented with aluminum foil 15 to 20 minutes. Roast will continue to rise about 5°F in temperature to reach 140°F for rare or 160°F for medium.
*Makes 10 to 12 servings*

*Favorite recipe from* **National Live Stock & Meat Board**

*Chicken Wellington*

# Chicken Wellington

6 large boneless skinless chicken breast
    halves (about 6 ounces each)
¾ teaspoon salt, divided
¼ teaspoon freshly ground black pepper,
    divided
¼ cup butter or margarine, divided
12 ounces mushrooms (button or crimini)
½ cup finely chopped shallots
2 tablespoons port wine or cognac
1 tablespoon fresh thyme leaves
1 package (17¼ ounces) frozen puff
    pastry, thawed
1 egg, separated
1 tablespoon country-style Dijon
    mustard
1 teaspoon milk

Sprinkle chicken with ¼ teaspoon salt and
⅛ teaspoon pepper. Melt 2 tablespoons
butter in large skillet over medium heat
until foamy. Cook 3 chicken breast halves
3 minutes; turn over. Cook 3 more minutes

until golden brown. (Chicken will be
almost cooked through but center will be
springy to the touch.) Transfer to plate;
cook remaining 3 chicken breast halves. Set
aside to cool slightly.

Process mushrooms in food processor until
finely chopped.

Melt remaining 2 tablespoons butter in
same skillet over medium heat until foamy.
Add mushrooms and shallots. Cook and
stir about 5 minutes or until mushrooms
release their liquid. Add wine, thyme,
remaining ½ teaspoon salt and ⅛ teaspoon
pepper and any juices that have
accumulated around chicken; simmer 10 to
12 minutes or until liquid evaporates,
stirring frequently. Cool.

Roll out each pastry sheet to 15 × 12-inch
rectangle on lightly floured surface with
rolling pin. Cut each rectangle into three
12 × 5-inch rectangles, creating 6 rectangles.
If desired, cut off small amount of pastry
from corners of each rectangle to use as
decoration.

Beat egg white in small bowl; brush over
pastry rectangles. Place 1 cooled chicken
breast on one side of each pastry rectangle.
Spread ½ teaspoon mustard over each
chicken breast, then spread each with
¼ cup cooled mushroom mixture. Fold
opposite half of pastry rectangle over
chicken. Fold edge of bottom dough over
top, pressing edges together to seal. Place
on ungreased baking sheet or jelly-roll pan.

Beat egg yolk with milk. Brush over surface
of pastry; decorate with pastry scraps, if
desired. Brush decorations with egg yolk
mixture. Cover loosely with plastic wrap.
Refrigerate until cold 1 to 4 hours before
baking.

Preheat oven to 400°F. Remove plastic
wrap. Bake Chicken Wellington 25 to 30
minutes or until deep golden brown and
temperature of chicken reaches 160°F.
Garnish, if desired. *Makes 6 servings*

# Rosemary Chicken with Asparagus Lemon Rice

¼ cup dry white wine
3 cloves garlic, minced
1 tablespoon finely chopped fresh rosemary
1 tablespoon vegetable oil
1 tablespoon low sodium soy sauce
1 teaspoon sugar
½ teaspoon black pepper
6 boneless skinless chicken breast halves (about 2¼ pounds)
  Nonstick cooking spray
3 cups cooked rice (cooked in low sodium chicken broth)
10 spears asparagus, blanched and cut into 1-inch pieces (¼ pound)
1 teaspoon grated lemon peel
1 teaspoon lemon pepper seasoning
½ teaspoon salt
  Lemon slices for garnish
  Fresh rosemary sprigs for garnish

Combine wine, garlic, rosemary, oil, soy sauce, sugar and black pepper in large shallow glass dish. Add chicken, turning to coat; cover and marinate in refrigerator at least 1 hour. Heat large skillet coated with cooking spray over medium-high heat until hot. Add chicken and marinade; cook 7 minutes on each side or until brown and no longer pink in center. Combine rice, asparagus, lemon peel, lemon pepper and salt in large bowl. To serve, spoon rice on individual serving plates. Cut chicken into strips; fan over rice. Garnish, if desired.

*Makes 6 servings*

*Favorite recipe from* **National Broiler Council**

# Salmon on a Bed of Leeks

3 to 4 leeks
2 teaspoons butter or margarine
½ cup dry white wine or vermouth
2 salmon fillets (6 to 8 ounces)
  Salt and black pepper to taste
2 tablespoons grated Gruyère cheese

Trim green tops and root ends from leeks; cut lengthwise into quarters, leaving ⅓ inch together at root end. Separate sections. Rinse under cold running water; drain well.

In 10-inch skillet, melt butter over medium heat. Add leeks; cook 2 to 3 minutes, stirring often, until leeks are wilted. Stir in wine; arrange salmon on leeks. Sprinkle with salt and pepper. Reduce heat to low. Cover; cook 5 minutes. Sprinkle cheese over salmon. Cover; cook another 3 to 5 minutes or until salmon is firm and opaque around edges and cheese is melted. Transfer to warm serving plate; serve immediately.       *Makes 2 servings*

*Favorite recipe from* **National Fisheries Institute**

*Salmon on a Bed of Leeks*

# Turkey-Olive Ragout en Crust

½ **pound boneless white or dark turkey meat, cut into 1-inch cubes**
1 **clove garlic, minced**
1 **teaspoon vegetable oil**
¼ **cup small whole frozen onions (about 10), thawed**
1 **medium red potato, skin on, cut into ½-inch cubes**
½ **cup reduced-sodium chicken broth or turkey broth**
½ **teaspoon dried parsley flakes**
⅛ **teaspoon dried thyme leaves**
1 **small bay leaf**
10 **frozen snow peas, thawed**
8 **whole, small pitted ripe olives**
1 **can (4 ounces) refrigerator crescent rolls**
½ **teaspoon dried dill weed**

1. Preheat oven to 375°F.

2. In medium skillet over medium heat, cook and stir turkey and garlic in oil 5 to 6 minutes or until turkey is no longer pink in center; remove and set aside. Add onions to skillet; cook and stir until lightly browned. Add potato, broth, parsley, thyme and bay leaf. Bring mixture to a boil. Reduce heat; cover and simmer 10 minutes or until potato is tender. Remove bay leaf; discard.

3. Add turkey to potato mixture. Stir in snow peas and olives. Divide mixture between 2 (1¾-cup) casserole dishes.

4. Divide crescent rolls into 2 rectangles; press perforations together to seal. If necessary, roll out each rectangle to make dough large enough to cover top of casseroles. Sprinkle dough with dill weed, pressing lightly into dough. Cut small decorative shape from center of each dough piece; discard or place on baking sheet and bake in oven with casseroles. Place dough over casseroles; trim dough to fit. Press dough to edges of each casserole to seal. Bake 7 to 8 minutes or until dough is golden brown. *Makes 2 servings*

**Lattice Crust:** With a pastry wheel or knife, cut each dough rectangle into 6 lengthwise strips. Arrange strips, lattice-fashion, over each casserole; trim dough to fit. Press ends of dough to edges of each casserole to seal.

**Note:** For a more golden crust, brush top of dough with beaten egg yolk before baking.

*Favorite recipe from **National Turkey Federation***

# Orange Glazed Chicken and Squash Bake

4 **broiler-fryer chicken legs**
½ **teaspoon salt**
¼ **teaspoon black pepper**
2 **small acorn squash, quartered lengthwise**
½ **cup orange marmalade**
1 **tablespoon lemon juice**
1 **teaspoon grated lemon peel**
¼ **teaspoon ground nutmeg**
¼ **teaspoon ground cinnamon**

Place chicken in single layer on wire rack in large shallow baking pan. Sprinkle salt and pepper over chicken. Place squash in medium baking dish. Add water to cover bottom of dish; cover with foil.

Bake chicken and squash in 375°F oven 25 minutes. Mix marmalade, lemon juice, lemon peel, nutmeg and cinnamon in small bowl. Brush marmalade mixture over chicken. Bake 20 minutes longer. Remove cover from squash. Brush remaining marmalade mixture over chicken and squash. Bake 10 minutes more or until chicken and squash are fork-tender.

*Makes 4 servings*

*Favorite recipe from **Delmarva Poultry Industry, Inc.***

*Turkey-Olive Ragout en Crust*

# Pork and Vegetable Stew with Noodles

1 pound lean boneless pork
2 tablespoons vegetable oil
3 cups beef broth
3 tablespoons chopped fresh parsley, divided
1 can (14½ ounces) stewed tomatoes
1 large carrot, sliced
3 green onions, sliced
2 teaspoons Dijon mustard
¼ teaspoon rubbed sage
⅛ teaspoon black pepper
3 cups uncooked noodles
1 teaspoon butter or margarine
2 tablespoons all-purpose flour
⅓ cup cold water
 Apples and fresh parsley for garnish

Cut pork into ¾-inch cubes. Heat oil in large saucepan over medium-high heat. Add meat; brown, stirring frequently. Carefully add beef broth. Stir in 1 tablespoon chopped parsley, tomatoes, carrot, onions, mustard, sage and pepper. Bring to a boil over high heat. Reduce heat to medium-low; simmer, uncovered, 30 minutes.

Meanwhile, cook noodles according to package directions; drain. Add reserved 2 tablespoons chopped parsley and butter; toss lightly. Keep warm until ready to serve.

Stir flour into cold water in cup until smooth. Stir into stew. Cook and stir over medium heat until slightly thickened. To serve, spoon noodles onto each plate. Ladle stew over noodles. Garnish, if desired.

*Makes 4 servings*

*Pork and Vegetable Stew with Noodles*

# Trout with Apples and Toasted Hazelnuts

⅓ cup whole hazelnuts or walnuts
5 tablespoons butter or margarine, divided
1 large Red Delicious apple, cored and cut into 16 wedges
2 butterflied rainbow trout fillets (about 8 ounces each)
 Salt and black pepper
3 tablespoons all-purpose flour
1 tablespoon lemon juice
1 tablespoon snipped fresh chives
 Lemon slices and fresh chives for garnish

Preheat oven to 350°F. To toast hazelnuts, spread in single layer on baking sheet. Bake 8 to 10 minutes or until skins split. Wrap hazelnuts in kitchen towel; set aside 5 minutes to cool slightly. Rub nuts in towel to remove as much of the papery skins as possible. Place hazelnuts in food processor. Process until coarsely chopped; set aside.

Melt 3 tablespoons butter in medium skillet over medium-high heat. Add apple; cook 4 to 5 minutes or until crisp-tender. Remove apple from skillet with slotted spoon; set aside.

Rinse trout and pat dry with paper towels. Sprinkle fish with salt and pepper, then coat in flour. Place fish in skillet. Cook 4 minutes or until golden and fish flakes easily when tested with fork, turning halfway through cooking time. Return apple to skillet. Reduce heat to low and keep warm. Melt remaining 2 tablespoons butter in small saucepan over low heat. Stir in lemon juice, chives and hazelnuts. Drizzle fish and apple with hazelnut mixture. Garnish, if desired.

*Makes 2 servings*

**Trout with Apples and Toasted Hazelnuts**

# Chicken Royale

**2 boneless skinless chicken breasts, halved**
**1 package (4 ounces) Boursin or other herb-flavored cheese, quartered**
**½ cup English walnuts, finely chopped**
**4 large spinach leaves, steamed slightly**
**½ teaspoon salt**
**½ teaspoon black pepper**
**½ cup dry white wine**
**½ cup bottled reduced calorie raspberry vinaigrette dressing***
**2 tablespoons margarine**
  **Hot cooked rice**

*If raspberry vinaigrette dressing is not available, substitute ¼ cup bottled reduced calorie red wine vinegar and oil dressing and ¼ cup seedless raspberry jam. Omit margarine.

Pound chicken breasts to ¼-inch thickness with flat side of meat mallet or rolling pin. Roll cheese in walnuts. Place 1 spinach leaf on each chicken breast; top with a cheese quarter. Fold chicken around spinach and cheese to form a mound. Sprinkle salt and pepper over chicken. Place chicken in baking pan. Cover; bake in 350°F oven 30 minutes or until chicken is fork-tender.

Mix wine and dressing in small skillet. Cook over medium heat until sauce is reduced by half; stir in margarine. Pour sauce over chicken. Serve with rice.

*Makes 4 servings*

*Favorite recipe from **Delmarva Poultry Industry, Inc.***

# Chicken Phyllo Wraps

Nonstick cooking spray
1 pound ground chicken
1 cup chopped fresh mushrooms
1 medium onion, chopped
3 cups cooked rice (cooked without salt and fat)
1 cup nonfat low salt ricotta cheese
1 package (10 ounces) chopped spinach, thawed and well drained
1 can (2¼ ounces) sliced black olives, drained
¼ cup pine nuts, toasted*
2 cloves garlic, minced
1 teaspoon dried oregano leaves
1 teaspoon lemon pepper
12 phyllo dough sheets

*To toast nuts, place on baking sheet. Bake at 350°F 5 to 7 minutes or until lightly browned.

Coat large skillet with cooking spray; heat over medium-high heat until hot. Add chicken, mushrooms and onion; cook and stir 2 to 4 minutes or until chicken is no longer pink and vegetables are tender. Reduce heat to medium. Add rice, ricotta cheese, spinach, olives, nuts, garlic, oregano and lemon pepper; cook and stir 3 to 4 minutes until well blended and thoroughly heated. Working with 1 phyllo sheet at a time, spray 1 sheet with cooking spray; fold sheet in half lengthwise. Place ¾ to 1 cup rice mixture on one end of phyllo strip. Fold left bottom corner over mixture, forming a triangle. Continue folding back and forth into triangles until end of strip. Repeat with remaining phyllo sheets and rice mixture. Place triangle, seam side down, on baking sheets coated with cooking spray. Coat top of each triangle with cooking spray. Bake at 400°F 15 to 20 minutes or until golden brown. Serve immediately. *Makes 12 servings*

*Favorite recipe from* **USA Rice Council**

*Chicken Phyllo Wrap*

# Baked Fish with Potatoes and Onions

1 pound baking potatoes, very thinly sliced
1 large onion, very thinly sliced
1 small red or green bell pepper, thinly sliced
  Salt
  Black pepper
½ teaspoon dried oregano leaves, divided
1 pound lean fish fillets, cut 1 inch thick
¼ cup butter or margarine
¼ cup all-purpose flour
2 cups milk
¾ cup (3 ounces) shredded Cheddar cheese

Preheat oven to 375°F.

Arrange ½ of the potatoes in buttered 3-quart casserole. Top with ½ of the onion and ½ of the bell pepper. Season with salt and black pepper. Sprinkle with ¼ teaspoon oregano. Arrange fish in 1 layer over vegetables. Arrange remaining potatoes, onion and bell pepper over fish. Season with salt, black pepper and remaining ¼ teaspoon oregano; set aside.

Melt butter in medium saucepan over medium heat. Stir in flour; cook until bubbly, stirring constantly. Gradually stir in milk. Cook until thickened, stirring constantly. Pour white sauce over casserole. Cover and bake at 375°F 40 minutes or until potatoes are tender. Sprinkle with cheese. Bake, uncovered, about 5 minutes more or until cheese is melted. *Makes 4 servings*

*Fruited Winter Pork Chop*

## Fruited Winter Pork Chops

 1 medium DOLE® Fresh Pineapple
 4 (1-inch-thick) pork chops, trimmed
16 DOLE® Pitted Prunes
   Salt and pepper to taste
 1 teaspoon vegetable oil
⅓ cup minced onion
 1 DOLE® Orange, peeled, sliced
 4 DOLE® Green Onions, sliced

**Orange Herb Sauce**

½ cup frozen DOLE® Pineapple Orange
    Juice concentrate, thawed
¼ cup water
 2 tablespoons white wine vinegar
 1 tablespoon grated orange peel
 1 teaspoon *each* dried basil leaves and
    mint leaves
 1 teaspoon chili powder
 1 teaspoon cornstarch
 2 large cloves garlic, pressed

•Twist crown from pineapple. Cut pineapple in half lengthwise. Refrigerate half for another use. Cut fruit from shell then crosswise into slices. Cut fruit into large chunks.

•Cut slit in side of each pork chop. Stuff each with 2 prunes. Cut remaining prunes into thirds. Season pork chops with salt and pepper. In large nonstick skillet, brown chops in oil. Add remaining prunes and onion. Cover; reduce heat and cook 8 minutes. Meanwhile, to prepare Orange Herb Sauce, combine orange juice concentrate, water, vinegar, orange peel, basil, mint, chili powder, cornstarch and garlic in small bowl. Stir until blended. Add sauce to pork chops. Cook, stirring, until sauce boils and thickens. Add pineapple, orange and green onions. Heat through.

*Makes 4 servings*

# COOKIES, BROWNIES & BARS

## Banana Crescents

½ cup DOLE® Chopped Almonds,
   toasted
6 tablespoons sugar, divided
½ cup margarine, cut into pieces
1½ cups plus 2 tablespoons all-purpose
   flour
⅛ teaspoon salt
1 extra-ripe, medium DOLE® Banana,
   peeled
2 to 3 ounces semisweet chocolate chips

•Pulverize almonds with 2 tablespoons
sugar in food processor.

•Beat margarine, almonds, remaining
4 tablespoons sugar, flour and salt.

•Purée banana; add to batter and mix until
well blended.

•Using 1 tablespoon batter, roll into log
then shape into crescent. Place on
ungreased cookie sheet. Bake in 375°F oven
25 minutes or until golden. Cool on wire
rack.

•Melt chocolate in microwavable dish at
50% power 1½ to 2 minutes, stirring once.
Dip ends of cookies in chocolate.
Refrigerate until chocolate hardens.

*Makes 2 dozen cookies*

## Yuletide Toffee Squares

4½ cups quick or old-fashioned oats,
   uncooked
1 cup packed brown sugar
¾ cup (1½ sticks) butter or margarine,
   melted
½ cup light corn syrup
1 tablespoon vanilla extract
½ teaspoon salt
2 cups (12-ounce package) NESTLÉ®
   TOLL HOUSE® Semi-Sweet
   Chocolate Morsels
⅔ cup chopped nuts

**COMBINE** oats, brown sugar, butter, corn
syrup, vanilla and salt in large bowl; mix
well. Firmly press mixture into greased
15 × 10-inch jelly-roll pan.

**BAKE** in preheated 400°F oven 18 minutes
or until mixture is browned and bubbly.
Remove from oven. Immediately sprinkle
chocolate morsels evenly over toffee. Let
stand 10 minutes.

**SPREAD** chocolate evenly over toffee;
sprinkle with nuts. Cool completely; cut
into squares. Store tightly covered in cool,
dry place.     *Makes about 6 dozen squares*

*Banana Crescents*

*Rugelach*

# Rugelach

1½ cups all-purpose flour
¼ teaspoon salt
¼ teaspoon baking soda
½ cup butter or margarine
 1 package (3 ounces) cream cheese,
   softened
⅓ cup plus ¼ cup granulated sugar,
   divided
 1 teaspoon grated lemon peel, divided
 1 cup ground toasted walnuts
 1 teaspoon ground cinnamon
 2 tablespoons honey
 1 tablespoon lemon juice
   Powdered sugar

Place flour, salt and baking soda in small bowl; combine.

Beat butter, cream cheese, ⅓ cup granulated sugar and ½ teaspoon lemon peel in large bowl with electric mixer at medium speed about 5 minutes or until light and fluffy, scraping down side of bowl once. Gradually add flour mixture. Beat at low speed until well blended, scraping down side of bowl once.

Form dough into three 5-inch discs; wrap in plastic wrap and refrigerate until firm, about 2 hours.

Preheat oven to 375°F. Grease cookie sheet; set aside.

Combine walnuts, remaining ¼ cup granulated sugar and cinnamon in medium bowl; set aside. Combine honey, remaining ½ teaspoon lemon peel and lemon juice in small bowl; set aside.

Working with 1 piece of dough at a time, remove plastic wrap and place dough on lightly floured surface. Roll out dough with lightly floured rolling pin to 10-inch circle. Keep remaining dough refrigerated.

Brush with ⅓ of the honey mixture. Sprinkle with ⅓ cup nut mixture. Lightly press nut mixture into dough.

Cut circle into 12 triangles with pizza cutter or sharp knife. Beginning with wide end of triangle, *tightly* roll up, jelly-roll fashion. Place cookies 1 inch apart on prepared cookie sheet.

Repeat with 2 remaining dough pieces and filling ingredients. Bake 10 to 12 minutes or until lightly golden brown. Let cookies stand on cookie sheets 1 minute. Remove cookies to wire rack; cool completely. Sprinkle with powdered sugar. Store tightly covered. *Makes 3 dozen*

# Milk Chocolate Florentine Cookies

²⁄₃ cup butter
 2 cups quick oats, uncooked
 1 cup granulated sugar
²⁄₃ cup all-purpose flour
¼ cup corn syrup
¼ cup milk
 1 teaspoon vanilla extract
¼ teaspoon salt
 2 cups (11½-ounce package) NESTLÉ®
   TOLL HOUSE® Milk Chocolate
   Morsels

In medium saucepan, melt butter; remove from heat. Stir in oats, sugar, flour, corn syrup, milk, vanilla and salt; mix well. Drop by level teaspoon about 3 inches apart onto foil-lined baking sheets. With rubber spatula, spread thinly. Bake in preheated 375°F oven for 6 to 8 minutes, until golden brown; cool. Peel foil from cookies. Over hot (not boiling) water, melt morsels, stirring until smooth. Spread thin layer of melted chocolate on flat side of half of the cookies. Top with remaining cookies.

*Makes about 3½ dozen sandwich cookies*

**Milk Chocolate Florentine Cookies**

# Orange-Glazed Date Bars

**Cookie Base**

1¼ cups firmly packed light brown sugar
 ¾ cup BUTTER FLAVOR* CRISCO®
   all-vegetable shortening *or* ¾
   BUTTER FLAVOR CRISCO® Stick
 2 tablespoons orange juice
 1 tablespoon vanilla
 1 tablespoon grated orange peel
 1 egg
1¾ cups all-purpose flour
 1 teaspoon salt
 ¾ teaspoon baking soda
 1 cup chopped dates
 1 cup walnuts

**Glaze**

1½ cups confectioners sugar
 2 tablespoons orange juice

*Butter Flavor Crisco is artificially flavored.

1. Heat oven to 350°F. Grease 13 × 9-inch baking pan. Place cooling rack on counter.

2. Place brown sugar, shortening, orange juice, vanilla and orange peel in large bowl. Beat at medium speed of electric mixer until well blended. Add egg; beat well.

3. Combine flour, salt and baking soda. Add to shortening mixture; beat at low speed just until blended. Stir in dates and walnuts.

4. Press dough into prepared pan.

5. Bake at 350°F for 20 to 25 minutes or until lightly browned and firm. *Do not overbake.* Cool completely on cooling rack.

6. For glaze, combine confectioners sugar and orange juice. Stir until smooth. Spread glaze over cookie base. Cut into 2 × 1½-inch bars. Garnish as desired.

*Makes 3 dozen bars*

# Gooey Caramel Chocolate Bars

2 cups all-purpose flour
1 cup granulated sugar
¼ teaspoon salt
2 cups butter or margarine, divided
1 cup packed light brown sugar
⅓ cup light corn syrup
1 cup (6 ounces) semisweet chocolate
    chips

Preheat oven to 350°F. Line 13 × 9-inch baking pan with foil. Combine flour, granulated sugar and salt in medium bowl; stir until blended. Cut in 14 tablespoons (1¾ sticks) butter until mixture resembles coarse crumbs. Press into bottom of prepared pan.

Bake 18 to 20 minutes until lightly browned around edges. Remove pan to wire rack; cool completely.

Combine 1 cup butter, brown sugar and corn syrup in heavy medium saucepan. Cook over medium heat 5 to 8 minutes until mixture boils, stirring frequently. Boil gently 2 minutes, without stirring. Immediately pour over cooled base; spread evenly to edges of pan with metal spatula. Cool completely.

Melt chocolate in double boiler over hot (not simmering) water. Stir in remaining 2 tablespoons butter. Pour over cooled caramel layer and spread evenly to edges of pan with metal spatula. Refrigerate 10 to 15 minutes until chocolate begins to set. Remove; cool completely. Cut into bars.

*Makes 3 dozen bars*

*Top to bottom: Oat-y Nut Bars (page 131) and Gooey Caramel Chocolate Bars*

# Oat-y Nut Bars

½ cup butter or margarine
½ cup honey
¼ cup corn syrup
¼ cup packed brown sugar
2¾ cups uncooked quick oats
⅔ cup raisins
½ cup salted peanuts

Preheat oven to 300°F. Grease 9-inch square baking pan. Melt butter with honey, corn syrup and brown sugar in medium saucepan over medium heat, stirring constantly. Bring to a boil; boil 8 minutes until mixture thickens slightly. Stir in oats, raisins and peanuts until well blended. Press evenly into prepared pan.

Bake 45 to 50 minutes until golden brown. Place pan on wire rack; score top into 2-inch squares. Cool completely. Cut into bars. *Makes about 16 bars*

# Raspberry Linzer Rounds

1¼ cups granulated sugar
1 cup BUTTER FLAVOR* CRISCO®
   all-vegetable shortening *or* 1
   BUTTER FLAVOR CRISCO® Stick
2 eggs
¼ cup light corn syrup or regular
   pancake syrup
1 teaspoon vanilla
1 teaspoon almond extract
3 cups all-purpose flour (plus 4
   tablespoons), divided
1 cup ground almonds (about 4 to
   5 ounces)
¾ teaspoon baking powder
½ teaspoon baking soda
½ teaspoon salt
½ cup seedless raspberry preserves,
   stirred
   Confectioners sugar

*Butter Flavor Crisco is artificially flavored.

1. Place granulated sugar and shortening in large bowl. Beat at medium speed of electric mixer until well blended. Add eggs, syrup, vanilla and almond extract; beat until blended and fluffy.

2. Combine 3 cups flour, ground almonds, baking powder, baking soda and salt. Add gradually to shortening mixture, beating at low speed until well blended.

3. Divide dough into 4 pieces; shape each piece into disk. Wrap with plastic wrap. Refrigerate several hours or until firm.

4. Heat oven to 375°F. Place sheets of foil on countertop for cooling cookies.

5. Sprinkle about 1 tablespoon flour on large sheet of waxed paper. Place disk of dough on floured paper; flatten slightly with hands. Turn dough over and cover with another large sheet of waxed paper. Roll dough to ¼-inch thickness. Remove top sheet of waxed paper. Cut out with 2- or 2½-inch floured scalloped round cookie cutter. Place 2 inches apart on ungreased baking sheet. Repeat with remaining dough. Cut out centers of half the cookies with ½- or ¾-inch round cookie cutter.

6. Bake one baking sheet at a time at 375°F for 5 to 7 minutes or until edges of cookies are lightly browned.** *Do not overbake.* Cool 2 minutes on baking sheet. Remove cookies to foil to cool completely.

7. Spread a small amount of raspberry jam on bottom of solid cookies; cover with cut-out cookies, bottom sides down, to form sandwiches. Sift confectioners sugar, if desired, over tops of cookies.

*Makes about 2 dozen cookies*

**Bake larger cookies 1 to 2 minutes longer.

# Spicy Gingerbread Cookies

½ cup firmly packed brown sugar
¾ cup (1½ sticks) butter or margarine, softened
⅔ cup light molasses
1 egg
1½ teaspoons grated lemon peel
2½ cups all-purpose flour
1¼ teaspoons ground cinnamon
1 teaspoon vanilla
1 teaspoon ground allspice
½ teaspoon ground ginger
½ teaspoon baking soda
½ teaspoon salt
¼ teaspoon baking powder
Frosting (recipe follows)

Combine brown sugar, butter, molasses, egg and lemon peel in large mixer bowl. Beat at medium speed with electric mixer until smooth and creamy. Add all remaining cookie ingredients. Continue beating at low speed until well mixed, 1 to 2 minutes. Cover; refrigerate at least 2 hours.

Preheat oven to 350°F. Grease cookie sheets. Roll out dough on well-floured surface, one half at a time (keep remaining dough refrigerated), to ¼-inch thickness. Cut with 3- to 4-inch cookie cutter. Place, 1 inch apart, on prepared cookie sheets. Bake 6 to 8 minutes or until no indentation remains when touched. Remove immediately to wire rack; cool completely.

*Makes about 4 dozen cookies*

## Frosting

4 cups powdered sugar
½ cup (1 stick) butter, softened
4 tablespoons milk
2 teaspoons vanilla
Food coloring (optional)

Combine powdered sugar, butter, milk and vanilla in small mixer bowl. Beat at low speed with electric mixer until fluffy, 1 to 2 minutes. If desired, color frosting with food coloring. Decorate cookies with frosting.

# Santa's Chocolate Cookies

1 cup margarine or butter
⅔ cup semisweet chocolate chips
¾ cup sugar
1 egg
½ teaspoon vanilla
2 cups all-purpose flour
Apricot jam, melted semisweet chocolate, chopped almonds, frosting, coconut or colored sprinkles

Preheat oven to 350°F. Melt margarine with ⅔ cup chocolate chips in small saucepan over low heat stirring until completely melted, or place in microwavable bowl and microwave at HIGH 2 to 2½ minutes, stirring after every minute. Combine chocolate mixture and sugar in large bowl. Add egg and vanilla; stir well. Add flour; stir well. Refrigerate, covered, 30 minutes or until firm.

Shape dough into 1-inch balls or 2-inch logs. Place 1 inch apart on ungreased cookie sheets. If desired, flatten balls with bottom of drinking glass; make a depression in center and fill with jam.

Bake 8 to 10 minutes or until set. Remove to wire racks; cool completely. Decorate as desired with melted chocolate, almonds, frosting, coconut and colored sprinkles.

*Makes about 3 dozen cookies*

*Spicy Gingerbread Cookies and Santa's Chocolate Cookies*

# Chocolate Clouds

3 egg whites
⅛ teaspoon cream of tartar
¾ cup sugar
1 teaspoon vanilla extract
2 tablespoons HERSHEY₅S Cocoa
1¾ cups (10-ounce package) HERSHEY₅S
    Semi-Sweet Chocolate Chunks *or*
    2 cups (12-ounce package)
    HERSHEY₅S Semi-Sweet Chocolate
    Chips

Preheat oven to 300°F. Cover cookie sheet with parchment paper or foil. In large bowl, beat egg whites and cream of tartar at high speed of electric mixer until soft peaks form. Gradually add sugar and vanilla, beating well after each addition until stiff peaks hold, sugar is dissolved and mixture is glossy. Sift cocoa onto egg white mixture; gently fold just until combined. Fold in chocolate chunks. Drop by heaping tablespoonfuls onto prepared cookie sheet. Bake 35 to 45 minutes or just until dry. Cool slightly; peel paper from cookies. Store, covered, at room temperature.

*Makes 30 cookies*

*Chocolate Clouds*

# Honey Nut Rugelach

1 cup butter or margarine, softened
3 ounces cream cheese, softened
½ cup honey, divided
2 cups all-purpose flour
1 teaspoon lemon juice
1 teaspoon ground cinnamon, divided
1 cup finely chopped walnuts
½ cup dried cherries or cranberries

Cream butter and cream cheese until fluffy. Add 3 tablespoons honey; mix well. Mix in flour until dough holds together. Shape dough into a ball. Wrap tightly with plastic wrap; refrigerate at least 2 hours. Divide dough into quarters. Place one quarter on lightly floured surface and roll into 9-inch circle. Combine 2 tablespoons honey and lemon juice; mix well. Brush dough with honey mixture; sprinkle ¼ teaspoon cinnamon over entire surface. Combine walnuts and cherries. Drizzle remaining honey over walnut mixture; mix well. Spread ¼ of the walnut mixture onto dough, leaving ½-inch border. Cut into 8 triangular pieces. Roll each piece starting at wide outer edge rolling towards tip. Gently bend ends to form crescent. Place rugelach on greased parchment paper-lined baking sheet; refrigerate at least 20 minutes. Repeat process with remaining dough and filling. Bake at 350°F 20 to 25 minutes or until golden brown. Cool on wire racks.

*Makes 32 cookies*

*Favorite recipe from **National Honey Board***

## Star Christmas Tree Cookies

### Cookies

½ cup CRISCO® all-vegetable shortening
⅓ cup butter or margarine, softened
2 egg yolks
1 teaspoon vanilla extract
1 package DUNCAN HINES® Moist Deluxe Yellow or Devil's Food Cake Mix
1 tablespoon water, divided

### Frosting

1 container (16 ounces) DUNCAN HINES® Creamy Homestyle Vanilla Frosting
Green food coloring
Red and green sugar crystals for garnish
Assorted colored candies and decors for garnish

Preheat oven to 375°F. For Cookies, combine shortening, butter, egg yolks and vanilla extract. Blend in cake mix gradually. Add 1 teaspoonful water at a time until dough is rolling consistency. Divide dough into 4 balls. Flatten one ball with hand; roll to ⅛-inch thickness on lightly floured surface. Cut with graduated star cookie cutters. Repeat using remaining dough. Bake large cookies together on ungreased baking sheet. Bake 6 to 8 minutes or until edges are light golden brown. Cool cookies 1 minute. Remove from baking sheet. Repeat with smaller cookies, testing for doneness at minimum baking time.

For Frosting, tint vanilla frosting with green food coloring. Frost cookies and stack beginning with largest cookies on bottom and ending with smallest cookies on top. Rotate cookies when stacking to alternate corners. Decorate as desired with colored sugar crystals and assorted colored candies and decors.      *Makes 2 to 3 dozen cookies*

*Star Christmas Tree Cookies*

## Frosty Cherry Cookies

½ cup (1 stick) butter or margarine
1 cup plus 3 tablespoons sugar, divided
1 egg, slightly beaten
½ teaspoon almond extract
1½ cups all-purpose flour
½ teaspoon salt
½ teaspoon baking soda
½ teaspoon baking powder
2 cups RICE CHEX® brand cereal, crushed to 1 cup
½ cup chopped green and red glacé cherries

Preheat oven to 350°F. In large bowl, combine butter and 1 cup sugar. Stir in egg and almond extract. Stir in flour, salt, baking soda and baking powder; mix well. Stir in cereal and cherries. Shape into ¾-inch balls. In small bowl, place remaining 3 tablespoons sugar. Roll balls in sugar. Place, 2 inches apart, on baking sheet. Bake 8 to 10 minutes or until bottoms are lightly browned.

*Makes 6 dozen cookies*

*Mini Chip Snowball Cookies*

# Mini Chip Snowball Cookies

1½ cups (3 sticks) butter, softened
¾ cup powdered sugar
1 tablespoon vanilla extract
½ teaspoon salt
3 cups all-purpose flour
2 cups (12-ounce package) NESTLÉ®
   TOLL HOUSE® Semi-Sweet
   Chocolate Mini Morsels
½ cup finely chopped pecans
   Powdered sugar

**BEAT** butter, sugar, vanilla and salt in large mixer bowl. Gradually beat in flour; stir in morsels and pecans. Shape level tablespoonfuls of dough into 1-inch balls. Place on ungreased baking sheets.

**BAKE** in preheated 375°F oven 10 to 12 minutes or until cookies are set and lightly browned. Remove from oven. Sift powdered sugar over hot cookies on baking sheet. Let stand 10 minutes; remove to wire racks to cool completely. Sprinkle with additional powdered sugar, if desired. Store in airtight containers.

*Makes 5 dozen cookies*

# Peppermint Refrigerator Slices

3 packages DUNCAN HINES® Golden
   Sugar Cookie Mix, divided
3 eggs, divided
3 to 4 drops red food coloring
¾ cup CRISCO® Oil or CRISCO®
   PURITAN® Canola Oil, divided
¾ teaspoon peppermint extract, divided
3 to 4 drops green food coloring

1. **For pink cookie dough,** combine ¼ cup oil, 1 egg, red food coloring and ¼ teaspoon peppermint extract in large bowl. Stir until evenly tinted. Add one cookie mix and stir until thoroughly blended. Set aside.

2. **For green cookie dough,** combine ¼ cup oil, 1 egg, green food coloring and ¼ teaspoon peppermint extract in large bowl. Stir until evenly tinted. Add one cookie mix and stir until thoroughly blended. Set aside.

3. **For plain cookie dough,** combine remaining cookie mix, ¼ cup oil, 1 egg and ¼ teaspoon peppermint extract in large bowl. Stir until thoroughly blended.

4. **To assemble,** divide each batch of cookie dough into four equal portions. Shape each portion into 12-inch-long roll on waxed paper. Lay 1 pink roll beside 1 green roll; press together slightly. Place 1 plain roll on top. Press rolls together to form 1 tri-colored roll; wrap in waxed paper or plastic wrap. Repeat with remaining rolls to form 3 more tri-colored rolls; wrap separately in waxed paper or plastic wrap. Refrigerate rolls for several hours or overnight.

5. Preheat oven to 375°F.

6. Cut chilled rolls into ¼-inch-thick slices. Place 2 inches apart on ungreased cookie sheets. Bake at 375°F for 7 to 8 minutes or until set but not browned. Cool 1 minute on cookie sheets. Remove to cooling racks. Cool completely. Store in airtight containers. *Makes about 15 dozen cookies*

# Spritz Christmas Trees

⅓ cup (3½ ounces) almond paste
1 egg
1 package DUNCAN HINES® Golden
Sugar Cookie Mix
¼ cup CRISCO® Oil or CRISCO®
PURITAN® Canola Oil
8 drops green food coloring
1 container DUNCAN HINES® Creamy
Homestyle Vanilla Frosting
Cinnamon candies, for garnish

1. Preheat oven to 375°F.

2. Combine almond paste and egg in large bowl. Beat at low speed with electric mixer until blended. Add oil and green food coloring. Beat until smooth and evenly tinted. Add cookie mix. Beat at low speed until thoroughly blended.

3. Fit cookie press with Christmas tree plate; fill with dough. Force dough through press, 2 inches apart, onto ungreased cookie sheets. Bake at 375°F for 6 to 7 minutes or until set but not browned. Cool 1 minute on cookie sheets. Remove to cooling racks. Cool completely.

4. To decorate, fill resealable plastic bag half full with vanilla frosting. Do not seal bag. Cut pinpoint hole in bottom corner of bag. Pipe small dot of frosting onto tip of one cookie tree and top with cinnamon candy. Repeat with remaining cookies. Pipe remaining frosting to form garland on cookie trees. Allow frosting to set before storing between layers of waxed paper in airtight container.

*Makes about 5 dozen cookies*

# Lemon Pecan Crescents

1 package DUNCAN HINES® Golden
Sugar Cookie Mix
2 eggs
¾ cup toasted pecans, chopped
¾ cup CRISCO® Oil or CRISCO®
PURITAN® Canola Oil
¼ cup all-purpose flour
1 tablespoon grated lemon peel
Confectioners' sugar

1. Preheat oven to 375°F.

2. Combine cookie mix, eggs, pecans, oil, flour and lemon peel in large bowl. Stir until thoroughly blended. Form level ½ measuring tablespoonfuls dough into crescent shapes. Place 2 inches apart on ungreased baking sheets. Bake 7 to 8 minutes or until set but not browned. Cool 2 minutes. Remove to cooling racks. Roll warm cookies in confectioners' sugar. Cool completely. Roll cookies again in confectioners' sugar.

*Makes about 6 dozen cookies*

*Clockwise from top left: Peppermint Refrigerator Slices (page 136), Lemon Pecan Crescents, Spritz Christmas Trees and Peanut Butter Stars (page 138)*

# Peanut Butter Stars

**1 package DUNCAN HINES® Peanut Butter Cookie Mix**
**1 egg**
**¼ cup CRISCO® Oil or CRISCO® PURITAN® Canola Oil**
**1 tablespoon water**
**1 package (3½ ounces each) chocolate sprinkles**
**1 package (7 ounces each) milk chocolate candy stars**

1. Preheat oven to 375°F.

2. Combine cookie mix, contents of peanut butter packet from Mix, egg, oil and water in large bowl. Stir until thoroughly blended. Shape dough into 1-inch balls. Roll in chocolate sprinkles. Place 2 inches apart on ungreased baking sheets. Bake at 375°F for 8 to 10 minutes or until set. Immediately place milk chocolate candy stars on top of hot cookies. Cool 1 minute on baking sheets. Remove to cooling racks. Cool completely. Store in airtight containers.          *Makes 4½ to 5 dozen cookies*

**Tip:** For evenly baked cookies, place baking sheets in center of oven, not touching the sides.

# Apple Lemon Bars

**Cookie Crust (recipe follows)**
**1 cup diced, peeled Golden Delicious apples**
**⅓ cup sugar**
**1 egg, beaten**
**2 tablespoons butter or margarine, melted**
**2 teaspoons grated lemon peel**
**¾ cup all-purpose flour**
**¼ teaspoon ground cinnamon**
**¼ teaspoon baking powder**
**¼ teaspoon salt**
**Lemon Glaze (recipe follows)**

Preheat oven to 350°F. Prepare Cookie Crust. Combine apples, sugar, egg, butter and lemon peel in large bowl; mix thoroughly. Combine flour, cinnamon, baking powder and salt in medium bowl; mix well. Stir flour mixture into apple mixture. Spread evenly over crust. Bake 25 minutes or until apples are tender. Cool in pan on wire rack. Brush with Lemon Glaze.
*Makes 16 bars*

**Cookie Crust:** Beat ½ cup butter or margarine, ¼ cup powdered sugar and 2 teaspoons grated lemon peel until creamy; blend in 1 cup flour. Press into bottom of ungreased 8-inch square baking pan. Bake at 350°F 15 to 18 minutes or until lightly browned.

**Lemon Glaze:** Combine ¾ cup powdered sugar and 1 tablespoon lemon juice; mix thoroughly.          *Makes about ⅓ cup*

*Favorite recipe from **Washington Apple Commission***

# Date-Nut Macaroons

**1 (8-ounce) package pitted dates, chopped**
**1½ cups flaked coconut**
**1 cup PLANTERS® Pecan Halves, chopped**
**¾ cup sweetened condensed milk (not evaporated milk)**
**½ teaspoon vanilla**

Preheat oven to 350°F.

In medium bowl, combine dates, coconut and nuts; blend in sweetened condensed milk and vanilla. Drop by rounded tablespoonfuls onto greased and floured cookie sheets. Bake for 10 to 12 minutes or until light golden brown. Carefully remove from cookie sheets; cool completely on wire racks. Store in airtight container.
*Makes about 2 dozen cookies*

*Date-Nut Macaroons*

## Walnut-Brandy Shortbread

1 cup butter
½ cup packed brown sugar
⅛ teaspoon salt
2 tablespoons brandy
1 cup all-purpose flour
1 cup finely chopped toasted California
    walnuts
    Granulated sugar

Cream butter with brown sugar and salt in large bowl; mix in brandy. Gradually add flour; stir in walnuts. Spread in ungreased 9-inch square pan. Refrigerate 30 minutes.

Pierce mixture all over with fork. Bake at 325°F about 55 minutes or until dark golden brown. If dough puffs up during baking, pierce again with fork. Sprinkle lightly with granulated sugar and cool. Cut into squares with sharp knife.

*Makes 36 squares*

*Favorite recipe from* **Walnut Marketing Board**

**Top to bottom: Walnut Macaroons, Walnut-Brandy Shortbread and Chocolate Walnut Truffles (page 166)**

## Walnut Macaroons

2⅔ cups flake coconut
1¼ cups coarsely chopped California
    walnuts
⅓ cup all-purpose flour
½ teaspoon cinnamon
¼ teaspoon salt
4 egg whites
1 teaspoon grated lemon peel
2 (1-ounce) squares semisweet chocolate

Combine coconut, walnuts, flour, cinnamon and salt in large bowl. Mix in egg whites and lemon peel.

Drop by teaspoonfuls onto lightly greased baking sheets. Bake at 325°F 20 minutes or until golden brown.

Microwave chocolate in microwavable bowl until melted, about 2½ minutes. Stir; dip macaroon bottoms in chocolate. Place on waxed paper to set.

*Makes about 3 dozen*

*Favorite recipe from* **Walnut Marketing Board**

## Toffee Spattered Sugar Stars

1¼ cups granulated sugar
1 cup BUTTER FLAVOR* CRISCO®
    all-vegetable shortening *or* 1
    BUTTER FLAVOR CRISCO® Stick
2 eggs
¼ cup light corn syrup or regular
    pancake syrup
1 tablespoon vanilla
3 cups all-purpose flour (plus
    4 tablespoons), divided
¾ teaspoon baking powder
½ teaspoon baking soda
½ teaspoon salt
1 package (6 ounces) milk chocolate
    English toffee chips, divided

*Butter Flavor Crisco is artificially flavored.

*Top to bottom: Pecan Cookies and Toffee Spattered Sugar Stars (page 140)*

1. Place sugar and shortening in large bowl. Beat at medium speed of electric mixer until well blended. Add eggs, corn syrup and vanilla; beat until well blended and fluffy.

2. Combine 3 cups flour, baking powder, baking soda and salt. Add gradually to shortening mixture, beating at low speed until well blended.

3. Divide dough into 4 equal pieces; shape each into disk. Wrap with plastic wrap. Refrigerate 1 hour or until firm.

4. Heat oven to 375°F. Place sheets of foil on countertop for cooling cookies.

5. Sprinkle about 1 tablespoon flour on large sheet of waxed paper. Place disk of dough on floured paper; flatten slightly with hands. Turn dough over; cover with another large sheet of waxed paper. Roll dough to ¼-inch thickness. Remove top sheet of waxed paper. Sprinkle about ¼ of toffee chips over dough. Roll lightly into dough. Cut out with floured star or round cookie cutter. Place 2 inches apart on ungreased baking sheet. Repeat with remaining dough and toffee chips.

6. Bake one baking sheet at a time at 375°F for 5 to 7 minutes or until cookies are lightly browned around edges. *Do not overbake.* Cool 2 minutes on baking sheet. Remove cookies to foil to cool completely.

*Makes about 3½ dozen cookies*

## Pecan Cookies

1¼ cups confectioners sugar
   1 cup BUTTER FLAVOR* CRISCO®
       all-vegetable shortening *or* 1
       BUTTER FLAVOR CRISCO® Stick
   2 eggs
   ¼ cup light corn syrup or regular
       pancake syrup
   1 tablespoon vanilla
   2 cups all-purpose flour
1½ cups finely chopped pecans
   ¾ teaspoon baking powder
   ½ teaspoon baking soda
   ½ teaspoon salt
       Confectioners sugar

*Butter Flavor Crisco is artificially flavored.

1. Heat oven to 350°F. Place sheets of foil on countertop for cooling cookies.

2. Place 1¼ cups confectioners sugar and shortening in large bowl. Beat at medium speed of electric mixer until well blended. Add eggs, corn syrup and vanilla; beat until well blended and fluffy.

3. Combine flour, pecans, baking powder, baking soda and salt. Add to shortening mixture; beat at low speed until well blended.

4. Shape dough into 1-inch balls. Place 2 inches apart on ungreased baking sheet.

5. Bake for 15 to 18 minutes or until bottoms of cookies are light golden brown. *Do not overbake.* Cool 2 minutes on baking sheet. Roll in confectioners sugar while warm. Remove cookies to foil to cool completely. Reroll in confectioners sugar prior to serving.

*Makes about 4 dozen cookies*

## Chocolate Dipped Brandy Snaps

½ cup (1 stick) butter
½ cup granulated sugar
⅓ cup dark corn syrup
½ teaspoon ground cinnamon
¼ teaspoon ground ginger
1 cup all-purpose flour
2 teaspoons brandy
1 cup (6 ounces) NESTLÉ® TOLL HOUSE® Semi-Sweet Chocolate Morsels
1 tablespoon shortening
⅓ cup finely chopped nuts

**MELT** butter, sugar, corn syrup, cinnamon and ginger in medium heavy saucepan over low heat, stirring until smooth. Remove from heat; stir in flour and brandy. Drop by rounded teaspoon onto ungreased baking sheets about 3 inches apart, baking no more than 6 at a time.

**BAKE** in preheated 300°F oven 10 to 14 minutes or until deep caramel color. Let stand 10 seconds. Remove from baking sheets and immediately roll around wooden spoon handle; cool.

**MICROWAVE** morsels and shortening in medium microwave-safe bowl on HIGH (100% power) 45 seconds; stir. Microwave at 10 to 20 second intervals, stirring until smooth. Dip cookies halfway in melted chocolate; shake off excess. Sprinkle with nuts; set on waxed paper-lined baking sheets. Chill 10 minutes or until chocolate is set. Store in airtight container in refrigerator.     *Makes about 3 dozen cookies*

*Chocolate Dipped Brandy Snaps*

## Banana Jumbles

2 extra-ripe, medium DOLE® Bananas, peeled
¾ cup packed brown sugar
½ cup creamy peanut butter
¼ cup margarine, softened
1 egg
1½ cups old-fashioned oats
1 cup all-purpose flour
1½ teaspoons baking powder
½ teaspoon salt
¾ cup DOLE® Raisins

•Mash bananas with fork. Measure 1 cup.

•Beat brown sugar, peanut butter and margarine in large bowl. Beat in egg and mashed bananas.

•Combine oats, flour, baking powder and salt. Stir into banana mixture until well combined. Stir in raisins.

•Drop by heaping tablespoonfuls onto cookie sheets coated with nonstick cooking spray. Shape cookies with back of spoon. Bake in 375°F oven 12 to 14 minutes until lightly browned. Cool on wire racks.
*Makes 18 cookies*

# Coffee Chip Drops

1¼ cups firmly packed light brown sugar
¾ cup **BUTTER FLAVOR\* CRISCO® all-vegetable shortening** *or* ¾ **BUTTER FLAVOR CRISCO® Stick**
2 tablespoons cold coffee
1 teaspoon vanilla
1 egg
1¾ cups all-purpose flour
1 tablespoon finely ground French roast or espresso coffee beans
1 teaspoon salt
¾ teaspoon baking soda
½ cup semisweet chocolate chips
½ cup milk chocolate chips
½ cup coarsely chopped walnuts
30 to 40 chocolate kiss candies, unwrapped

\*Butter Flavor Crisco is artificially flavored.

1. Heat oven to 375°F. Place sheets of foil on countertop for cooling cookies.

2. Place brown sugar, shortening, coffee and vanilla in large bowl. Beat at medium speed of electric mixer until well blended. Add egg; beat well.

3. Combine flour, ground coffee, salt and baking soda. Add to shortening mixture; beat at low speed just until blended. Stir in chocolate chips and walnuts.

4. Drop dough by rounded measuring tablespoonfuls 2 inches apart onto ungreased baking sheets.

5. Bake one baking sheet at a time at 375°F for 8 to 10 minutes or until cookies are lightly browned and just set. *Do not overbake.* Place 1 candy in center of each cookie. Cool 2 minutes on baking sheet. Remove cookies to foil to cool completely.
*Makes about 3 dozen cookies*

# Apple Crumb Squares

2 cups QUAKER® Oats (Quick or Old Fashioned), uncooked
1½ cups all-purpose flour
1 cup packed brown sugar
1 teaspoon ground cinnamon
½ teaspoon salt (optional)
½ teaspoon baking soda
¼ teaspoon ground nutmeg
¾ cup butter or margarine, melted
1 cup commercially prepared applesauce
½ cup chopped nuts

Preheat oven to 350°F. In large bowl, combine all ingredients except applesauce and nuts; mix until crumbly. Reserve 1 cup oats mixture. Press remaining oats mixture onto bottom of greased 13 × 9-inch pan. Bake 13 to 15 minutes; cool. Spread applesauce over partially baked crust; sprinkle with nuts. Sprinkle reserved 1 cup oats mixture over top. Bake 13 to 15 minutes or until golden brown. Cool in pan on wire rack; cut into 2-inch squares.
*Makes about 24 squares*

*Apple Crumb Squares*

# Holiday Shortbread with Variations

**1 cup (2 sticks) butter**
**½ cup sugar**
**2½ cups all-purpose flour**
**¼ teaspoon salt**

Preheat oven to 375°F. Cream butter in large mixer bowl until fluffy. Add sugar; beat until light and fluffy. Gradually blend in flour and salt. Roll out on lightly floured surface to 11 × 7-inch rectangle, ½ inch thick. Cut into 1-inch squares. Bake on ungreased cookie sheets 12 to 15 minutes or until lightly golden. Cool completely on wire racks. Store at room temperature in container with tight fitting lid.

*Makes about 6 dozen*

**Anise Stars:** Prepare Basic Shortbread, stirring in ¾ teaspoon anise extract and ¼ teaspoon nutmeg with flour and salt. Wrap dough in plastic wrap. Refrigerate 1 to 2 hours. Roll dough to ¼-inch thickness on lightly floured surface. Cut into star shape using floured cutter. Bake in preheated 375°F oven on ungreased cookie sheets 13 to 15 minutes or until lightly golden. Cool completely on wire rack. Decorate with red and green frosting and small silver dragées. *Makes 3 to 4 dozen*

**Rum Raisin Balls:** Prepare Basic Shortbread, stirring in 1 cup golden seedless raisins and 1 teaspoon rum extract with flour and salt. Form into 1-inch balls. Bake in preheated 375°F oven on ungreased cookie sheets 15 to 18 minutes or until lightly golden. Remove from cookie sheets; cool completely on wire racks. Dust lightly with confectioners' sugar before serving.

*Makes 5 dozen*

**Noel Tarts:** Prepare Basic Shortbread, stirring in 1 teaspoon vanilla with flour and salt. Press rounded tablespoonfuls of dough into 1¾-inch muffin cups. Bake in

preheated 375°F oven 18 to 20 minutes or until lightly golden. Cool in pan 10 minutes. Carefully remove from pan; cool completely on wire rack. Fill as desired with pie filling, pudding, mincemeat, etc.

*Makes 3 dozen*

**Chocolate-Frosted Almond Bars:** Prepare Basic Shortbread, reducing flour to 2 cups. Add ½ cup finely ground almonds and 1 teaspoon almond extract with flour and salt. Press into unbuttered 13 × 9-inch baking pan. Bake in preheated 375°F oven 20 to 25 minutes or until lightly golden. Cool completely in pan on wire rack. Frost with 1 package (6 ounces) semisweet chocolate morsels, melted and combined with ½ cup dairy sour cream and 1 teaspoon vanilla. Cut into bars. Decorate with sliced almonds. *Makes 4 dozen*

*Favorite recipe from* **American Dairy Association**

# No-Fuss Bar Cookies

**24 graham cracker squares**
**1 cup semisweet chocolate chips**
**1 cup flaked coconut**
**¾ cup coarsely chopped walnuts**
**1 can (14 ounces) sweetened condensed milk (NOT evaporated milk)**

Preheat oven to 350°F. Grease 13 × 9-inch baking pan; set aside. Place graham crackers in food processor. Process until crackers form fine crumbs. Combine graham cracker crumbs, chocolate chips, coconut and walnuts in medium bowl. Stir in milk until blended. Spread batter evenly in prepared pan. Bake 15 to 18 minutes or until edges are golden brown. Cool completely on wire rack; cut into 2¼ × 2¼-inch bars. *Makes 20 bars*

*Top to bottom: Anise Stars, Rum Raisin Balls, Noel Tarts and Chocolate-Frosted Almond Bars*

*Peanut Butter Reindeer*

# Peanut Butter Reindeer

### Cookies

    1 package DUNCAN HINES® Peanut
        Butter Cookie Mix
    1 egg
    ¼ cup CRISCO® Oil or CRISCO®
        PURITAN® Canola Oil
    4 teaspoons all-purpose flour, divided

### Assorted Decorations

    Miniature semisweet chocolate chips
    Vanilla milk chips
    Candy-coated semisweet chocolate
      chips
    Colored sprinkles

1. For Cookies, combine cookie mix, peanut butter packet from mix, egg and oil in large bowl. Stir until thoroughly blended. Form dough into ball; divide in half. Place 2 teaspoons flour in gallon size (10⁹⁄₁₆ × 11-inch) resealable plastic bag. Place dough in center of bag (do not seal). Roll dough with rolling pin out to edges of bag. Slide bag onto baking sheet. Repeat with remaining 2 teaspoons flour, second plastic bag and remaining dough ball. Chill in refrigerator at least 1 hour.

2. Preheat oven to 375°F.

3. Use scissors to cut one bag down center and across ends. Turn plastic back to uncover dough. Dip reindeer cookie cutter in flour after each cut. Transfer cutout cookies using floured pancake turner to ungreased baking sheets. Decorate as desired making eyes, mouth, nose and tail with assorted decorations. Bake at 375°F for 5 to 7 minutes or until set but not browned. Cool 2 minutes on baking sheets. Remove to cooling racks. Cool completely. Repeat with remaining chilled dough. Store cookies between layers of waxed paper in airtight container.

*Makes about 4 dozen cookies*

**Tips:** Reroll dough by folding plastic back over dough.

To use as ornaments, press end of drinking straw in top of each unbaked cookie to make hole. Press straw through cookies again after baking. String ribbon through holes of cooled cookies. Tie at top.

# Chocolate Gingerbread Boys and Girls

**2 cups (12-ounce package) NESTLÉ® TOLL HOUSE® Semi-Sweet Chocolate Morsels, divided**
**2¾ cups GOLD MEDAL® All-Purpose Flour**
**1 teaspoon baking soda**
**½ teaspoon salt**
**½ teaspoon ground ginger**
**½ teaspoon ground cinnamon**
**3 tablespoons butter or margarine, softened**
**3 tablespoons granulated sugar**
**½ cup molasses**
**¼ cup water**
**1 container (16 ounces) prepared vanilla frosting, colored as desired or colored icing in tubes**

**MICROWAVE** 1½ cups morsels in medium microwave-safe bowl on HIGH (100% power) 1 minute; stir. Microwave at 10 to 20 second intervals, stirring until smooth; cool to room temperature. Combine flour, baking soda, salt, ginger and cinnamon in medium bowl.

**BEAT** butter and sugar in small mixer bowl until creamy; beat in molasses and melted chocolate. Gradually add flour mixture alternately with water, beating until smooth. Cover and chill 1 hour or until firm.

**ROLL** ½ of the dough to ¼-inch thickness on floured surface with floured rolling pin. Cut into gingerbread boy and girl shapes; place on ungreased baking sheets. Repeat with remaining dough.

**BAKE** in preheated 350°F oven 5 to 6 minutes or until edges are set but centers are slightly soft. Let stand 2 minutes. Remove to wire racks to cool completely.

**DECORATE** with colored frosting and melted chocolate.

**TO PIPE CHOCOLATE,** place remaining ½ cup morsels in heavy-duty plastic bag. Microwave on HIGH 45 seconds; knead. Microwave 10 seconds; knead until smooth. Cut tiny corner from bag; squeeze to pipe.
*Makes about 2½ dozen cookies*

# Double Crunch Biscotti

**⅓ cup vegetable oil**
**¾ cup sugar**
**3 eggs, beaten**
**½ teaspoon almond extract**
**½ teaspoon vanilla**
**2½ cups all-purpose flour**
**2 cups ALMOND DELIGHT® brand cereal, crushed to 1 cup**
**2 teaspoons baking powder**
**12 ounces chocolate, melted (optional)**
**¼ cup chopped almonds (optional)**

Preheat oven to 350°F. Lightly grease cookie sheet. In large bowl, combine oil and sugar. Beat in eggs, almond extract and vanilla. Gradually stir in flour, cereal and baking powder. Divide dough in half. Place each half of dough on prepared cookie sheet, shaping each into a 3½ × 11-inch log. Bake 25 to 28 minutes or until lightly browned. Remove from oven; immediately cut into ½-inch-thick slices. Place slices, cut side down, on clean ungreased cookie sheet. Bake 13 minutes, turning cookies over after 8 minutes. Cool on wire rack. If desired, spread chocolate on one end of each cookie; sprinkle with almonds. *Makes 44 cookies*

*Cinnamon Crinkles Cookies*

## Cinnamon Crinkles Cookies

**Toppings**

2 tablespoons sugar
½ teaspoon ground cinnamon
2 eggs, separated
1 teaspoon water

**Cookies**

¾ cup butter or margarine, softened
1 teaspoon vanilla extract
1 package DUNCAN HINES® Moist Deluxe French Vanilla Flavor Cake Mix
48 whole almonds or pecans halves for garnish (optional)

1. Preheat oven to 375°F.

2. **For Toppings,** combine sugar and cinnamon in small bowl; set aside. Combine egg whites and water in another small bowl; beat lightly with fork. Set aside.

3. **For Cookies,** combine butter, egg yolks and vanilla extract in large bowl. Blend in cake mix gradually. Stir until thoroughly blended. Roll 1 level measuring teaspoon dough into ball. Dip half the ball into egg white mixture then into cinnamon-sugar mixture. Place ball sugar-side-up on ungreased baking sheet. Press nut on top. Repeat with remaining dough placing balls 2 inches apart. Bake at 375°F for 9 to 10 minutes or until puffed and edges are light golden brown. Cool 2 minutes on baking sheets. Remove to cooling rack. Store in airtight container.       *Makes 48 cookies*

**Note:** Cookies will flatten after removing from oven.

## Chocolate Cherry Oatmeal Fancies

½ cup sliced almonds
1¼ cups firmly packed light brown sugar
¾ cup BUTTER FLAVOR* CRISCO® all-vegetable shortening *or* ¾ BUTTER FLAVOR CRISCO® Stick
1 egg
⅓ cup milk
1 teaspoon vanilla
½ teaspoon almond extract
3 cups quick oats, uncooked
1 cup all-purpose flour
½ teaspoon baking soda
½ teaspoon salt
6 ounces white baking chocolate, coarsely chopped
6 ounces semisweet chocolate, coarsely chopped
½ cup coarsely chopped red candied cherries or well-drained, chopped maraschino cherries

*Butter Flavor Crisco is artificially flavored.

1. Heat oven to 350°F. Spread almonds on baking sheet. Bake at 350°F for 5 to 7 minutes or until almonds are golden brown. Cool completely; reserve.

2. *Increase oven temperature to 375°F.* Grease baking sheets. Place sheets of foil on countertop for cooling cookies.

3. Place brown sugar, shortening, egg, milk, vanilla and almond extract in large bowl. Beat at medium speed of electric mixer until well blended.

4. Combine oats, flour, baking soda and salt. Add to shortening mixture; beat at low speed just until blended. Stir in white chocolate, semisweet chocolate, cherries and reserved almonds.

5. Drop by rounded tablespoonfuls 2 inches apart onto prepared baking sheets.

6. Bake one baking sheet at a time at 375°F for 10 to 12 minutes or until cookies are lightly browned. *Do not overbake.* Cool 2 minutes on baking sheet. Remove cookies to foil to cool completely.

*Makes about 4 dozen cookies*

# Southwestern Bizcochitos

## Cookies

1¼ cups granulated sugar
  1 cup BUTTER FLAVOR* CRISCO®
    all-vegetable shortening *or* 1
    BUTTER FLAVOR CRISCO® Stick
  2 eggs
¼ cup light corn syrup or regular
    pancake syrup
  1 tablespoon vanilla
  1 tablespoon grated orange peel
  2 teaspoons anise seed
  3 cups all-purpose flour (plus 4
    tablespoons), divided
¾ teaspoon baking powder
½ teaspoon baking soda
½ teaspoon salt

## Topping

⅓ cup granulated sugar
  1 tablespoon cinnamon
    Milk

*Butter Flavor Crisco is artificially flavored.

1. For cookies, place 1¼ cups sugar and shortening in large bowl. Beat at medium speed of electric mixer until well blended. Add eggs, corn syrup, vanilla, orange peel and anise seed; beat until well blended and fluffy.

2. Combine 3 cups flour, baking powder, baking soda and salt. Add gradually to shortening mixture, beating at low speed until well blended. Wrap dough in plastic wrap. Refrigerate 1 hour or overnight.

3. Divide dough into 4 equal pieces; shape each into a disk. Wrap with plastic wrap. Refrigerate 1 hour or until firm.

4. Heat oven to 375°F. Place sheets of foil on countertop for cooling cookies.

5. Sprinkle about 1 tablespoon of flour on large sheet of waxed paper. Place disk of dough on floured paper; flatten slightly with hands. Turn dough over; cover with another large sheet of waxed paper. Roll dough to ¼-inch thickness. Remove top sheet of waxed paper. Cut out with floured cookie cutter. Place 2 inches apart on ungreased baking sheet. Repeat with remaining dough.

6. For topping, combine ⅓ cup sugar and cinnamon. Brush cookies with milk. Sprinkle cookies with sugar mixture.

7. Bake one baking sheet at a time at 375°F for 7 to 9 minutes or until cookies are lightly set. *Do not overbake.* Cool 2 minutes on baking sheet. Remove cookies to foil to cool completely.

*Makes about 4½ dozen cookies*

# Jammy Pinwheels

1¼ cups granulated sugar
  1 cup BUTTER FLAVOR* CRISCO®
    all-vegetable shortening *or* 1
    BUTTER FLAVOR CRISCO® Stick
  2 eggs
¼ cup light corn syrup or regular
    pancake syrup
  1 tablespoon vanilla
  3 cups all-purpose flour (plus 2
    tablespoons), divided
¾ teaspoon baking powder
½ teaspoon baking soda
½ teaspoon salt
  1 cup apricot, strawberry or seedless
    raspberry jam

*Butter Flavor Crisco is artificially flavored.

1. Place sugar and shortening in large bowl. Beat at medium speed of electric mixer until well blended. Add eggs, corn syrup and vanilla; beat until well blended and fluffy.

2. Combine 3 cups flour, baking powder, baking soda and salt. Add gradually to shortening mixture, beating at low speed until well blended.

3. Divide dough in half. Pat each half into thick rectangle. Sprinkle about 1 tablespoon flour on large sheet of waxed paper. Place rectangle of dough on floured paper. Turn dough over; cover with another large sheet of waxed paper. Roll dough into an 8 × 12-inch rectangle about ⅛ inch thick. Trim edges. Slide dough and waxed paper onto ungreased baking sheets. Refrigerate 20 minutes or until firm. Repeat with remaining dough.

4. Heat oven to 375°F. Grease baking sheets. Place sheets of foil on countertop for cooling cookies.

5. Place chilled dough rectangle on work surface. Remove top sheet of waxed paper. Cut dough into 2-inch squares. Place squares 2 inches apart on prepared baking sheets. Make a 1-inch diagonal cut from each corner of square almost to center. Place 1 teaspoon jam in center. Lift every other corner and bring together in center of cookie. Repeat with remaining dough.

6. Bake at 375°F for 7 to 10 minutes or until edges of cookies are golden brown. *Do not overbake.* Cool 2 minutes on baking sheet. Remove cookies to foil to cool completely.
*Makes about 4 dozen cookies*

# Christmas Spirits

 32 chocolate creme sandwich cookies
1¼ cups toasted California walnuts
¾ cup powdered sugar, divided
  2 tablespoons instant coffee powder,
    divided
  2 tablespoons light corn syrup
⅓ cup brandy, coffee liqueur or rum

Break up cookies and place in food processor; process until cookies form fine crumbs (about 2 cups crumbs). Add walnuts, ½ cup powdered sugar and 1½ tablespoons coffee powder. Process until thoroughly combined. Add corn syrup; gradually mix in brandy until mixture forms a thick paste. Form into 1-inch balls.

Combine remaining ¼ cup powdered sugar and 1½ teaspoons coffee powder. Roll balls in sugar mixture to coat. Cookies may be stored loosely packed between sheets of waxed paper or aluminum foil in airtight container for up to 2 weeks.
*Makes about 48 cookies*

*Favorite recipe from* **Walnut Marketing Board**

*Clockwise from top left: Jammy Pinwheels, Chocolate Cherry Oatmeal Fancies (page 148) and Southwestern Bizcochitos (page 149)*

# Fudge-Topped Brownies

2 cups sugar
1 cup margarine or butter, melted
1 cup unsifted flour
⅔ cup unsweetened cocoa
½ teaspoon baking powder
½ cup milk
2 eggs
3 teaspoons vanilla extract
1 cup chopped nuts, optional
2 cups (12 ounces) semisweet chocolate chips
1 (14-ounce) can EAGLE® Brand Sweetened Condensed Milk (NOT evaporated milk)
Dash salt

Preheat oven to 350°. In large mixer bowl, combine sugar, margarine, flour, cocoa, baking powder, milk, eggs and 1½ teaspoons vanilla; beat well. Stir in nuts, if desired. Spread in greased 13 × 9-inch baking pan. Bake 40 minutes or until brownies begin to pull away from sides of pan. Just before brownies are done, in large heavy saucepan over low heat, melt chips with sweetened condensed milk, remaining 1½ teaspoons vanilla and salt, stirring frequently until smooth. Remove from heat. Immediately spread over hot brownies. Cool. Chill. Cut into bars. Store covered at room temperature.        *Makes 36 to 40 brownies*

# Walnut-Granola Clusters

¼ cup butter
1 (10½-ounce) package miniature marshmallows
½ teaspoon ground cinnamon
3 cups rolled oats
2 cups chopped California walnuts
1 cup coconut
2 (1-ounce) squares semisweet chocolate

Microwave butter in large microwavable bowl 40 seconds or until melted. Stir in marshmallows and cinnamon. Microwave 1½ minutes until melted, stirring halfway through cooking. Quickly stir in oats, walnuts and coconut. With wet hands, form small balls and place on waxed paper-lined baking sheets.

Microwave chocolate in microwavable measuring cup until melted, about 2½ minutes. Stir and lightly drizzle over clusters.        *Makes 5 dozen*

*Favorite recipe from **Walnut Marketing Board***

# Walnut-Orange Chocolate Chippers

1½ cups all-purpose flour
½ cup packed brown sugar
½ cup granulated sugar
1½ teaspoons baking powder
½ teaspoon salt
⅓ cup butter, softened
2 eggs, slightly beaten
2 cups (12 ounces) semisweet chocolate chips
1 cup coarsely chopped California walnuts
2 tablespoons grated orange peel

Combine flour, brown sugar, granulated sugar, baking powder and salt in large bowl; mix in butter and eggs. Add remaining ingredients and mix thoroughly (batter will be stiff). Spread dough evenly into greased and floured 9-inch square pan (use wet hands to smooth). Bake at 350°F 25 minutes or until golden brown. Cool; cut into squares.        *Makes 36 squares*

*Favorite recipe from **Walnut Marketing Board***

*Clockwise from top: Walnut-Orange Chocolate Chippers (page 152), Walnut-Apple Dumpling Bars and Walnut-Granola Clusters (page 152)*

# Walnut-Apple Dumpling Bars

6 tablespoons (¾ stick) butter or
    margarine
1 cup packed light brown sugar
1 cup all-purpose flour
1½ teaspoons ground cinnamon
1 teaspoon baking powder
2 eggs
1½ cups coarsely chopped walnuts
1 Granny Smith or Pippin apple,
    coarsely grated* (about 1 cup lightly
    packed)
    Powdered sugar

*It is not necessary to peel or core the apple. Simply use a hand grater, turning the apple as you go, until only the core remains.

Melt butter in 3-quart saucepan. Add sugar. Stir until sugar is melted and mixture begins to bubble; cool. In medium bowl combine flour, cinnamon and baking powder; mix to blend thoroughly. Beat eggs into butter mixture in saucepan, 1 at a time, then add flour mixture. Mix in walnuts and apple. Turn into buttered and floured 9-inch square baking pan; smooth top. Bake in 350°F oven 25 to 35 minutes or until wooden pick inserted in center comes out clean and edges begin to pull away from sides of pan. Cool completely on rack. Sprinkle with powdered sugar. Cut into 24 bars about 3 × 1 inches.      *Makes 27 bars*

# Moist Pumpkin Cookies

½ cup butter or margarine, softened
1 cup packed brown sugar
½ cup granulated sugar
1½ cups canned pumpkin (not pumpkin pie filling)
1 egg
1 teaspoon vanilla
2¼ cups all-purpose flour
1¼ teaspoons ground cinnamon
1 teaspoon baking powder
½ teaspoon baking soda
½ teaspoon salt
½ teaspoon ground nutmeg
¾ cup raisins
½ cup chopped walnuts
   Powdered Sugar Glaze (recipe follows)

Preheat oven to 350°F. Beat butter and sugars in large bowl until creamy. Beat in pumpkin, egg and vanilla until light and fluffy. Mix in flour, cinnamon, baking powder, baking soda, salt and nutmeg until blended. Stir in raisins and walnuts. Drop heaping tablespoonfuls of dough 2 inches apart onto ungreased cookie sheets.

Bake 12 to 15 minutes until set. Cool 2 minutes on cookie sheets. Remove to wire racks; cool completely. Drizzle Powdered Sugar Glaze onto cookies. Let glaze set. Store between layers of waxed paper in airtight containers.

*Makes about 3½ dozen cookies*

**Powdered Sugar Glaze:** Combine 1 cup powdered sugar and 2 tablespoons milk in small bowl until well blended.

# Sugar Cookie Wreaths

1 package DUNCAN HINES® Golden Sugar Cookie Mix
1 egg
¼ cup CRISCO® Oil or CRISCO® PURITAN® Canola Oil
1 tablespoon water
   Green food coloring
   Candied or maraschino cherry pieces

1. Preheat oven to 375°F.

2. Combine cookie mix, egg, oil and water in large bowl. Stir until thoroughly blended.

3. Tint dough with green food coloring. Stir until desired color. Form into balls the size of miniature marshmallows. For each wreath, arrange 9 or 10 balls, with sides touching, into a ring. Place wreaths 2 inches apart on ungreased baking sheets. Flatten slightly with fingers. Place small piece of candied cherry on each ball.

4. Bake at 375°F for 5 to 7 minutes or until set but not browned. Cool 1 minute on baking sheets. Remove to cooling racks. Cool completely. Store in airtight container.

*Makes 4 dozen cookies*

**Tip:** Instead of tinting dough green, coat balls with green sugar crystals.

*Sugar Cookie Wreaths*

# Double Mint Brownies

1 package DUNCAN HINES® Chocolate
Lover's Chewy Recipe Fudge
Brownie Mix, Family Size
1 egg
⅓ cup water
⅓ cup CRISCO® Oil or CRISCO®
PURITAN® Canola Oil
½ teaspoon peppermint extract
24 chocolate-covered peppermint patties
(1½ inches *each*)
1 cup confectioners' sugar, divided
4 teaspoons milk, divided
Red food coloring
Green food coloring

1. Preheat oven to 350°F. Grease bottom of
13 × 9 × 2-inch pan. Combine brownie
mix, egg, water, oil and peppermint extract
in large bowl. Stir with spoon until well
blended, about 50 strokes. Spread in pan.
Bake brownies following package
directions. Place peppermint patties on
warm brownies. Cool completely.

2. Combine ½ cup confectioners' sugar,
2 teaspoons milk and 1 drop red food
coloring in small bowl. Stir until smooth.
Place in small resealable plastic bag; set
aside. Repeat with remaining ½ cup
confectioners' sugar, remaining 2 teaspoons
milk and 1 drop green food coloring. Cut
pinpoint hole in bottom corner of each bag.
Drizzle pink and green glazes over
brownies as shown. Allow glazes to set
before cutting into bars.

*Makes 24 brownies*

**Tip:** To prevent overdone edges and
underdone center, wrap foil strips around
outside edges of pan (do not cover bottom
or top). Bake as directed.

*Double Mint Brownies*

# Snow Puff Cookies

1 cup (2 sticks) butter or margarine,
softened
1 cup sifted powdered sugar
2 teaspoons vanilla
2 cups all-purpose flour
1 cup WHEAT CHEX® brand cereal,
crushed to ⅓ cup
½ teaspoon salt
Powdered sugar

Preheat oven to 325°F. In large bowl,
combine butter and sugar until well
blended. Stir in vanilla. Stir in flour, cereal
and salt, mixing well. Using level
tablespoon, shape dough into 1-inch balls.
Place on ungreased baking sheet. Bake 14 to
16 minutes or until bottoms are lightly
browned. Cool. Roll in powdered sugar.

*Makes 3 dozen cookies*

# CANDIES & CONFECTIONS

## Jolly Bourbon Balls

1 package (12 ounces) vanilla wafers,
   finely crushed (3 cups)
1 cup finely chopped nuts
1 cup powdered sugar, divided
1 cup (6 ounces) semisweet chocolate
   chips
½ cup light corn syrup
⅓ cup bourbon or rum

Combine crushed wafers, nuts and ½ cup powdered sugar in large bowl; set aside.

Melt chocolate with corn syrup in top of double boiler set over simmering (not boiling) water. Stir in bourbon until smooth. Pour chocolate mixture over crumb mixture; stir to combine thoroughly. Shape scant 1 tablespoonful of mixture into 1-inch ball. Repeat with remaining mixture. Roll balls in your palms to form uniform round shapes; place on waxed paper.

Place remaining ½ cup powdered sugar in shallow bowl. Roll balls in powdered sugar; place in petit four or candy cases. Store in airtight containers at least 3 days before serving for flavors to mellow. (May be stored up to 2 weeks.)

*Makes about 48 candies*

## Merri-Mint Truffles

1 package (10 ounces) mint chocolate
   chips
⅓ cup whipping cream
¼ cup butter or margarine
1 container (3½ ounces) chocolate
   sprinkles

Melt chocolate chips with cream and butter in heavy medium saucepan over low heat, stirring occasionally. Pour into pie pan. Refrigerate about 2 hours or until mixture is fudgy, but soft.

Shape about 1 tablespoonful of mixture into 1¼-inch ball. Repeat with remaining mixture. Roll balls in your palms to form uniform round shapes; place on waxed paper.

Place sprinkles in shallow bowl. Roll balls in sprinkles; place in petit four or candy cases. (If coating mixture won't stick because truffle has set, roll between your palms until outside is soft.) Store in airtight container up to 3 days in refrigerator or several weeks in freezer.

*Makes about 24 truffles*

*Top box (left to right): Merri-Mint Truffles, Easy Orange Truffles (page 158) and Jolly Bourbon Balls*

# Easy Orange Truffles

1 cup (6 ounces) semisweet chocolate
    chips
2 squares (1 ounce each) unsweetened
    chocolate, chopped
1½ cups powdered sugar
 ½ cup butter or margarine, softened
1 tablespoon grated orange peel
1 tablespoon orange-flavored liqueur
2 squares (1 ounce each) semisweet
    chocolate, grated *or* cocoa

Melt chocolate chips and unsweetened chocolate in heavy small saucepan over very low heat, stirring constantly; set aside.

Combine powdered sugar, butter, orange peel and liqueur in small bowl. Beat with electric mixer until combined. Beat in cooled chocolate. Pour into pie pan. Refrigerate about 30 minutes or until mixture is fudgy and can be shaped into balls.

Shape scant 1 tablespoonful of mixture into 1-inch ball. Repeat with remaining mixture. Roll balls in your palms to form uniform round shapes; place on waxed paper.

Sprinkle grated chocolate or cocoa in shallow bowl. Roll balls in grated chocolate or cocoa; place in petit four or candy cases. (If coating mixture won't stick because truffle has set, roll between your palms until outside is soft.) Store in airtight container up to 3 days in refrigerator or several weeks in freezer.

*Makes about 34 truffles*

**Tip:** Truffles are coated with cocoa, powdered sugar, nuts, sprinkles or cookie crumbs to add flavor and prevent the truffle from melting in your fingers.

# Cherry Merry Christmas Crunch

2 cups walnut halves
1 cup candied red and green cherries,
    cut in half
2 tablespoons butter or margarine
1 teaspoon salt
1 teaspoon maple extract
 ¼ teaspoon cherry extract
2 cups sugar
 ¾ cup light corn syrup
 ¼ cup maple syrup

Generously grease baking sheet. Combine walnuts, cherries, butter, salt and extracts in medium bowl; set aside. Combine sugar, corn syrup and maple syrup in heavy large saucepan. Bring to a boil. Cook over medium heat until mixture reaches 300°F on candy thermometer (hard-crack stage). Remove from heat; stir in walnut mixture. Quickly pour onto prepared pan. Cool completely. Break into pieces.

*Makes about 2 pounds candy*

*Top to bottom: Cherry Merry Christmas Crunch and Eggnog Gift Fudge (page 159)*

*German Chocolate Fudge Swirl*

# Eggnog Gift Fudge

¾ cup prepared eggnog
2 tablespoons light corn syrup
2 tablespoons butter or margarine
2 cups sugar
1 teaspoon vanilla

Butter 8-inch square pan. Lightly butter inside of heavy medium saucepan. Combine eggnog, corn syrup, butter and sugar in prepared saucepan. Cook over medium heat, stirring constantly, until sugar dissolves and mixture comes to a boil. Wash down side of pan with pastry brush frequently dipped in hot water to remove sugar crystals. Add candy thermometer. Continue to cook until mixture reaches 238°F (soft-ball stage). Pour into large heatproof bowl. Cool to lukewarm (about 110°F). Add vanilla; beat with heavy-duty electric mixer until thick. Spread into prepared pan. Score fudge into 36 squares. Refrigerate until firm. Cut into squares. Wrap in plastic wrap and top with bows as shown in photo on page 158.

*Makes 36 pieces*

# German Chocolate Fudge Swirl

**Filling**

¾ cup flaked coconut
¾ cup chopped nuts
2 tablespoons undiluted CARNATION®
    Evaporated Milk

**Fudge**

1½ cups granulated sugar
⅔ cup undiluted CARNATION®
    Evaporated Milk
2 tablespoons butter or margarine
¼ teaspoon salt
2 cups (4 ounces) miniature
    marshmallows
1½ cups NESTLÉ® TOLL HOUSE®
    Semi-Sweet Chocolate Morsels
1 teaspoon vanilla

**FOR FILLING: MIX** coconut, nuts and 2 tablespoons evaporated milk in small bowl.

**FOR FUDGE: LINE** 15 × 10-inch jelly-roll pan with heavily buttered waxed paper.

**COMBINE** sugar, ⅔ cup evaporated milk, butter and salt in medium saucepan. Bring to a boil over medium heat, stirring constantly. Boil 4 to 5 minutes, stirring constantly; remove from heat.

**STIR** in marshmallows, morsels and vanilla. Stir vigorously for 1 minute or until marshmallows melt completely.

**POUR** into prepared pan, spreading evenly (if fudge is difficult to spread, let stand for 1 minute). Sprinkle with filling. Let cool about 5 minutes. Starting with long side of pan, roll up fudge jelly-roll style, using waxed paper to assist, if necessary. Wrap fudge roll in waxed paper. Cool and cut into slices. *Makes about 2 pounds*

*Clockwise from top left: Easy Caramel Pop Corn Balls, Almond Butter Crunch Pop Corn and Rocky Road Peanut Butter Pop Corn Bars*

## Rocky Road Peanut Butter Pop Corn Bars

  3 quarts popped JOLLY TIME® Pop Corn
½ cup raisins
  1 cup light corn syrup
  1 tablespoon butter or margarine
½ cup peanut butter chips
⅓ cup chunky or creamy peanut butter
¾ cup miniature marshmallows
½ cup peanuts
½ cup semisweet chocolate chips
  1 teaspoon vegetable shortening

Place pop corn and raisins in large bowl. In medium saucepan, heat corn syrup and butter to a boil. Boil 3 minutes. Remove from heat. Stir in peanut butter chips and peanut butter. Stir until smooth. Pour mixture over pop corn, tossing gently to coat all pieces. Press into buttered 9-inch square baking pan. Sprinkle marshmallows and peanuts over top, pressing lightly into pop corn mixture. Melt chocolate chips and shortening over very low heat. Drizzle over top. Cool several hours before serving. Cut into 2¼ × 1-inch bars. *Makes 36 bars*

## Easy Caramel Pop Corn Balls

2½ quarts popped JOLLY TIME® Pop Corn
  1 package (14 ounces) light caramels
¼ cup light corn syrup
  2 tablespoons water

Keep pop corn warm in 200°F oven. Melt caramels in heavy saucepan over low heat, stirring occasionally, about 15 minutes. Add corn syrup and water and mix until smooth. Slowly pour over pop corn in large bowl or pan, mixing well. Shape into balls.
*Makes 10 medium pop corn balls*

**Microwave Directions:** Microwave caramels and water in large microwavable bowl on HIGH 2 to 3 minutes or until mixture is smooth, stirring after every minute. Add corn syrup and mix until smooth. Proceed as directed.

## Almond Butter Crunch Pop Corn

½ cup butter or margarine
  1 cup granulated sugar
¼ cup light corn syrup
¼ teaspoon salt
½ teaspoon vanilla
½ teaspoon butter extract
¼ teaspoon baking soda
2½ quarts popped JOLLY TIME® Pop Corn
1½ cups whole almonds, toasted*

*To toast almonds, spread on large cookie sheet and bake at 325°F 15 to 20 minutes.

Melt butter in medium saucepan. Stir in sugar, corn syrup and salt. Bring to a boil, stirring constantly. Boil 8 minutes, stirring once, over lowest heat possible to maintain a boil. Remove from heat; stir in vanilla, butter extract and baking soda. Gradually pour over popped pop corn and almonds, mixing well. Turn into large shallow baking pan. Bake at 250°F 30 minutes, mixing well after 15 minutes. Allow to cool completely. Break apart and store in tightly covered container. *Makes about 3 quarts*

## Creamy Caramels

½ cup slivered or chopped toasted almonds (optional)
1 cup butter or margarine, cut into small pieces
1 can (14 ounces) sweetened condensed milk
2 cups sugar
1 cup light corn syrup
1½ teaspoons vanilla

Line 8-inch square baking pan with foil, extending edges over sides of pan. Lightly grease foil; sprinkle almonds over bottom of pan, if desired.

Melt butter in heavy 2-quart saucepan over low heat. Add milk, sugar and corn syrup. Stir over low heat until sugar is dissolved and mixture comes to a boil. Carefully clip candy thermometer to side of pan (do not let bulb touch bottom of pan). Cook over low heat about 30 minutes or until thermometer registers 240°F (soft-ball stage), stirring occasionally. Immediately remove from heat and stir in vanilla. Pour mixture into prepared pan. Cool completely.

Lift caramels out of pan using foil; remove foil. Place on cutting board; cut into 1-inch squares with sharp knife. Wrap each square in plastic wrap. Store in airtight container.

*Makes about 2½ pounds or 64 caramels*

## Traditional Christmas Fudge

2 tablespoons butter or margarine
⅔ cup undiluted CARNATION® Evaporated Milk
1½ cups granulated sugar
¼ teaspoon salt
2 cups (4 ounces) miniature marshmallows
1½ cups (9 ounces) NESTLÉ® TOLL HOUSE® Semi-Sweet Chocolate Morsels
½ cup chopped pecans or walnuts
1 teaspoon vanilla

**COMBINE** butter, evaporated milk, sugar and salt in medium, heavy saucepan. Bring to a boil over medium heat, stirring constantly. Boil for 4 to 5 minutes, stirring constantly. Remove from heat.

**STIR** in marshmallows, morsels, pecans and vanilla. Stir vigorously 1 minute or until marshmallows are melted. Pour into foil-lined 8-inch square baking pan. Sprinkle with additional pecans, if desired. Chill until firm. *Makes about 2 pounds*

**Milk Chocolate Fudge:** Substitute 2 cups (11½-ounce package) NESTLÉ® TOLL HOUSE® Milk Chocolate Morsels for Semi-Sweet Morsels.

**Butterscotch Fudge:** Substitute 2 cups (12-ounce package) NESTLÉ® TOLL HOUSE® Butterscotch Flavored Morsels for Semi-Sweet Morsels.

**Mint Chocolate Fudge:** Substitute 1½ cups (10-ounce package) NESTLÉ® TOLL HOUSE® Mint-Chocolate Morsels for Semi-Sweet Morsels.

# Christmas Fudge

3 cups sugar
1 cup PET® Evaporated Milk
½ cup butter
2 cups semisweet chocolate chips
1 jar (7 to 7½ ounces) marshmallow creme
1 teaspoon vanilla
1 cup crushed peppermint candies

1. Butter 13 × 9 × 2-inch baking pan.

2. In heavy 3-quart saucepan, combine sugar, evaporated milk and butter. Bring to a full rolling boil over high heat, stirring constantly.

3. Reduce heat to medium and boil 6 minutes (234°F), stirring constantly.

4. Remove from heat and stir in chocolate chips, marshmallow creme and vanilla.

5. Stir in peppermint candies.

6. Pour into prepared pan. Cool until firm.

*Makes 117 (1-inch) pieces*

# Caramel-Marshmallow Apples

1 package (14 ounces) caramels
1 cup miniature marshmallows
1 tablespoon water
5 or 6 small apples

1. Line baking sheet with buttered waxed paper; set aside.

2. Combine caramels, marshmallows and water in medium saucepan. Cook over medium heat, stirring constantly, until caramels melt. Cool slightly while preparing apples.

3. Rinse and thoroughly dry apples. Insert flat sticks in stem ends of apples.

4. Dip each apple in caramel mixture, coating apples. Remove excess caramel mixture by scraping apple bottoms across rim of saucepan. Place on prepared baking sheet. Refrigerate until firm.

*Makes 5 or 6 apples*

**Caramel-Nut Apples:** Roll coated apples in chopped nuts before refrigerating.

**Caramel-Chocolate Apples:** Drizzle melted milk chocolate over coated apples before refrigerating.

# Almond-Coconut Balls

1 can (7 ounces) almond paste
1 cup flaked coconut
⅓ cup powdered sugar
1 to 2 teaspoons water
7 ounces pastel-colored confectionery coating

Line baking sheet with buttered waxed paper; set aside.

Combine almond paste, coconut and sugar in medium bowl. Stir in water if mixture is dry.

For each candy, shape 1 scant tablespoonful of mixture into 1-inch ball. Place balls on prepared baking sheet. Refrigerate until set, about 30 minutes.

Melt confectionery coating in saucepan set over hot, not boiling, water, stirring constantly.

Dip balls in coating to cover. Remove excess coating by scraping bottom of ball across rim of saucepan. Return to baking sheet. Reheat coating if it gets too thick. Refrigerate until set, about 30 minutes.

*Makes about 24 balls*

*Christmas Fudge*

# Festive Popcorn Treats

6 cups popped popcorn
½ cup sugar
½ cup light corn syrup
¼ cup peanut butter
　　Green food coloring
¼ cup red cinnamon candies

Line baking sheet with waxed paper. Pour popcorn into large bowl. Combine sugar and corn syrup in medium saucepan. Bring to a boil over medium heat, stirring constantly; boil 1 minute. Remove from heat. Add peanut butter and green food coloring; stir until peanut butter is completely melted. Pour over popcorn; stir to coat well. Lightly butter hands and shape popcorn mixture into trees as shown in photo. While trees are still warm, press red cinnamon candies into trees. Place on prepared baking sheet; let stand until firm, about 30 minutes. *Makes 6 servings*

*Clockwise from left: Festive Popcorn Treats, Good Luck Meringue Mushrooms and Tiger Stripes (page 165)*

# Good Luck Meringue Mushrooms

2 egg whites
　　Pinch cream of tartar
½ cup sugar
½ cup semisweet chocolate chips, melted
　　Unsweetened cocoa

Preheat oven to 250°F. Beat egg whites in small bowl until foamy. Add cream of tartar and beat until soft peaks form. Add sugar, 2 tablespoons at a time, beating until stiff and glossy. Line baking sheets with parchment paper. Spoon mixture into pastry bag fitted with large writing tip. Pipe 1-inch rounds to make mushroom caps. Smooth tops with wet fingertips. Pipe 1-inch-high cones to make stems. (Pipe an equal number of caps and cones.) Bake about 30 minutes or until firm. Turn oven off; let stand in oven 1 hour. Remove from oven; cool completely. Make small hole in center of flat side of each cap with sharp knife. Fill hole with melted chocolate. Insert stem into hole. Set aside until chocolate sets. Sift cocoa through fine sieve over mushroom caps. *Makes about 2½ dozen*

**Note:** These can be made ahead and stored, loosely covered, at room temperature for up to 1 week. Avoid making on humid days as meringue may become moist and sticky.

## Tiger Stripes

1 package (12 ounces) semisweet
   chocolate chips
3 tablespoons chunky peanut butter,
   divided
2 (2-ounce) white chocolate baking bars

Line 8-inch square pan with foil. Grease
lightly. Melt semisweet chocolate and
2 tablespoons peanut butter in small
saucepan over low heat; stir well. Pour half
of chocolate mixture into prepared pan. Let
stand 10 to 15 minutes to cool slightly. Melt
white baking bars with remaining 1
tablespoon peanut butter in small saucepan
over low heat. Spoon half of white
chocolate mixture over dark chocolate
mixture. Drop remaining dark and white
chocolate mixtures by spoonfuls over
mixture in pan. Using small metal spatula
or knife, pull through the chocolates to
create tiger stripes. Freeze about 1 hour or
until firm. Remove from pan; peel off foil.
Cut into 36 pieces. Refrigerate until ready
to serve. *Makes 36 pieces*

## Double Chocolate-Creme Fudge

1 can (12 ounces) evaporated milk
2 cups (11½ ounces) milk chocolate
   chips
1 cup (6 ounces) semisweet chocolate
   chips
1 jar (7 ounces) marshmallow creme
¼ cup butter or margarine
4 cups sugar
   Dash salt
1 teaspoon vanilla
2½ to 3 cups chopped pecans, divided

Butter 13 × 9-inch pan; set aside. Lightly
butter side of heavy large saucepan.

*Top to bottom: Double Chocolate-Creme Fudge and Sour Cream Fudge (page 166)*

Combine evaporated milk, chips,
marshmallow creme, butter, sugar and salt
in prepared saucepan. Cook over medium
heat, stirring constantly, until sugar
dissolves and mixture comes to a boil.
Wash down side of pan with pastry brush
frequently dipped in hot water to remove
sugar crystals.

Add candy thermometer. Stir mixture
occasionally. Continue to cook until
mixture reaches soft-ball stage (238°F). Pour
into large heatproof mixer bowl. Cool to
lukewarm. Add vanilla and beat with
heavy-duty electric mixer until thick. Beat
in 1 cup chopped pecans when candy starts
to lose its gloss. Immediately spread into
prepared pan. Sprinkle remaining chopped
pecans over fudge; gently press into fudge.
Score fudge into squares. Refrigerate until
firm. Cut into squares. Refrigerate.

*Makes about 4 pounds*

## Sour Cream Fudge

¾ cup sour cream
¼ cup milk
2 tablespoons corn syrup
2 tablespoons butter or margarine
2 cups sugar
1 teaspoon vanilla
½ cup walnut halves (optional)

Butter 8-inch square pan; set aside. Lightly butter side of heavy medium saucepan.

Combine sour cream, milk, corn syrup, butter and sugar in prepared saucepan. Cook over medium heat, stirring constantly, until sugar dissolves and mixture comes to a boil. Wash down side of pan with pastry brush frequently dipped in hot water to remove sugar crystals.

Add candy thermometer. Continue to cook until mixture reaches soft-ball stage (238°F).

Pour into large heatproof mixer bowl. Cool to lukewarm (about 110°F).

Add vanilla and beat with heavy-duty electric mixer until thick. Spread into prepared pan. Score fudge into small squares. Refrigerate until firm. Cut into squares. Place walnut half on each piece. Refrigerate. *Makes about 1¼ pounds*

## Chocolate Walnut Truffles

1 cup heavy cream
16 ounces semisweet chocolate, cut into small pieces
2 tablespoons butter
1 cup finely chopped walnuts
4 tablespoons coffee liqueur
Grated chocolate, shredded coconut and finely chopped walnuts

Bring heavy cream to a boil in large saucepan over medium heat; add chocolate. Stir with wooden spoon until mixture is smooth and thick; stir in butter. Pour into large bowl; cool. Stir in walnuts and liqueur; refrigerate until firm. Form into 1-inch balls and roll in chocolate, coconut or walnuts; refrigerate until set. Store in airtight container in refrigerator.

*Makes 3½ dozen truffles*

*Favorite recipe from* **Walnut Marketing Board**

## Chocolate-Coated Almond Toffee

1 cup (2 sticks) butter or margarine
1 cup sugar
3 tablespoons water
1 tablespoon corn syrup
½ cup toasted chopped almonds
6 squares BAKER'S® Semi-Sweet Chocolate, melted
⅓ cup toasted finely chopped almonds

**COOK** butter, sugar, water and corn syrup in heavy 2-quart saucepan over medium heat until mixture boils, stirring constantly. Boil gently, stirring frequently, 10 to 12 minutes or until golden brown and very thick. (Or until ½ teaspoon of mixture will form a hard, brittle thread when dropped in 1 cup cold water.)

**REMOVE** from heat. Stir in ½ cup almonds. Spread evenly into well-buttered 15½ × 10½ × 1-inch baking pan. Let stand until almost cool to the touch.

**SPREAD** melted chocolate over toffee; sprinkle with ⅓ cup almonds. Let stand until chocolate is firm. Break into pieces.

*Makes about 1½ pounds candy*

**Prep Time:** 30 minutes

*Coffee Liqueur Pecan Fudge*

# Coffee Liqueur Pecan Fudge

3 cups miniature marshmallows
2 cups (12-ounce package) NESTLÉ®
   TOLL HOUSE® Semi-Sweet
   Chocolate Morsels
2 ounces NESTLÉ® Unsweetened
   Chocolate Baking Bars, coarsely
   chopped
⅔ cup undiluted CARNATION®
   Evaporated Milk
1⅓ cups granulated sugar
¼ cup butter
1 cup coarsely chopped pecans
¼ cup coffee liqueur

In large bowl, combine marshmallows, morsels and unsweetened chocolate. In heavy 2-quart saucepan, combine evaporated milk, sugar and butter. Bring to a boil over medium heat, stirring frequently; boil for 6 minutes, stirring constantly. Pour over marshmallow mixture; stir until marshmallows and chocolate are completely melted and mixture is smooth. Stir in pecans and liqueur. Pour into buttered 8-inch square baking pan; cool. Chill until firm. Cut into 36 squares.          *Makes 2½ pounds*

# Sugared Nuts

1 cup sugar
½ cup water
2½ cups unsalted mixed nuts
1 teaspoon vanilla

Grease baking sheet; set aside.

Combine sugar and water in medium saucepan. Cook, stirring constantly, over medium heat until sugar dissolves.

Add nuts and vanilla. Cook, stirring occasionally, until water evaporates and nuts are sugary, about 12 minutes.

Spread on prepared baking sheet, separating nuts. Let stand until cooled.
          *Makes about 1 pound*

# Rich Chocolate Sauce

1 cup whipping cream
⅓ cup light corn syrup
1 cup (6 ounces) semisweet chocolate
   chips
1 to 2 tablespoons dark rum (optional)
1 teaspoon vanilla

Place cream and corn syrup in heavy 2-quart saucepan. Stir over medium heat until mixture boils. Remove from heat. Stir in chocolate, rum, if desired, and vanilla until chocolate is melted. Cool 10 minutes. Serve warm or pour into clean glass jars and seal tightly. Store up to 6 months in refrigerator. Reheat sauce over low heat before serving.

          *Makes about 1¾ cups sauce*

## Citrus Candied Nuts

1 egg white
1½ cups whole almonds
1½ cups pecan halves
1 cup powdered sugar
2 tablespoons lemon juice
2 teaspoons grated orange peel
1 teaspoon grated lemon peel
⅛ teaspoon ground nutmeg

Preheat oven to 300°F. Generously grease 15½ × 10½ × 1-inch jelly-roll pan. Beat egg white in medium bowl with electric mixer at high speed until soft peaks form. Add almonds and pecans; stir until coated. Stir in remaining ingredients. Turn out onto prepared pan, spreading nuts in single layer.

Bake 30 minutes, stirring after 20 minutes. *Turn off oven.* Let nuts stand in oven 15 minutes. Immediately remove nuts from pan to sheet of foil. Cool completely. Store up to 2 weeks in airtight container.

*Makes about 3 cups nuts*

## Gooey Hot Fudge Sauce

2 cups (12 ounces) semisweet chocolate chips
2 tablespoons butter
½ cup half-and-half
1 tablespoon corn syrup
⅛ teaspoon salt
½ teaspoon vanilla

Melt chocolate and butter with half-and-half, corn syrup and salt in heavy 2-quart saucepan over low heat, stirring until smooth. Remove from heat; let stand 10 minutes. Stir in vanilla. Serve warm or pour into clean glass jars and seal tightly. Store up to 6 months in refrigerator. Reheat sauce in double-boiler over hot (not boiling) water before serving, if desired.

*Makes about 1½ cups sauce*

## Elegant Cream Cheese Mints

Chocolate Topping (recipe follows), optional
1 package (3 ounces) cream cheese, softened
3 tablespoons butter or margarine, softened
½ teaspoon vanilla
¼ to ½ teaspoon desired food coloring
¼ teaspoon peppermint extract
1 pound powdered sugar (3½ to 4 cups)
⅓ cup granulated sugar

Line large cookie sheet with waxed paper. Prepare Chocolate Topping; keep warm.

Beat cream cheese, butter, vanilla, food coloring and peppermint extract in large bowl with electric mixer at medium speed until smooth, scraping side of bowl once. Gradually beat in powdered sugar at low speed until well combined, scraping side of bowl several times. (If necessary, stir in remaining powdered sugar with wooden spoon or knead candy on work surface sprinkled lightly with powdered sugar.)

Place granulated sugar in shallow bowl. Roll 2 teaspoons of cream cheese mixture into a ball. Roll ball in granulated sugar until coated. Flatten ball with fingers or fork to make a patty. Place patty on prepared cookie sheet. Repeat with remaining cream cheese mixture and sugar. Drizzle patties with topping, if desired. Refrigerate until firm. Store in airtight container in refrigerator.

*Makes about 1½ pounds or 40 (1-inch) mints*

**Chocolate Topping:** Place ½ cup semisweet chocolate chips and 1 tablespoon vegetable shortening in 1-cup microwavable glass measuring cup. Microwave on HIGH about 2 minutes or until melted, stirring after 1½ minutes.

*Top to bottom: Citrus Candied Nuts and Elegant Cream Cheese Mints*

*Popcorn Crunchies*

## Popcorn Crunchies

12 cups popped popcorn (about ¾ cup
    unpopped)
1½ cups sugar
 ⅓ cup water
 ⅓ cup corn syrup
 2 tablespoons butter or margarine
 1 teaspoon vanilla

Preheat oven to 250°F. Grease large shallow roasting pan. Add popcorn. Keep warm in oven while preparing caramel mixture.

Place sugar, water and corn syrup in heavy 2-quart saucepan. Stir over low heat until sugar has dissolved and mixture comes to a boil. Carefully clip candy thermometer to side of pan (do not let bulb touch bottom of pan). Cook over low heat about 10 minutes or until thermometer registers 280°F, without stirring. Occasionally wash down any sugar crystals that form on side of the pan using pastry brush dipped in warm water. Immediately remove from heat. Stir in butter and vanilla until smooth.

Pour hot syrup mixture slowly over warm popcorn, turning to coat kernels evenly. Set aside until cool enough to handle but warm enough to shape. Butter hands. Working quickly, lightly press warm mixture into 2-inch balls. Cool completely. Store in airtight container.

*Makes about 14 popcorn balls*

**Tips:** If making Popcorn Crunchies to eat, insert lollipop sticks while still warm; set aside to cool completely. Cover with decorative plastic wrap. If making Popcorn Crunchies for tree ornaments, cool balls completely and wrap each ball with enough decorative plastic wrap to pull wrap together at top. Secure with a ribbon which can be formed into a bow or a loop for hanging.

## Honey Nut White Fudge

2 tablespoons butter or margarine
⅔ cup undiluted CARNATION®
    Evaporated Milk
1½ cups granulated sugar
2 cups (4 ounces) miniature
    marshmallows
2 cups (12-ounce package) NESTLÉ®
    TOLL HOUSE® Premier White
    Morsels
1½ cups honey roasted peanuts, divided
2 teaspoons vanilla

COMBINE butter, evaporated milk and sugar in medium, heavy saucepan. Bring to a *full rolling boil* over medium heat, stirring constantly. Boil 4½ to 5 minutes, stirring constantly. Remove from heat.

STIR in marshmallows, morsels, *1 cup* peanuts and vanilla. Stir vigorously for 1 minute or until marshmallows are melted. Pour into foil-lined 9-inch square baking pan. Coarsely chop *remaining ½ cup* peanuts; sprinkle over fudge and lightly press. Chill until firm. Remove foil before cutting into squares.

*Makes about 1¾ pounds fudge*

## Easy Chocolate Truffles

1 package (8 ounces) PHILADELPHIA
    BRAND® Cream Cheese, softened
3 cups powdered sugar
1½ packages (12 ounces) BAKER'S®
    Semi-Sweet Chocolate, melted
1½ teaspoons vanilla
    Ground nuts, unsweetened cocoa or
    BAKER'S® ANGEL FLAKE®
    Coconut, toasted

BEAT cream cheese until smooth. Gradually add sugar, beating until well blended. Add melted chocolate and vanilla; mix well. Refrigerate about 1 hour. Shape into 1-inch balls. Roll in nuts, cocoa or coconut. Store in refrigerator.

*Makes about 5 dozen candies*

**Prep Time:** 15 minutes
**Chill Time:** 1 hour

**Variation:** To flavor truffles with liqueurs, omit vanilla. Divide truffle mixture into thirds. Add 1 tablespoon liqueur (almond, coffee or orange) to each third mixture; mix well.

## Chocolate Fondue

⅔ cup KARO® Light or Dark Corn Syrup
½ cup heavy cream
8 squares (1 ounce each) semisweet
    chocolate
    Assorted fresh fruit

In medium saucepan, combine corn syrup and cream. Bring to a boil over medium heat. Remove from heat. Add chocolate; stir until completely melted. Serve warm as a dip for fruit. *Makes 1½ cups fondue*

**Prep Time:** 10 minutes

**Microwave Directions:** In medium microwavable bowl, combine corn syrup and cream. Microwave at HIGH (100% power) 1½ minutes or until boiling. Add chocolate; stir until completely melted. Serve as directed.

**Note:** Chocolate Fondue can be made a day ahead. Store covered in refrigerator and reheat before serving.

# Old-Fashioned Fudge

3 cups sugar
1 cup PET® Evaporated Milk
½ cup butter
2 cups semisweet chocolate chips
1 jar (7 to 7½ ounces) marshmallow creme
1 cup chopped nuts (optional)
1 teaspoon vanilla

1. Butter 13 × 9 × 2-inch baking pan.

2. In heavy 3-quart saucepan, combine sugar, evaporated milk and butter. Bring to a full rolling boil over high heat, stirring constantly.

3. Reduce heat to medium and boil 5 minutes (approximately 234°F), stirring constantly.

4. Remove from heat and stir in chocolate chips, marshmallow creme, nuts and vanilla.

5. Pour into prepared pan and cool until firm. *Makes 117 (1-inch) pieces*

# Penuche

¼ cup butter
2½ cups packed brown sugar
¾ cup PET® Evaporated Milk
2 tablespoons light corn syrup
1 teaspoon vanilla
1 cup chopped pecans (optional)

1. Butter 8-inch square baking pan.

2. In heavy 3-quart saucepan, melt butter. Add sugar, evaporated milk and corn syrup; stir well. Bring to a full rolling boil over medium heat, stirring constantly.

3. Cover pan and continue boiling very gently over low heat 2 minutes. Remove cover and scrape side of pan with rubber spatula.

4. Continue boiling, uncovered, over low heat until mixture reaches 236°F, gently scraping side of saucepan occasionally. (DO NOT SCRAPE BOTTOM OF PAN.)

5. Pour mixture into nonmetallic bowl. Do not scrape side or bottom of saucepan. Place candy thermometer in mixture. Place bowl in ½ inch of lukewarm water. Cool mixture to 110°F *without stirring*.

6. Add vanilla. Beat until mixture thickens and starts to lose its gloss. Stir in pecans, if desired. Pour into buttered pan. Cool until firm. Store in covered container.
*Makes 64 (1-inch) pieces*

# White Truffles

2 pounds EAGLE™ Brand Vanilla-Flavored Candy Coating
1 (14-ounce) can EAGLE® Brand Sweetened Condensed Milk (NOT evaporated milk)
1 tablespoon vanilla extract
1 pound EAGLE™ Brand Chocolate-Flavored Candy Coating, melted *or* ¾ cup unsweetened cocoa

In large heavy saucepan over low heat, melt vanilla candy coating with sweetened condensed milk, stirring frequently until smooth. Remove from heat; stir in vanilla. Cool. Shape into 1-inch balls. With wooden pick, partially dip each ball into melted chocolate candy coating or roll in cocoa. Place on waxed paper-lined baking sheets until firm. Store covered at room temperature or in refrigerator.
*Makes about 8 dozen truffles*

**Microwave Directions:** In 2-quart glass measure with handle, combine vanilla candy coating and sweetened condensed milk. Cook on HIGH (100% power) 3 to 3½ minutes or until coating melts, stirring after each 1½ minutes. Proceed as directed.

# Double Decker Fudge

1 cup REESE'S® Peanut Butter Chips
1 cup HERSHEY'S Semi-Sweet
  Chocolate Chips or HERSHEY'S
  MINI CHIPS® Semi-Sweet
  Chocolate
2¼ cups sugar
1 jar (7 ounces) marshmallow creme
¾ cup evaporated milk
¼ cup (½ stick) butter or margarine
1 teaspoon vanilla extract

Line 8-inch square pan with foil, extending foil over edges of pan. In medium bowl, place peanut butter chips. In second medium bowl, place chocolate chips. In heavy 3-quart saucepan, combine sugar, marshmallow creme, evaporated milk and butter. Cook over medium heat, stirring constantly, until mixture comes to a boil; boil 5 minutes, stirring constantly. Remove from heat; stir in vanilla. Immediately stir half of the hot mixture (1½ cups) into peanut butter chips until chips are completely melted; quickly spread into prepared pan. Stir remaining hot mixture into chocolate chips until chips are completely melted. Quickly spread over top of peanut butter layer. Cool to room temperature; refrigerate until firm. Use foil to lift fudge out of pan; peel off foil. Cut into 1-inch squares. Store tightly covered in refrigerator.

*Makes 5 dozen pieces or about 2 pounds fudge*

**Peanut Butter Fudge:** Omit chocolate chips; place 1⅔ cups (10-ounce package) REESE'S® Peanut Butter Chips in large bowl. Cook fudge mixture as directed; add to chips, stirring until chips are completely melted. Pour into prepared pan; cool to room temperature.

**Chocolate Fudge:** Omit peanut butter chips; place 2 cups (12-ounce package) HERSHEY'S Semi-Sweet Chocolate Chips or HERSHEY'S MINI CHIPS® Semi-Sweet Chocolate in large bowl. Cook fudge mixture as directed; add to chips, stirring until chips are completely melted. Pour into prepared pan; cool to room temperature.

*Top to bottom: Semi-Sweet Chocolate Fudge and Double Decker Fudge*

# Semi-Sweet Chocolate Fudge

4 cups sugar
1 jar (7 ounces) marshmallow creme
1½ cups (12-ounce can) evaporated milk
1 tablespoon butter or margarine
4 cups (24-ounce package) HERSHEY'S
  Semi-Sweet Chocolate Chips

Line 13 × 9 × 2-inch pan with foil extending over edges of pan. Butter foil lightly. In heavy 4-quart saucepan, stir together sugar, marshmallow creme, evaporated milk and butter. Cook over medium heat, stirring constantly, until mixture comes to a full rolling boil; boil and stir 5 minutes. Remove from heat; immediately add chocolate chips, stirring until smooth. Pour into prepared pan; cool until firm. Using foil to lift fudge out of pan, remove. Peel off foil. Cut into squares. Store in airtight container in cool, dry place.

*Makes about 8 dozen squares*

# Caramels

2 cups sugar
2 cups light corn syrup
⅛ teaspoon salt
½ cup butter
2 cups PET® Evaporated Milk
1 cup chopped nuts (optional)
1 teaspoon vanilla

1. Butter 9-inch square baking pan.

2. In heavy 3-quart saucepan, combine sugar, corn syrup and salt. Cook over medium-high heat until mixture reaches firm-ball stage (244°F), stirring constantly.

3. Stir in butter.

4. Very slowly add evaporated milk so that mixture does not stop boiling. Cook rapidly to firm-ball stage again, approximately 30 minutes, stirring constantly.

5. Stir in nuts and vanilla. Pour into prepared pan without scraping sides of saucepan. Cool until firm.

*Makes 81 (1-inch) pieces*

**Marble Caramels:** After pouring caramel mixture into baking pan, sprinkle with ⅓ cup semisweet chocolate chips. Let stand until soft enough to spread, 1 to 2 minutes. Swirl chocolate through caramels using metal spatula or knife. Cool until firm.

**Mocha Caramels:** Follow caramel recipe, except add 2 tablespoons instant coffee crystals to corn syrup mixture before cooking.

# Fast 'n' Fabulous Dark Chocolate Fudge

½ cup KARO® Light or Dark Corn Syrup
⅓ cup evaporated milk
3 cups (18 ounces) semisweet chocolate chips
¾ cup confectioners' sugar, sifted
2 teaspoons vanilla
1 cup coarsely chopped nuts (optional)

Line 8-inch square baking pan with plastic wrap. In 3-quart microwavable bowl combine corn syrup and evaporated milk; stir until well blended. Microwave on HIGH (100% power) 3 minutes. Stir in chocolate chips until melted. Stir in confectioners' sugar, vanilla and nuts. With wooden spoon, beat until thick and glossy. Spread into prepared pan. Refrigerate 2 hours or until firm.    *Makes 25 squares*

**Prep Time:** 10 minutes, plus chilling

**Marvelous Marble Fudge:** Omit nuts. Prepare as directed; spread into prepared pan. Drop ⅓ cup Skippy® creamy peanut butter over fudge in small dollops. With small spatula, swirl fudge to marbleize. Continue as directed.

**Double Peanut Butter Chocolate Fudge:** Prepare as directed. Stir in ⅓ cup Skippy® Super Chunk peanut butter. Spread in prepared pan. Drop additional ⅓ cup peanut butter over fudge in small dollops. With small spatula, swirl fudge to marbleize. Continue as directed.

*Plate (top to bottom): Marble Caramels and Caramels*

# Baked Caramel Corn

6 quarts popped JOLLY TIME® Pop
  Corn
1 cup butter or margarine
2 cups firmly packed brown sugar
½ cup light or dark corn syrup
1 teaspoon salt
1 teaspoon vanilla
½ teaspoon baking soda

Preheat oven to 250°F. Coat bottom and
sides of large roasting pan with nonstick
cooking spray. Place pop corn in prepared
pan. In heavy pan, slowly melt butter; stir
in brown sugar, corn syrup and salt. Bring
to a boil, stirring constantly. Boil, without
stirring, 5 minutes. Remove from heat; stir
in vanilla and baking soda. Gradually pour
over pop corn, mixing well. Bake 1 hour,
stirring every 15 minutes. Remove from
oven; cool completely. Break apart and
store in tightly covered container.

*Makes about 6 quarts*

*Top to bottom: Old-Fashioned Pop Corn
Balls and Baked Caramel Corn*

# Old-Fashioned Pop Corn Balls

2 quarts popped JOLLY TIME® Pop
  Corn
1 cup sugar
⅓ cup light or dark corn syrup
⅓ cup water
¼ cup butter or margarine
½ teaspoon salt
1 teaspoon vanilla

Keep pop corn warm in 200°F oven while
preparing syrup. In 2-quart saucepan,
combine sugar, corn syrup, water, butter
and salt. Cook over medium heat, stirring
constantly, until mixture comes to a boil.
Continue cooking without stirring until
temperature reaches 270°F on candy
thermometer or until small amount of
syrup dropped into very cold water
separates into threads that are hard but not
brittle. Remove from heat. Add vanilla; stir
just enough to mix through hot syrup.
Slowly pour over popped pop corn, stirring
to coat every kernel. Cool just enough to
handle. With Jolly Time® Pop Corn Ball
Maker or buttered hands, shape into balls.

*Makes 12 medium pop corn balls*

# Layered Mint Chocolate Fudge

2 cups (12 ounces) semi-sweet chocolate
  chips
1 (14-ounce) can EAGLE® Brand
  Sweetened Condensed Milk
  (NOT evaporated milk)
2 teaspoons vanilla extract
6 ounces EAGLE™ Brand Vanilla-
  Flavored Candy Coating
1 tablespoon peppermint extract
  Green or red food coloring, optional

In large heavy saucepan over low heat, melt chips with *1 cup* sweetened condensed milk, stirring frequently until smooth; add vanilla. Spread *half* the mixture into aluminum foil-lined 8- or 9-inch square pan; chill 10 minutes or until firm. Reserve remaining chocolate mixture at room temperature. In separate heavy saucepan over low heat, melt candy coating with remaining sweetened condensed milk (mixture will be thick). Add peppermint extract and food coloring if desired. Spread over chilled chocolate layer; chill 10 minutes or until firm. Spread reserved chocolate mixture over mint layer. Chill 2 hours or until firm. Place fudge on cutting board; peel off foil and cut into squares. Store loosely covered at room temperature.

*Makes about 1¾ pounds*

## Louisiana Cream Pralines

2⅓ cups packed brown sugar
¾ cup PET® Evaporated Milk
1 tablespoon butter
⅛ teaspoon salt
2 cups pecan halves
1 teaspoon vanilla

1. Butter baking sheet.

2. In heavy 2-quart saucepan, combine sugar, evaporated milk, butter and salt. Cook and stir over low heat until sugar is dissolved.

3. Add pecans. Cook over medium heat until candy thermometer reaches 234°F, about 9 minutes, stirring constantly.

4. Remove from heat; stir in vanilla. Cool 5 minutes without stirring.

5. Stir vigorously until mixture thickens and loses its gloss, about 5 minutes.

6. Drop quickly by tablespoonfuls onto buttered baking sheet. Cool. Store in covered container. *Makes 2½ to 3 dozen*

## Creamy Caramel Sauce

1 cup granulated sugar
1 cup whipping cream
½ cup packed light brown sugar
⅓ cup corn syrup
1 teaspoon vanilla

Place granulated sugar, cream, brown sugar and corn syrup in heavy 2-quart saucepan. Stir over low heat until mixture boils. Carefully clip candy thermometer to side of pan (do not let bulb touch bottom of pan). Cook, stirring occasionally, about 20 minutes or until thermometer registers 238°F. Immediately remove from heat. Stir in vanilla. Cool about 15 minutes. Serve warm or pour into clean glass jars and seal tightly. Store up to 6 months in refrigerator. Reheat sauce over low heat before serving.

*Makes about 2 cups sauce*

## Microwave Fudge

½ cup butter
3 cups sugar
¾ cup PET® Evaporated Milk
2 cups semisweet chocolate chips
1 jar (7 to 7½ ounces) marshmallow creme
1 teaspoon vanilla

1. Butter 13 × 9 × 2-inch baking pan.

2. Place butter in microwave-safe 3-quart bowl. Microwave on HIGH (100% power) 1 minute or until melted.

3. Stir in sugar and milk. Microwave on HIGH 11 minutes, stirring every 2 minutes (approximately 234°F).

4. Stir in chocolate chips, marshmallow creme and vanilla.

5. Pour into prepared pan. Cool until firm. Store in covered container.

*Makes 117 (1-inch) pieces*

# DESSERTS

## Peanut Chocolate Surprise Pie

½ cup (1 stick) butter, melted
1 cup sugar
2 eggs
½ cup all-purpose flour
½ cup chopped peanuts
½ cup chopped walnuts
½ cup semisweet chocolate chips
¼ cup bourbon
1 teaspoon vanilla
1 (9-inch) unbaked deep-dish pie shell
Whipped cream for garnish
Chocolate shavings for garnish

Preheat oven to 350°F. Cream butter and sugar in large bowl. Add eggs and beat until well mixed. Gradually add flour; stir in nuts, chocolate chips, bourbon and vanilla. Spread mixture evenly in unbaked pie shell. Bake 40 minutes. Cool pie on wire rack. Garnish, if desired.

*Makes one 9-inch pie*

## Apple Pumpkin Desserts

1 (21-ounce) can apple pie filling
1 (16-ounce) can pumpkin (about 2 cups)
1 (14-ounce) can EAGLE® Brand Sweetened Condensed Milk (NOT evaporated milk)
2 eggs
1 teaspoon ground cinnamon
½ teaspoon ground nutmeg
½ teaspoon salt
1 cup gingersnap crumbs (about 18 cookies)
2 tablespoons margarine or butter, melted

Preheat oven to 400°. Spoon equal portions of apple pie filling into 8 to 10 lightly greased custard cups. In large mixer bowl, combine pumpkin, sweetened condensed milk, eggs, cinnamon, nutmeg and salt; mix well. Spoon equal portions over apple pie filling. Combine crumbs and margarine. Sprinkle over pumpkin mixture. Place cups in 15 × 10-inch baking pan. Bake 10 minutes. *Reduce oven temperature to 350°;* bake 15 minutes longer or until set. Cool. Serve warm. Garnish as desired. Refrigerate leftovers.

*Makes 8 to 10 servings*

*Peanut Chocolate Surprise Pie*

*Chocolate Almond Confection Cake*

# Chocolate Almond Confection Cake

### Cake

  1 package (7 ounces) pure almond paste
½ cup CRISCO® Oil or CRISCO®
    PURITAN® Canola Oil, divided
  3 eggs
  1 package DUNCAN HINES® Moist
    Deluxe Devil's Food Cake Mix
1⅓ cups water

### Glaze

  1 package (6 ounces) semisweet
    chocolate chips
  3 tablespoons cherry jelly or seedless
    red raspberry jam
  2 tablespoons butter or margarine
  1 tablespoon light corn syrup
    Natural sliced almonds, for garnish
    Candied whole maraschino cherries or
    fresh raspberries, for garnish

1. Preheat oven to 350°F. Grease and flour 10-inch Bundt® or tube pan.

2. **For cake,** combine almond paste and 2 tablespoons oil in large bowl. Beat at medium speed with electric mixer until blended. Add remaining oil, 2 tablespoons at a time, until blended. Add 1 egg; beat at medium speed until blended. Add remaining 2 eggs; beat until smooth. Add cake mix and water; beat at medium speed for 2 minutes. Pour into prepared pan. Bake at 350°F for 50 to 55 minutes or until toothpick inserted in center comes out clean. Cool in pan 25 minutes. Invert onto cooling rack. Cool completely.

3. **For glaze,** place chocolate chips, cherry jelly, butter and corn syrup in microwave-safe medium bowl. Microwave at HIGH (100% power) for 1 to 1½ minutes. Stir until melted and smooth. Glaze top of cake. Garnish with sliced almonds and candied maraschino cherries.

*Makes 12 to 16 servings*

**Tip:** This recipe may also be prepared in the food processor. Place almond paste in work bowl with knife blade. Process until finely chopped. Add cake mix, eggs, water and oil. Process for 1 minute or until smooth. Bake and cool as directed.

# Lemon Meringue Torte

### Meringue

  4 egg whites
¼ teaspoon cream of tartar
  1 cup sugar

### Lemon Layer

  4 egg yolks
½ cup sugar
¼ cup fresh lemon juice
    Grated peel of 1 lemon
  1 cup whipping cream
    Candied lemon peel and salad burnett
    (optional)

Preheat oven to 275°F. To prepare meringue, beat egg whites and cream of tartar in medium bowl with electric mixer at medium speed until foamy. Gradually beat in 1 cup sugar on high speed until stiff peaks form. Draw 9-inch circle on heavy brown paper. Place on baking sheet; spread meringue inside circle to form 8- to 9-inch round. Bake 1 hour. *Turn off oven;* cool completely in oven.

Meanwhile, to prepare lemon layer, beat egg yolks in top of double boiler. Stir in ½ cup sugar, juice and grated peel. Place over hot, not boiling, water; cook 5 to 8 minutes or until thickened, stirring constantly. Remove top of double boiler; cover and set aside to cool.

Place cooled meringue round on serving plate. Spread with thin lemon layer. Refrigerate until set. Just before serving, whip cream and spread over lemon filling. Garnish with candied peel and salad burnett, if desired. Refrigerate leftovers.

*Makes 8 servings*

*Favorite recipe from* **Bob Evans Farms**®

**Rice Pudding with Dried Fruits and Nutmeg**

# Rice Pudding with Dried Fruits and Nutmeg

⅔ **cup CAROLINA®, MAHATMA®, RIVER® or WATER MAID® rice**
⅛ **teaspoon salt**
4 **cups water**
3 **eggs *or* 3 ounces egg substitute**
2 **cups milk**
¾ **cup sugar**
2 **teaspoons vanilla**
½ **teaspoon freshly grated nutmeg**
1 **package unflavored gelatin**
¼ **cup cold water**
1 **cup raisins, chopped dried apricots, dried peaches and other dried fruit**
1 **cup cream, light sour cream or light vanilla yogurt**
 **Additional freshly grated nutmeg for garnish**
 **Fresh fruit for garnish**
 **Coconut for garnish**

In large saucepan, combine rice and salt with 4 cups water; bring to a boil. Reduce heat; simmer until most of the liquid is absorbed, stirring occasionally. In medium bowl, whisk together eggs, milk, sugar, vanilla and nutmeg. Stir egg mixture into rice mixture and cook on low heat until thickened. *Do not boil.* In small bowl, sprinkle gelatin over ¼ cup cold water and let soften 10 minutes. Add gelatin mixture to rice mixture; stir. Add dried fruit; cover and refrigerate, stirring occasionally.

Whip cream until soft peaks form; fold into rice mixture. Refrigerate 2 to 3 hours. Garnish, if desired. *Makes 8 servings*

# Early American Pumpkin Pie

1½ cups cooked pumpkin, canned or fresh
1 cup whole or 2% milk
1 cup sugar
2 eggs, beaten
1 tablespoon butter or margarine, melted
½ teaspoon ground cinnamon
¼ teaspoon salt
¼ teaspoon ground ginger
¼ teaspoon ground nutmeg
1 (9-inch) unbaked pie shell
  Sweetened whipped cream or whipped topping (optional)
Fresh currants (optional)

Preheat oven to 425°F. Combine all ingredients except pie shell, cream and currants in large bowl; blend well. Pour into pie shell. Bake 45 to 50 minutes or until knife inserted into filling comes out clean. Serve with whipped cream and garnish with currants, if desired. Refrigerate leftovers. *Makes 6 to 8 servings*

*Favorite recipe from* **Bob Evans Farms®**

# Tiramisù

6 egg yolks
½ cup sugar
⅓ cup Cognac or brandy
2 cups (15 ounces) SARGENTO® Old Fashioned Ricotta Cheese
1 cup whipping cream, whipped
32 ladyfingers, split in half
3 teaspoons instant coffee dissolved in ¾ cup of boiling water
1 tablespoon unsweetened cocoa
  Chocolate curls (optional)

*Tiramisù*

In top of double boiler, whisk together egg yolks, sugar and Cognac. Place pan over simmering water. Cook, whisking constantly, until mixture is thickened, about 2 to 3 minutes. Cool. Beat yolk mixture and ricotta cheese in large bowl with electric mixer at medium speed until blended. Fold in whipped cream.

Place half of the ladyfingers in bottom of 13 × 9-inch pan, cut side up. Brush with half of coffee; spread with half of ricotta mixture. Repeat layers. Refrigerate 2 hours. Just before serving, dust with cocoa; cut into squares. Garnish with chocolate curls. *Makes 16 servings*

**Tip:** To prepare chocolate curls, combine ½ cup semisweet chocolate chips with 2 teaspoons vegetable shortening in 2-cup bowl. Microwave at HIGH 1 minute. Stir until chocolate is completely melted. Spread evenly into a thin layer on a small cookie sheet. Cool. Hold small spatula upside down at a 45° angle to cookie sheet. Run spatula across chocolate, allowing chocolate to curl.

# Butter Pecan Banana Cake

**Cake**

- 1 package DUNCAN HINES® Moist Deluxe Butter Recipe Golden Cake Mix
- 4 eggs
- 1 cup mashed, ripe bananas (about 3 medium)
- ¾ cup CRISCO® Oil or CRISCO® PURITAN® Canola Oil
- ½ cup sugar
- ¼ cup milk
- 1 teaspoon vanilla extract
- 1 cup chopped pecans

**Frosting**

- 1 cup coarsely chopped pecans
- ¼ cup butter or margarine
- 1 container (16 ounces) DUNCAN HINES® Creamy Homestyle Vanilla Frosting

1. Preheat oven to 325°F. Grease and flour 10-inch Bundt® or tube pan.

2. **For cake,** combine cake mix, eggs, bananas, oil, sugar, milk and vanilla extract in large bowl. Beat at low speed with electric mixer until moistened. Beat at medium speed for 2 minutes. Stir in 1 cup chopped pecans. Pour into prepared pan. Bake at 325°F for 50 to 60 minutes or until toothpick inserted in center comes out clean. Cool in pan 25 minutes. Invert onto cooling rack. Cool completely.

3. **For frosting,** place 1 cup coarsely chopped pecans and butter in skillet. Cook on medium heat, stirring until pecans are toasted. Stir into frosting. Cool until spreading consistency. Frost cake.

*Makes 12 to 16 servings*

# Cranberry 'n' Barley Pudding

- 2 cups cooked barley
- ½ cup chopped dried cranberries
- 1⅓ cups milk
- ½ cup packed brown sugar
- 2 eggs
- 1 tablespoon butter or margarine, softened
- 1 teaspoon vanilla
- ½ teaspoon ground cinnamon
- ⅛ teaspoon salt

Preheat oven to 325°F. Combine barley and cranberries in medium bowl; set aside. Combine milk, brown sugar, eggs, butter, vanilla, cinnamon and salt in large bowl; beat well. Stir in barley mixture. Pour into greased 2-quart casserole. Bake 50 minutes or until set. Serve hot or cold with cream or your favorite topping.

*Makes 6 to 8 servings*

*Favorite recipe from* **North Dakota Barley Council**

*Butter Pecan Banana Cake*

# Bûche de Noël

¾ cup cake flour
½ teaspoon baking powder
½ teaspoon salt
5 eggs, separated
1 cup granulated sugar, divided
1 teaspoon vanilla
½ cup powdered sugar
1 cup semisweet chocolate chips
¾ cup heavy cream
1 tablespoon rum
    Cocoa Frosting (recipe follows)
    White Chocolate Curls (recipe follows)
2 teaspoons unsweetened cocoa powder
    (optional)

Preheat oven to 375°F. Grease 15½ × 10½-inch jelly-roll pan; line pan with waxed paper. Grease again; set aside.

Place flour, baking powder and salt in small bowl; stir to combine.

Beat egg yolks and ⅔ cup granulated sugar in small bowl with electric mixer at high speed about 5 minutes or until thick and lemon colored, scraping down side of bowl once. Beat in vanilla; set aside.

Beat egg whites until foamy. Gradually beat in remaining ⅓ cup granulated sugar, 1 tablespoon at a time, until stiff peaks form.

Fold flour mixture into egg yolk mixture. Fold flour mixture into egg white mixture.

Spread mixture into prepared pan. Bake 12 to 15 minutes or until cake springs back when lightly touched with finger. Meanwhile, lightly sift powdered sugar over clean dish towel.

Loosen warm cake from edges of pan; invert onto prepared towel. Remove pan; carefully peel off paper. Gently roll up in towel from short end, jelly-roll fashion. Let cool completely on wire rack.

*Bûche de Noël*

For chocolate filling, place chocolate chips and cream in heavy 2-quart saucepan. Heat over low heat until chocolate is melted, stirring frequently. Pour into small bowl; stir in rum. Cover and refrigerate about 1½ hours or until filling is spreading consistency, stirring occasionally.

Prepare Cocoa Frosting; refrigerate until ready to use. Prepare White Chocolate Curls; refrigerate until ready to use. Unroll cake; remove towel. Spread cake with chocolate filling to within ½ inch of edge; reroll cake. Spread Cocoa Frosting over cake roll. Garnish with White Chocolate Curls. Sprinkle with cocoa, if desired. *Makes 12 servings*

## Cocoa Frosting

1 cup heavy cream
½ cup powdered sugar, sifted
2 tablespoons unsweetened cocoa
    powder, sifted
1 teaspoon vanilla

Beat heavy cream, powdered sugar, cocoa and vanilla with electric mixer at medium speed until soft peaks form. Refrigerate until ready to use. *Makes about 2 cups*

## White Chocolate Curls

1 package (8 ounces) white chocolate,
    coarsely chopped
1 tablespoon vegetable shortening

Melt together chocolate and shortening. Pour melted chocolate mixture onto back of baking pan. Quickly spread chocolate into a very thin layer. Refrigerate about 10 minutes or until firm, but still pliable. When chocolate is just firm, use small straight-edge metal spatula. Holding spatula at a 45° angle, push spatula firmly along baking pan, under chocolate, so chocolate curls as it is pushed. (If chocolate is too firm to curl, let stand a few minutes at room temperature.) Transfer curls to waxed paper. Store in cool, dry place until ready to use.

# Individual Orange Soufflés

Nonstick cooking spray
3 oranges
1½ tablespoons cornstarch
3 tablespoons orange-flavored liqueur
6 egg whites
⅛ teaspoon salt
6 tablespoons sugar
1½ tablespoons sliced almonds (optional)
1½ tablespoons powdered sugar (optional)

Preheat oven to 450°F. Spray 6 individual soufflé dishes (8 to 10 ounces each) with cooking spray. Place dishes on jelly-roll pan; set aside.

Grate enough orange peel to equal 1½ teaspoons.

Cut peel and membrane from oranges; section oranges over 1-quart saucepan. Dice oranges. There will be 1½ cups juice and pulp. Stir in cornstarch until smooth. Cook and stir over medium heat until mixture comes to a boil and thickens slightly. Remove from heat. Stir in liqueur and reserved orange peel.

Beat egg whites and salt with electric mixer at high speed in large bowl until soft peaks form. Gradually beat in sugar, 1 tablespoon at a time, until stiff peaks form and sugar is dissolved. Fold ¼ of egg white mixture into orange mixture. Fold all of orange mixture into remaining egg white mixture. Spoon into prepared dishes. Sprinkle with almonds, if desired. Immediately bake 12 to 15 minutes or until soufflés are puffed and browned. Sprinkle with powdered sugar, if desired. Serve immediately.

*Makes 6 servings*

# Chocolate Cherry Torte

1 package DUNCAN HINES® Moist Deluxe Devil's Food Cake Mix
1 can (21 ounces) cherry pie filling
¼ teaspoon almond extract
1 container (8 ounces) frozen whipped topping, thawed and divided
¼ cup toasted sliced almonds, for garnish (see Tip)

1. Preheat oven to 350°F. Grease and flour two 9-inch round cake pans.

2. Prepare, bake and cool cake following package directions for basic recipe. Combine cherry pie filling and almond extract in small bowl. Stir until blended.

3. To assemble, place one cake layer on serving plate. Spread with 1 cup whipped topping, then half the cherry pie filling mixture. Top with second cake layer. Spread with remaining pie filling to within 1½ inches of cake edge. Decorate cake edge with remaining whipped topping. Garnish with sliced almonds.

*Makes 12 to 16 servings*

**Tip:** To toast almonds, spread in a single layer on baking sheet. Bake at 325°F for 4 to 6 minutes or until fragrant and golden.

*Chocolate Cherry Torte*

## Almond Fudge Banana Cake

3 extra-ripe, medium DOLE® Bananas, peeled
1½ cups sugar
½ cup margarine, softened
3 eggs
3 tablespoons amaretto liqueur *or*
    ½ to 1 teaspoon almond extract
1 teaspoon vanilla
1⅓ cups all-purpose flour
⅓ cup unsweetened cocoa powder
1 teaspoon baking soda
½ teaspoon salt
½ cup DOLE® Chopped Almonds, toasted, ground

Banana Chocolate Glaze

1 extra-ripe, small DOLE® Banana, puréed
1 square (1 ounce) semisweet chocolate, melted

• Mash bananas.

• Beat sugar and margarine until light and fluffy. Beat in eggs, liqueur and vanilla.

• Combine dry ingredients. Stir in almonds. Add to beaten sugar mixture alternately with bananas. Beat well.

• Turn batter into greased 10-inch Bundt pan. Bake in 350°F oven 45 to 50 minutes or until wooden toothpick inserted in center comes out nearly clean and cake pulls away from sides of pan. Cool 10 minutes. Remove cake from pan to wire rack to cool completely. Drizzle glaze over top and down sides of cake.

*Makes 16 to 20 servings*

**Banana Chocolate Glaze:** With wire whisk, beat puréed banana into melted chocolate.

*Almond Fudge Banana Cake*

## Orange Pecan Pie

3 eggs
½ cup GRANDMA'S® Molasses Unsulphured
½ cup light corn syrup
¼ cup orange juice
1 teaspoon grated orange peel
1 teaspoon vanilla
1½ cups whole pecans
1 (9-inch) unbaked pie shell
    Whipped cream

Preheat oven to 350°F. In large bowl, beat eggs. Add molasses, corn syrup, orange juice, orange peel and vanilla; beat until well blended. Stir in pecans. Pour into unbaked pie shell. Bake 40 to 50 minutes or until filling is set. Cool. Serve with whipped cream.     *Makes 8 servings*

# Classic Sour Cream Cheesecake

1½ cups shortbread cookie crumbs (about 24 cookies)
2 tablespoons margarine or butter, melted
3 (8-ounce) packages cream cheese, softened
1 (14-ounce) can EAGLE® Brand Sweetened Condensed Milk (NOT evaporated milk)
4 eggs
1 (8-ounce) container BORDEN® or MEADOW GOLD® Sour Cream
1 tablespoon vanilla extract

Preheat oven to 350°. Combine crumbs and margarine; press firmly onto bottom of 9-inch springform pan. In large mixer bowl, beat cheese until fluffy. Gradually beat in sweetened condensed milk until smooth. Beat in eggs then sour cream and vanilla. Pour into prepared pan. Bake 50 to 55 minutes or until lightly browned around edge (center will be slightly soft). Cool. Chill. Just before serving, remove side of springform pan. Garnish with cherry pie filling, if desired. Refrigerate leftovers.

*Makes one 9-inch cheesecake*

*Orange Carrot Cake*

# Orange Carrot Cake

1 cup margarine or butter, softened
1 cup GRANDMA'S® Molasses Unsulphured
4 eggs
½ cup orange juice
1 cup all-purpose flour
1 cup whole wheat flour
2 teaspoons baking soda
1 teaspoon ground cinnamon
½ teaspoon salt
2 cups shredded carrots
½ cup chopped walnuts

Frosting

1 (3-ounce) package cream cheese, softened
1½ cups powdered sugar
2 tablespoons margarine or butter, softened
1 teaspoon grated orange peel

Preheat oven to 350°F. Grease two 8- or 9-inch round cake pans. In large bowl, combine margarine, molasses, eggs and orange juice; mix well. Stir in flours, baking soda, cinnamon and salt; mix well. Stir in carrots and walnuts. Pour into prepared pans. Bake at 350°F 30 to 35 minutes or until wooden toothpick inserted in center comes out clean. Cool 15 minutes; remove from pans. Cool completely.

In small bowl, combine all frosting ingredients; beat until smooth. Place one cake layer on serving plate; spread with frosting. Top with second layer; spread with frosting. If desired, garnish with additional grated orange peel or walnuts.

*Makes 12 servings*

*All-American Pineapple & Fruit Trifle*

# All-American Pineapple & Fruit Trifle

1 DOLE® Fresh Pineapple
1 cup frozen sliced peaches, thawed
1 cup frozen strawberries, thawed, sliced
1 cup frozen raspberries, thawed
1 (10-inch) angel food cake
1 package (4-serving size) instant sugar free vanilla pudding mix
⅓ cup cream sherry
½ cup frozen whipped topping, thawed

• Twist crown from pineapple. Cut pineapple in half lengthwise. Refrigerate 1 half for another use. Cut fruit from shell. Cut fruit into thin wedges. Reserve 3 wedges for garnish; combine remaining with peaches and berries.

• Cut cake in half. Freeze half for another use. Tear cake into chunks.

• Prepare pudding according to package directions.

• In 2-quart glass bowl, layer half of each: cake, sherry, fruit mixture and pudding.

Repeat layers once. Cover; refrigerate 1 hour or overnight.

• Just before serving, garnish with whipped topping and reserved pineapple wedges.
*Makes 8 to 10 servings*

# Chocolate Angel Food Dessert

1 package DUNCAN HINES® Angel Food Cake Mix
16 large marshmallows
½ cup milk
1 package (11 ounces) milk chocolate chips
1 pint whipping cream
¼ cup semisweet chocolate chips
1½ teaspoons CRISCO® all-vegetable shortening

1. Preheat oven to 375°F. Prepare, bake and cool cake following package directions.

2. Melt marshmallows and milk in heavy saucepan over low heat. Remove from heat; stir in milk chocolate chips until melted. Cool to room temperature. Beat whipping cream in large bowl until stiff peaks form. Fold cooled chocolate mixture into whipped cream. Refrigerate until spreading consistency.

3. To assemble, split cake horizontally into 3 even layers. Place 1 cake layer on serving plate. Spread with one-fourth of frosting. Repeat with second layer. Top with third layer. Frost sides and top with remaining frosting. Refrigerate.

4. For drizzle, place semisweet chocolate chips and shortening in 1-cup glass measuring cup. Microwave at MEDIUM (50% power) for 1 minute. Stir until smooth. Drizzle melted chocolate around outer top edge of cake, allowing mixture to run down sides unevenly. Refrigerate until ready to serve. *Makes 12 to 16 servings*

# Glazed Cranberry Mini-Cakes

⅓ cup butter or margarine, softened
⅓ cup granulated sugar
⅓ cup packed light brown sugar
1 egg
1¼ teaspoons vanilla extract
1⅓ cups all-purpose flour
¾ teaspoon baking powder
¼ teaspoon baking soda
¼ teaspoon salt
2 tablespoons milk
1¼ cups coarsely chopped fresh
    cranberries
½ cup coarsely chopped walnuts
1⅔ cups HERSHEY₀'S Vanilla Milk Chips,
    divided
    Vanilla Glaze (recipe follows)
    Additional fresh cranberries (optional)

Heat oven to 350°F. Lightly grease or paper-line small muffin cups (1¾ inches in diameter). In large mixer bowl, beat butter, granulated sugar, brown sugar, egg and vanilla until light and fluffy. Stir together flour, baking powder, baking soda and salt; gradually blend into butter mixture. Add milk; stir until blended. Stir in cranberries, walnuts and ⅔ cup vanilla milk chips (reserve remaining chips for glaze). Fill muffin cups ⅞ full with batter. Bake 18 to 20 minutes or until wooden pick inserted in center comes out clean. Cool 5 minutes; remove from pans to wire rack. Cool completely. Prepare Vanilla Glaze; drizzle over top of mini-cakes. Garnish with additional cranberries, if desired. Refrigerate 10 minutes to set glaze.

*Makes about 3 dozen mini-cakes*

**Vanilla Glaze:** In small microwave-safe bowl, place remaining 1 cup HERSHEY₀'S Vanilla Milk Chips; sprinkle 2 tablespoons vegetable oil over chips. Microwave at HIGH (100% power) 30 seconds; stir vigorously. If necessary, microwave at HIGH additional 30 seconds or just until chips are melted when stirred.

# Grasshopper Cheesecake

1½ cups creme-filled chocolate sandwich
    cookie crumbs (about 18 cookies)
3 tablespoons margarine or butter,
    melted
4 (8-ounce) packages cream cheese,
    softened
1 (14-ounce) can EAGLE® Brand
    Sweetened Condensed Milk
    (NOT evaporated milk)
4 eggs
3 tablespoons unsweetened cocoa
2 teaspoons vanilla extract
3 tablespoons green crème de menthe
    liqueur
2 tablespoons white crème de cacao
    liqueur
    Chocolate Glaze (recipe follows)

Preheat oven to 300°. Combine crumbs and margarine; press firmly onto bottom of 9-inch springform pan. In large mixer bowl, beat cheese until fluffy. Gradually beat in sweetened condensed milk until smooth. Add eggs; mix well. Divide batter in half (about 3 cups each); beat cocoa and vanilla into one half. Pour into prepared pan. Stir liqueurs into remaining batter. Spoon evenly over chocolate batter. Bake 1 hour and 10 minutes or until center is set. Turn off oven and allow cheesecake to cool 1 hour in oven with door slightly open. Remove from oven; cool thoroughly. Remove side of springform pan. Spread top with Chocolate Glaze, letting excess glaze drip down sides. Chill thoroughly. Garnish as desired. Refrigerate leftovers.

*Makes one 9-inch cheesecake*

**Chocolate Glaze:** In small saucepan over low heat, melt 3 (1-ounce) squares semi-sweet chocolate with ⅓ cup BORDEN® or MEADOW GOLD® Whipping Cream, *unwhipped.* Cook and stir until thickened and smooth. Immediately spread over warm cheesecake. *Makes about ½ cup*

*Glazed Cranberry Mini-Cakes*

## Cassata

2 cups (15 ounces) SARGENTO®
    Part-Skim Ricotta Cheese
¼ cup sugar
3 tablespoons orange liqueur
⅓ cup finely chopped mixed candied
    fruit
¼ cup chopped almonds
1¼ cups semisweet mini chocolate chips,
    divided
1 prepared pound cake (10¾ ounces)
1 teaspoon instant coffee dissolved in
    ¼ cup boiling water
6 tablespoons unsalted butter or
    margarine, cut into 8 pieces, chilled
Chopped almonds (optional)

Combine ricotta cheese, sugar and liqueur in large bowl; beat until light and fluffy, about 3 minutes. Fold in candied fruit, almonds and ¼ cup chocolate chips; set aside.

*Cassata*

Cut pound cake in half horizontally using sharp serrated knife. Cut each half again horizontally. Place top of pound cake, top side down, on serving platter. Spread one-third of the ricotta mixture evenly over cake. Repeat procedure twice. Top with remaining cake layer; press slightly to compact layers. Cover with plastic wrap; refrigerate at least 2 hours.

Meanwhile, place remaining 1 cup chocolate chips and coffee mixture in top of double boiler set over hot, not boiling, water. Stir constantly until chocolate is melted. Add butter pieces, 1 at a time, stirring constantly, until all butter is added and melted. Remove from heat; refrigerate until spreading consistency, about 2 to 2½ hours.

Spread top and sides of cake with frosting. Sprinkle top with chopped almonds, if desired. *Makes 12 servings*

**Tip:** Cake can be made 1 day in advance, covered with plastic wrap and refrigerated. Let stand at room temperature about 30 minutes before slicing.

## Chocolate Truffle Tart

**Crust**

⅔ cup all-purpose flour
½ cup powdered sugar
½ cup ground walnuts
6 tablespoons butter or margarine,
    softened
⅓ cup NESTLÉ® Baking Cocoa

**Filling**

1¼ cups heavy whipping cream
¼ cup granulated sugar
2 cups (12-ounce package) NESTLÉ®
    TOLL HOUSE® Semi-Sweet
    Chocolate Morsels
2 tablespoons seedless raspberry jam
    Sweetened whipped cream (optional)
    Fresh raspberries (optional)

To prepare crust, beat flour, powdered sugar, walnuts, butter and cocoa in large mixer bowl until a soft dough forms. Press dough onto bottom and side of ungreased 9- or 9½-inch fluted tart pan with removable bottom.

Bake in preheated 350°F oven for 12 to 14 minutes or until puffed. Cool completely on wire rack.

To prepare filling, heat cream and granulated sugar in medium saucepan just until boiling, stirring occasionally. Remove from heat. Stir in morsels and jam; let stand for 5 minutes. Whisk until chocolate mixture is smooth. Transfer to small mixer bowl. Cover; chill for 45 to 60 minutes or until mixture is cool and slightly thickened.

Beat for 20 to 30 seconds, just until color lightens slightly. Spoon into crust. Chill until firm. Remove rim of pan; garnish with whipped cream and raspberries.

*Makes one 9-inch tart*

**Note:** May be made in 9-inch pie plate following directions.

## Kahlua® Chocolate Decadence

½ cup butter
8 ounces (8 squares) semisweet baking chocolate, divided
3 extra large eggs
¾ cup granulated sugar
1¼ cups finely ground walnuts or pecans
2 tablespoons all-purpose flour
5 tablespoons KAHLUA® Liqueur, divided
1 teaspoon vanilla
Sifted powdered sugar
Raspberries, strawberries, chocolate nonpareil candy or coffee beans for garnish

*Kahlua® Chocolate Decadence*

Preheat oven to 325°F. In small saucepan over medium heat, or in microwave-safe bowl on HIGH (100% power), melt butter and 6 ounces chocolate, stirring until blended. Remove from heat; cool. In large bowl, beat eggs and granulated sugar at high speed of electric mixer about 3 minutes or until light and lemon colored. Stir together walnuts and flour; gradually beat into egg mixture.

Stir 3 tablespoons Kahlua® and vanilla into cooled chocolate mixture; gradually beat into egg mixture until well combined. Pour batter into 9-inch springform pan. Bake 35 to 45 minutes or until top is set. Cool cake in pan.

Remove side of pan; place cake on serving plate. Sprinkle top with powdered sugar. Melt remaining 2 ounces chocolate as previously directed. Stir together melted chocolate and remaining 2 tablespoons Kahlua®; drizzle over cake. Decorate with raspberries, if desired.

*Makes 1 (9-inch) cake*

*Golden Holiday Fruitcake*

## Golden Holiday Fruitcake

1½ cups butter or margarine, softened
1½ cups sugar
  6 eggs
  2 tablespoons fresh lemon juice
  2 teaspoons grated lemon peel
  3 cups all-purpose flour
  2 teaspoons baking powder
½ teaspoon baking soda
¼ teaspoon salt
1½ cups golden raisins
1½ cups pecan halves
1½ cups red and green candied pineapple
    chunks
  1 cup dried apricot halves, cut in half
  1 cup halved red candied cherries
  1 cup halved green candied cherries
    Light corn syrup
    Candied and dried fruit for garnish

Preheat oven to 325°F. Grease and flour 10-inch tube pan. Beat butter in large bowl with electric mixer at medium speed until creamy. Add sugar; beat until light and fluffy. Add eggs, 1 at a time, beating well after each addition. Stir in lemon juice and peel. Combine flour, baking powder, baking soda and salt in large bowl. Reserve ½ cup flour mixture. Gradually blend remaining flour mixture into butter mixture on low speed. Combine raisins, pecans, pineapple, apricots and cherries in large bowl. Toss fruit mixture with reserved ½ cup flour mixture. Stir fruit mixture into butter mixture. Spoon evenly into prepared pan.

Bake 80 to 90 minutes until wooden pick inserted in center comes out clean. Cool in pan 15 minutes. Remove from pan to wire rack; cool completely. Store up to 1 month tightly covered at room temperature. (If desired, cake may be stored wrapped in a wine- or brandy-soaked cloth in airtight container. Cake may be frozen up to 2 months.)

Before serving, lightly brush surface of cake with corn syrup. Arrange candied and dried fruit decoratively on top. Brush fruit with corn syrup.

*Makes one 10-inch round fruitcake*

## Frosty Holiday Grapes

½ cup sugar
  2 envelopes unflavored gelatin
10 small California grape clusters
    Water

Combine sugar and gelatin; mix well. Dip grape clusters in water; shake off excess water. Sprinkle sugar mixture through sieve over wet grapes. Place on waxed paper about 45 minutes or until dry.

*Makes 10 servings*

*Favorite recipe from **California Table Grape Commission***

# Fruit Flower

1 small DOLE® Fresh Pineapple
1 DOLE® Cantaloupe
1 DOLE® Banana, peeled
½ cup sliced DOLE® Strawberries
½ cup low fat vanilla yogurt
1 teaspoon honey
¼ teaspoon grated lime peel
2 teaspoons chopped mint leaves

• Twist crown from pineapple. Cut pineapple lengthwise in half. Refrigerate 1 half for another use. Cut remaining half in quarters. Cut fruit from shells. Trim off core; slice into ¼-inch wedges (fan shape).

• Cut cantaloupe in half. Refrigerate 1 half for another use. Cut remaining half in quarters. Trim off rind; slice ¼ inch thick (crescent shape).

• Diagonally slice banana.

• Arrange fruit in alternating circles on large plate, leaving room in center for strawberries.

• Combine remaining ingredients. Serve with fruit.          *Makes 4 servings*

*Individual Cheesecake Cups*

# Individual Cheesecake Cups

**Crust**

 1 package DUNCAN HINES® Moist Deluxe Yellow or Devil's Food Cake Mix
¼ cup butter or margarine, melted

**Cheese Filling**

 2 packages (8 ounces each) cream cheese, softened
 3 eggs
¾ cup sugar
 1 teaspoon vanilla extract

**Topping**

1½ cups dairy sour cream
¼ cup sugar
 1 can (21 ounces) cherry pie filling (optional)

1. Preheat oven to 350°F. Place 2½-inch foil or paper liners in 24 muffin cups.

2. **For crust,** combine cake mix and melted butter in large bowl. Beat at low speed with electric mixer for 1 minute. Mixture will be crumbly. Divide mixture evenly into muffin cups. Level but do not press.

3. **For filling,** combine cream cheese, eggs, ¾ cup sugar and vanilla extract in medium bowl. Beat at medium speed with electric mixer until smooth. Spoon evenly into muffin cups. Bake at 350°F for 20 minutes or until set.

4. **For topping,** combine sour cream and ¼ cup sugar in small bowl. Spoon evenly over cheesecakes. Return to oven for 5 minutes. Cool completely. Garnish each cheesecake with cherry pie filling, if desired. Refrigerate until ready to serve.
          *Makes 24 servings*

# Black Forest Cake

2 cups plus 2 tablespoons all-purpose
    flour
2 cups granulated sugar
¾ cup cocoa
1½ teaspoons baking powder
¾ teaspoon baking soda
¾ teaspoon salt
3 eggs
1 cup milk
½ cup vegetable oil
1 tablespoon vanilla
    Cherry Topping (recipe follows)
    Frosting (recipe follows)

Preheat oven to 350°F. Grease and flour 2 (9-inch) round cake pans. Cover bottoms with waxed paper.

Combine dry ingredients in large bowl. Add eggs, milk, oil and vanilla; beat until well blended. Pour evenly into prepared pans. Bake 35 minutes or until wooden pick inserted in centers comes out clean. While cake is baking, prepare Cherry Topping; cool. Cool layers in pans on wire racks 10 minutes. Loosen edges; remove from pans to racks. Remove waxed paper; cool completely.

Split each cake layer in half horizontally. Tear 1 split layer into crumbs; set aside.

Prepare Frosting; reserve 1½ cups for decorating cake; set aside.

Brush loose crumbs off cake layers. To assemble, place 1 cake layer on serving plate. Spread with 1 cup Frosting; top with ¾ cup Cherry Topping. Top with second cake layer; repeat layers of Frosting, Cherry Topping and cake, ending with cake.

Frost side of cake with remaining Frosting. Pat reserved crumbs onto Frosting on side of cake. Spoon reserved 1½ cups Frosting into pastry bag fitted with star decorator tip. Pipe around top and bottom edges of cake. Spoon remaining Cherry Topping onto top of cake. Serve or refrigerate cake.

*Makes 1 (3-layer) cake*

# Cherry Topping

2 (20-ounce) cans tart pitted cherries,
    undrained
1 cup granulated sugar
¼ cup cornstarch
1 teaspoon vanilla

Drain cherries, reserving ½ cup juice. Combine reserved juice, cherries, sugar and cornstarch in 2-quart saucepan. Cook over low heat until thickened, stirring constantly. Stir in vanilla. Cool; set aside.

# Frosting

3 cups whipping cream
⅓ cup powdered sugar

Beat together whipping cream and powdered sugar in chilled medium bowl at high speed of electric mixer until stiff peaks form.

# Apple Yogurt Trifle

1 Granny Smith apple, cored and finely
    chopped
2 (8-ounce) containers low fat cherry
    yogurt
½ cup plus 2 tablespoons crunch nutlike
    cereal nuggets

Evenly divide half the chopped apple pieces among four parfait dishes or tall glasses. Divide yogurt from one 8-ounce container among dishes. Add 2 tablespoons cereal to each trifle, then top with layers of remaining yogurt, chopped apple and a sprinkle of cereal on top. Refrigerate at least 15 to 20 minutes before serving to allow cereal to soften slightly.

*Makes 4 servings*

*Favorite recipe from **Washington Apple Commission***

*Black Forest Cake*

*Pumpkin Chiffon Cake*

# Pumpkin Chiffon Cake

**Cake**
1 package DUNCAN HINES® Moist
    Deluxe Spice Cake Mix
3 eggs
1 cup water
1 tablespoon CRISCO® Oil or CRISCO®
    PURITAN® Canola Oil
1½ cups solid pack pumpkin, divided

**Filling**
2 cups whipping cream, chilled
½ cup sugar
1 cup Sugared Pecans, chopped (recipe
    follows)
    Sugared Pecan halves, for garnish

1. Preheat oven to 350°F. Grease and flour two 8-inch round cake pans.

2. **For cake,** combine cake mix, eggs, water and oil in large bowl. Beat at low speed with electric mixer until moistened. Beat at medium speed for 2 minutes. Fold in 1 cup pumpkin. Pour batter into pans. Bake and cool cake following package directions.

3. **For filling,** place whipping cream and sugar in large bowl. Beat at high speed with electric mixer until stiff peaks form. Fold in remaining ½ cup pumpkin and chopped Sugared Pecans.

4. To assemble, level cake layers. Split each cake layer in half horizontally. Place 1 cake layer on serving plate. Spread with one-fourth of the filling. Repeat layering 3 more times. Garnish with Sugared Pecan halves.
*Makes 12 to 16 servings*

## Sugared Pecans

1 cup sugar
1 tablespoon ground cinnamon
1 teaspoon salt
1 egg white
1 tablespoon water
1 pound pecan halves

1. Preheat oven to 300°F.

2. Combine sugar, cinnamon and salt in small bowl; set aside.

3. Place egg white and water in medium bowl. Beat with electric mixer at medium speed until frothy but not stiff. Pour pecans into egg white mixture; stir until coated. Add sugar mixture; stir until evenly coated. Spread on cookie sheet. Bake at 300°F for 45 minutes, stirring every 15 minutes. Cool completely.

# Peppermint Cheesecake

**Crust**

1¼ cups vanilla wafer crumbs
 3 tablespoons melted margarine

**Filling**

 4 cups (30-ounces) SARGENTO® Light
   Ricotta Cheese
 ½ cup sugar
 ½ cup half-and-half
 ¼ cup all-purpose flour
 1 teaspoon vanilla
 ¼ teaspoon salt
 3 eggs
16 peppermint candies (½ cup crushed
   pieces)
   Fresh mint leaves (optional)

Lightly grease sides of 8- or 9-inch
springform pan. Combine crumbs and
margarine; mix well. Press evenly over
bottom of pan. Refrigerate while preparing
filling.

Combine ricotta cheese, sugar, half-and-
half, flour, vanilla and salt in large bowl;
beat with electric mixer until smooth. Add
eggs, 1 at a time; beat until smooth. Place
candies in heavy plastic bag. Crush with
meat mallet or hammer. Reserve ¼ cup
larger pieces for garnish; stir remaining
crushed candies into batter. Pour batter
over crust.

Bake at 350°F 1 hour or until center is just
set. Turn off oven; cool in oven with door
propped open 30 minutes. Remove to wire
cooling rack; loosen cake from rim of pan
with metal spatula. Cool completely;
refrigerate at least 4 hours. Immediately
before serving, garnish cake around top
edge with reserved crushed candies and
mint leaves, if desired.     *Makes 8 servings*

*Left to right: Mini-Cheesecakes
(page 200) and Peppermint Cheesecake*

# Cherry Angel Cream Cake

1 (10- to 12-ounce) prepared angel food
   cake, frozen (for easy slicing)
1 (14-ounce) can EAGLE® Brand
   Sweetened Condensed Milk
   (NOT evaporated milk)
1 cup cold water
1 teaspoon almond extract
1 (4-serving size) package instant vanilla
   flavor pudding mix
2 cups (1 pint) BORDEN® or MEADOW
   GOLD® Whipping Cream, whipped
2 (21-ounce) cans cherry or peach pie
   filling

Cut cake into ¼-inch slices; arrange half the
slices on bottom of 13 × 9-inch baking dish.
In large mixer bowl, combine sweetened
condensed milk, water and almond extract;
mix well. Add pudding mix; beat well.
Chill 5 minutes. Fold in whipped cream.
Spread half the cream mixture over cake
slices; top evenly with one can pie filling.
Top with remaining cake slices, cream
mixture and pie filling. Cover; chill 4 hours
or until set. Cut into squares to serve.
Refrigerate leftovers.

*Makes 12 to 16 servings*

# Walnut Brownie Cheesecake

### Crust

1¼ cups finely crushed chocolate wafer crumbs (about 25 cookies)

3 tablespoons melted margarine

### Filling

4 cups (30 ounces) SARGENTO® Light Ricotta Cheese

1¼ cups packed light brown sugar

½ cup half-and-half

⅓ cup unsweetened cocoa powder

¼ cup all-purpose flour

1 teaspoon vanilla

¼ teaspoon salt

3 eggs

½ cup (2 ounces) coarsely chopped walnuts

Confectioners' sugar (optional)

Lightly grease sides of 8- or 9-inch springform pan. Combine crumbs and margarine; mix well. Press evenly over bottom of pan. Refrigerate while preparing filling. Combine ricotta cheese, brown sugar, half-and-half, cocoa, flour, vanilla and salt in large bowl; beat with electric mixer until smooth. Add eggs, 1 at a time; beat until smooth. Stir in walnuts. Pour batter over crust.

Bake at 350°F 1 hour and 10 minutes or until center is just set. Turn off oven; cool in oven with door propped open 30 minutes. Remove to wire cooling rack; loosen cake from rim of pan with metal spatula. Cool completely; refrigerate at least 4 hours. If desired, sift confectioners' sugar over cheesecake immediately before serving.

*Makes 8 servings*

**Four Mini-Cheesecakes:** Line 24 medium (2½-inch) muffin cups with cupcake papers. Sprinkle scant 1 tablespoon crust mixture into each cup; pat lightly with fingertips.

Pour scant ⅓ cup cheesecake batter over crumb mixture. Bake 350°F 30 minutes or until set. Remove to wire cooling rack; cool completely. Cover and chill at least 2 hours. Garnish as desired immediately before serving.

# Chocolate Intensity

### Cake

1 package (8 ounces) NESTLÉ® Unsweetened Chocolate Baking Bars

1½ cups granulated sugar

½ cup butter, softened

3 eggs

2 teaspoons vanilla

⅔ cup all-purpose flour

Powdered sugar (optional)

### Coffee Crème Anglaise Sauce

4 egg yolks

⅓ cup granulated sugar

1 tablespoon TASTER'S CHOICE® Freeze Dried Instant Coffee

1½ cups milk

1 teaspoon vanilla

*Chocolate Intensity*

**FOR CAKE:** In small heavy saucepan over low heat, melt baking bars, stirring until smooth. Remove from heat; cool to lukewarm. In small bowl, beat 1½ cups sugar, butter, eggs and 2 teaspoons vanilla about 4 minutes or until thick and pale yellow. Beat in melted chocolate. Gradually beat in flour. Spread into greased 9-inch springform pan. Bake in preheated 350°F oven 25 to 28 minutes. Wooden pick inserted in center will be moist. Cool in pan on wire rack 15 minutes. Remove side of pan; cool completely. Sprinkle with powdered sugar, if desired. Cut into 10 or 12 servings. Serve with 3 to 4 tablespoons sauce.

**FOR COFFEE CRÈME ANGLAISE SAUCE:** In small bowl, whisk egg yolks. In medium saucepan, combine ⅓ cup sugar and coffee; stir in milk. Cook over medium heat, stirring constantly, until mixture comes to a simmer. Remove from heat. Gradually whisk ½ of hot milk mixture into yolks; return to saucepan. Continue cooking, stirring constantly 3 to 4 minutes or until mixture is slightly thickened. Strain into small bowl; stir in 1 teaspoon vanilla. Cover with plastic wrap; refrigerate.

*Makes one 9-inch cake*

# Kahlua® Black Forest Cake

1 package (18.25 ounces) chocolate fudge cake mix with pudding
3 eggs
¾ cup water
½ cup KAHLUA® Liqueur
⅓ cup vegetable oil
1 can (16 ounces) vanilla or chocolate frosting
1 can (21 ounces) cherry filling and topping
  Chocolate shavings or chocolate sprinkles for garnish (optional)

*Kahlua® Black Forest Cake*

Preheat oven to 350°F. Grease and flour 2 (9-inch) cake pans; set aside. In large mixer bowl, prepare cake mix according to package directions, using eggs, water, Kahlua® and oil. Pour batter into prepared pans. Bake 25 to 35 minutes or until toothpick inserted in center comes out clean. Cool cake in pans 10 minutes; turn layers out onto wire racks to cool completely.

Place one cake layer bottom side up on serving plate. Spread thick layer of frosting in circle, 1½ inches around outer edge of cake. Spoon half of cherry filling into center of cake layer to frosting edge. Top with second cake layer, bottom side down. Repeat with frosting and remaining cherry filling. Spread remaining frosting around side of cake. Decorate with chocolate shavings or sprinkles, if desired.

*Makes 1 (9-inch) cake*

## Classic Pecan Pie

3 eggs
1 cup sugar
1 cup KARO® Light or Dark Corn Syrup
2 tablespoons MAZOLA® margarine or
   butter, melted
1 teaspoon vanilla
1½ cups pecans
   Easy-As-Pie Crust (recipe follows) *or*
   1 (9-inch) frozen deep dish pie
   crust*

*To use prepared frozen pie crust: Do not thaw. Preheat oven and a cookie sheet. Pour filling into frozen crust. Bake on cookie sheet.

Preheat oven to 350°F. In medium bowl with fork beat eggs slightly. Add sugar, corn syrup, margarine and vanilla; stir until well blended. Stir in pecans. Pour into prepared pie crust

Bake 50 to 55 minutes or until knife inserted halfway between center and edge comes out clean. Cool on wire rack.

*Makes 8 servings*

**Almond Amaretto Pie:** Substitute 1 cup sliced almonds for pecans. Add 2 tablespoons almond flavored liqueur and ½ teaspoon almond extract to filling.

## Easy-As-Pie Crust

Single Pie Crust
1¼ cups unsifted flour
⅛ teaspoon salt
½ cup MAZOLA® margarine
2 to 3 tablespoons cold water

In medium bowl combine flour and salt. With pastry blender or 2 knives, cut in margarine until mixture resembles fine crumbs. Sprinkle water over mixture while tossing to blend well. Press dough firmly into ball. On lightly floured surface, roll

into 12-inch circle. Fit loosely into 9-inch pie plate. Trim and flute edge. Fill and bake according to recipe.

**Bake Pie Shell:** Preheat oven to 450°F. Pierce pie crust thoroughly with fork. Bake 12 to 15 minutes or until light golden brown.

## Oreo® Cheesecake

1 (20-ounce) package OREO® Chocolate
   Sandwich Cookies
⅓ cup BLUE BONNET® 75% Vegetable
   Oil Spread, melted
3 (8-ounce) packages cream cheese,
   softened
¾ cup sugar
4 eggs, at room temperature
1 cup dairy sour cream
1 teaspoon vanilla
   Whipped cream for garnish

Preheat oven to 350°F. Finely roll 30 cookies; coarsely chop 20 cookies. In medium bowl, combine finely rolled cookie crumbs and spread. Press on bottom and 2 inches up side of 9-inch springform pan; set aside.

In large bowl with electric mixer at medium speed, beat cream cheese and sugar until creamy. Blend in eggs, sour cream and vanilla; fold in chopped cookies. Spread mixture into prepared crust. Bake at 350°F 60 minutes or until set.

Cool on wire rack at room temperature. Chill at least 4 hours. Halve remaining cookies; remove side of pan. To serve, garnish with whipped cream and cookie halves.

*Makes 12 servings*

*Top to bottom: Almond Amaretto Pie and*
*Classic Pecan Pie*

# Walnut Holiday Cake

2 tablespoons dark rum
4 single graham cracker squares
5 eggs, separated
2 cups powdered sugar
1 teaspoon grated orange peel
¼ teaspoon cream of tartar
3½ cups finely ground toasted California walnuts
¼ cup grated semisweet chocolate
6 squares (1 ounce each) semisweet chocolate
6 tablespoons butter or margarine
1 tablespoon honey
California walnut halves for garnish

In small bowl, pour rum over graham crackers. When crackers are softened, mash with fork.

In large bowl, beat egg yolks at medium speed until lemon colored. Add sugar and orange peel; beat at high speed until thick, about 3 minutes. Beat cracker mixture into yolk mixture. In separate large bowl, beat egg whites with cream of tartar at high speed until stiff, but not dry, peaks form. Gently fold beaten whites, ground walnuts and grated chocolate into yolk mixture.

*Walnut Holiday Cake*

Grease 9-inch springform pan; line bottom with waxed paper and grease again. Pour batter into prepared pan. Bake in preheated 350°F oven 45 to 50 minutes or until toothpick inserted into center comes out clean and small crack appears on surface. Let cool completely in pan on wire rack. Remove side of springform pan. Invert cake onto serving plate; remove bottom of pan and waxed paper. Place strips of waxed paper under cake to cover plate.

In top of double boiler set over simmering water, melt chocolate squares and butter; stir to blend. Stir in honey. Pour chocolate mixture over cake; let stand until slightly cool. Spread over top and side of cake. Remove waxed paper strips. Garnish, if desired. When firm, cut into thin wedges.

*Makes 16 servings*

*Favorite recipe from* **Walnut Marketing Board**

# Decadent Turtle Cheesecake

2 cups crushed chocolate cookies or vanilla wafers (about 8 ounces cookies)
¼ cup (½ stick) butter, melted
2½ packages (8 ounces each) cream cheese, softened
1 cup sugar
1½ tablespoons all-purpose flour
1½ teaspoons vanilla
¼ teaspoon salt
3 eggs
2 tablespoons whipping cream
Caramel and Chocolate Toppings (page 205)
¾ cup chopped toasted pecans

Preheat oven to 450°F. For crust, combine cookie crumbs and butter; press onto bottom of 9-inch springform pan.

For filling, beat cream cheese in large bowl with electric mixer until creamy. Beat in sugar, flour, vanilla and salt; mix well. Add eggs, one at a time, beating well after each addition. Blend in cream. Pour over crust.

Bake 10 minutes; *reduce oven temperature to 200°F.* Continue baking 35 to 40 minutes or until set. Loosen cake from rim of pan; cool completely before removing rim of pan. Meanwhile, prepare Caramel and Chocolate Toppings.

Drizzle cake with toppings. Refrigerate. Sprinkle with pecans before serving.

*Makes one 9-inch cheesecake*

**Caramel Topping:** Combine ½ (14-ounce) bag caramels and ¼ cup whipping cream in small saucepan; stir over low heat until smooth.

**Chocolate Topping:** Combine 4 squares (1 ounce each) semisweet chocolate *or* 4 ounces semisweet chocolate chips, 1 teaspoon butter and 2 tablespoons whipping cream in small saucepan; stir over low heat until smooth.

# Almond Orange Splendor

1 package DUNCAN HINES® Angel
    Food Cake Mix
⅔ cup water
⅔ cup orange juice
1 cup toasted natural sliced almonds,
    chopped, divided
1 teaspoon grated orange peel
½ teaspoon orange extract
    Sorbet or frozen nonfat yogurt
    (optional)

*Almond Orange Splendor*

1. Preheat oven to 375°F.

2. Combine Egg White Mixture (blue "A" packet) from Mix with water and orange juice in large bowl. Beat at low speed with electric mixer for 1 minute. Beat at high speed for 5 to 10 minutes or until stiff peaks form.

3. Add Cake Flour Mixture (red "B" packet) following package directions. Fold in ½ cup chopped almonds, orange peel and orange extract. Pour into ungreased 10-inch tube pan. Run knife through batter to remove air bubbles. Sprinkle remaining ½ cup chopped almonds over top. Bake and cool cake following package directions. Slice and serve with scoop of sorbet or frozen yogurt. *Makes 12 to 16 servings*

**Note:** This recipe contains no cholesterol.

*Top to bottom: Traditional Pumpkin Pie and Streusel Apple Mince Pie*

# Traditional Pumpkin Pie

1 (9-inch) unbaked pastry shell
1 (16-ounce) can pumpkin (about 2 cups)
1 (14-ounce) can EAGLE® Brand Sweetened Condensed Milk (NOT evaporated milk)
2 eggs
1 teaspoon ground cinnamon
½ teaspoon ground ginger
½ teaspoon ground nutmeg
½ teaspoon salt

Preheat oven to 425°. In large mixer bowl, combine all ingredients except pastry shell; mix well. Pour into pastry shell. Bake 15 minutes. *Reduce oven temperature to 350°;* bake 35 to 40 minutes longer or until knife inserted 1 inch from edge comes out clean. Cool. Garnish as desired. Refrigerate leftovers.                *Makes one 9-inch pie*

**Maple Pecan Topping Variation:** In small saucepan, combine ½ cup Borden® or Meadow Gold® Whipping Cream, unwhipped, and ½ cup Cary's®, Maple Orchards® or MacDonald's™ Pure Maple Syrup; bring to a boil. Boil rapidly 5 minutes or until thickened; stir occasionally. Add ¼ cup chopped toasted pecans. Spread on warm pumpkin pie.
                *Makes about ¾ cup*

# Streusel Apple Mince Pie

1 (9-inch) unbaked pastry shell
3 medium all-purpose apples, cored, pared and thinly sliced
½ cup plus 3 tablespoons unsifted flour
2 tablespoons margarine or butter, melted
1 (27-ounce) jar NONE SUCH® Ready-to-Use Mincemeat (Regular or Brandy & Rum)
¼ cup firmly packed light brown sugar
1 teaspoon ground cinnamon
⅓ cup cold margarine or butter
¼ cup chopped nuts

Place rack in lowest position in oven; preheat oven to 425°. In large bowl, toss apples with *3 tablespoons* flour and *melted* margarine; arrange in pastry shell. Top with mincemeat. In medium bowl, combine remaining *½ cup* flour, sugar and cinnamon; cut in cold margarine until crumbly. Add nuts; sprinkle over mincemeat. Bake 10 minutes. *Reduce oven temperature to 375°;* bake 25 minutes longer or until golden. Cool. Garnish as desired.
                *Makes one 9-inch pie*

**Tip:** One 9-ounce package None Such® Condensed Mincemeat, reconstituted as package directs, can be substituted for None Such® Ready-to-Use Mincemeat.

# Triple Chocolate Fantasy

## Cake

1 package DUNCAN HINES® Moist
    Deluxe Devil's Food Cake Mix
3 eggs
1⅓ cups water
½ cup CRISCO® Oil or CRISCO®
    PURITAN® Canola Oil
½ cup ground walnuts

## Chocolate Glaze

1 package (12 ounces) semisweet
    chocolate chips
¼ cup plus 2 tablespoons butter or
    margarine
¼ cup coarsely chopped walnuts

## White Chocolate Glaze

3 ounces white chocolate, coarsely
    chopped
1 tablespoon CRISCO® all-vegetable
    shortening

1. Preheat oven to 350°F. Grease and flour 10-inch Bundt® pan.

2. **For cake,** combine cake mix, eggs, water, oil and ground walnuts in large bowl. Beat at medium speed with electric mixer for 2 minutes. Pour into pan. Bake at 350°F for 45 to 55 minutes or until toothpick inserted in center comes out clean. Cool in pan 25 minutes. Invert onto serving plate. Cool completely.

3. **For chocolate glaze,** combine chocolate chips and butter in small heavy saucepan. Heat on low heat until chips are melted. Stir constantly until shiny and smooth. (Glaze will be very thick.) Spread hot glaze over cooled cake. Sprinkle with coarsely chopped walnuts.

4. **For white chocolate glaze,** combine white chocolate and shortening in small heavy saucepan. Heat on low heat until melted, stirring constantly. Drizzle hot glaze over top and sides of cake.

*Makes 12 to 16 servings*

# Little Banana Upside-Down Cakes

3 tablespoons margarine, melted
3 tablespoons flaked coconut, toasted
3 tablespoons DOLE® Chopped
    Almonds, toasted
2 tablespoons brown sugar
1 firm, large DOLE® Banana, peeled,
    sliced
¼ cup cake flour
¼ teaspoon baking powder
    Pinch salt
1 egg
3 tablespoons granulated sugar
1 teaspoon rum extract

• Divide margarine, coconut, almonds, brown sugar and banana among 3 (¾-cup) soufflé dishes.

• Combine flour, baking powder and salt.

• Beat egg and granulated sugar until thick and pale. Beat in rum extract. Fold in flour mixture. Pour batter evenly over coconut mixture.

• Bake in 350°F oven 15 to 20 minutes. Invert onto serving plates.

*Makes 3 servings*

*Triple Chocolate Fantasy*

# Chocolate Mini-Puffs

½ cup water
¼ cup (½ stick) butter or margarine
⅛ teaspoon salt
½ cup all-purpose flour
 2 eggs
    Chocolate Mousse Filling (recipe
      follows)
    Chocolate Glaze (recipe follows) or
      powdered sugar

Heat oven to 400°F. In medium saucepan, heat water, butter and salt to a full rolling boil; reduce heat to low. Add flour all at once; beat with wooden spoon until mixture forms a ball. Remove from heat; cool slightly. Add eggs, one at a time, beating with wooden spoon until mixture is smooth. Drop by scant teaspoonfuls onto ungreased cookie sheet. Bake 25 to 30 minutes or until puffed and golden brown. Remove from oven; cool on wire rack. Prepare Chocolate Mousse Filling and Chocolate Glaze. Fill puffs with filling. Replace tops. Drizzle puffs with glaze. Refrigerate until ready to serve.

*Makes about 2 to 2½ dozen mini-puffs*

## Chocolate Mousse Filling

 1 teaspoon unflavored gelatin
 1 tablespoon cold water
 2 tablespoons boiling water
½ cup sugar
¼ cup HERSHEY'S Cocoa
 1 cup chilled whipped cream
 1 teaspoon vanilla extract

In small bowl, sprinkle gelatin over cold water; let stand 1 minute to soften. Add boiling water; stir until gelatin is completely dissolved and mixture is clear. Cool slightly. In small cold mixer bowl, stir together sugar and cocoa; add whipped cream and vanilla. Beat at medium speed, scraping bottom of bowl occasionally, until stiff; pour in gelatin mixture and beat until well blended. Refrigerate at least 30 minutes before using.

*Makes about 2 cups filling*

**Chocolate Glaze:** In small saucepan over low heat, melt 2 tablespoons butter or margarine; add 2 tablespoons HERSHEY'S Cocoa and 2 tablespoons water. Cook and stir over low heat until smooth and slightly thickened; do not boil. Remove from heat; cool slightly. Gradually blend in 1 cup powdered sugar and ½ teaspoon vanilla extract; beat with wire whisk until smooth and slightly thickened.

*Makes about ¾ cup glaze*

# West Coast Brandied Rice

 1 cup firmly packed brown sugar
½ cup butter or margarine
 2 apples, cored and chopped
 1 cup golden raisins
½ cup brandy
 5 cups cooked brown rice*
 1 cup chopped walnuts
1½ teaspoons ground cinnamon
 1 pint vanilla ice cream

*Medium- or long-grain white rice may be substituted.

Combine brown sugar and butter in large skillet. Cook over medium heat until sugar is dissolved. Stir in apples, raisins and brandy. Cook until apples are crisp-tender, stirring constantly. Fold in rice, walnuts and cinnamon. Serve topped with vanilla ice cream. *Makes 8 servings*

*Favorite recipe from **USA Rice Council***

*Chocolate Mini-Puffs*

# Fudge Truffle Cheesecake

1½ cups vanilla wafer crumbs (about 45 wafers)
½ cup confectioners' sugar
⅓ cup unsweetened cocoa
⅓ cup margarine or butter, melted
3 (8-ounce) packages cream cheese, softened
1 (14-ounce) can EAGLE® Brand Sweetened Condensed Milk (NOT evaporated milk)
2 cups (12 ounces) semi-sweet chocolate chips *or* 8 (1-ounce) squares semi-sweet chocolate, melted
4 eggs
¼ cup coffee-flavored liqueur, optional
2 teaspoons vanilla extract

Preheat oven to 300°. Combine crumbs, sugar, cocoa and margarine; press firmly onto bottom of 9-inch springform pan. In large mixer bowl, beat cheese until fluffy. Gradually beat in sweetened condensed milk until smooth. Add melted chocolate then all remaining ingredients; mix well. Pour into prepared pan. Bake 1 hour and 5 minutes or until center is set. Cool. Chill. Just before serving, remove side of springform pan. Garnish as desired. Refrigerate leftovers.

*Makes one 9-inch cheesecake*

# Pumpkin Bread Pudding

½ loaf (8 ounces) raisin bread, cut into cubes
1 cup solid pack pumpkin
½ cup packed brown sugar
½ cup liquid egg substitute *or* 2 eggs
1 teaspoon vanilla
1 teaspoon freshly grated ginger
1 (12-ounce) can evaporated skimmed milk
⅓ cup California walnuts, chopped

Preheat oven to 400°F. Place bread cubes in 9-inch pie plate or baking dish coated with nonstick cooking spray.

Combine pumpkin, brown sugar, egg substitute, vanilla and ginger in medium bowl. Stir in evaporated milk and pour over cubed bread, tossing to coat bread cubes.

Sprinkle with walnuts. Bake 25 to 30 minutes or until knife inserted near center comes out clean. Cut into wedges and serve.                    *Makes 8 servings*

*Favorite recipe from* **Walnut Marketing Board**

# Sour Cream Mince Pie

1 (9-inch) unbaked pastry shell
1 (9-ounce) package NONE SUCH® Condensed Mincemeat, crumbled
1 cup apple juice or water
1 tablespoon flour
1 medium all-purpose apple, cored, pared and chopped
2 cups (1 pint) BORDEN® or MEADOW GOLD® Sour Cream
2 eggs
2 tablespoons sugar
1 teaspoon vanilla extract
2 to 3 tablespoons chopped nuts

Place rack in lowest position in oven; preheat oven to 425°. In small saucepan, combine mincemeat and apple juice. Bring to a boil; boil briskly 1 minute. In medium bowl, stir flour and apple to coat; stir in mincemeat mixture. Pour into pastry shell. Bake 25 minutes. Meanwhile, in small mixer bowl, combine sour cream, eggs, sugar and vanilla; beat until smooth. Pour evenly over mincemeat mixture. Sprinkle with nuts. *Reduce oven temperature to 325°;* bake 20 minutes longer or until set. Cool. Chill thoroughly. Garnish as desired. Refrigerate leftovers.

*Makes one 9-inch pie*

*Linzer Torte*

## Linzer Torte

½ cup toasted whole almonds
1½ cups all-purpose flour
1 teaspoon ground cinnamon
¼ teaspoon salt
¾ cup granulated sugar
½ cup butter or margarine
½ teaspoon grated lemon peel
1 egg
¾ cup raspberry or apricot jam
Powdered sugar

Place almonds in food processor; process until almonds are ground, but not pasty. Measure enough to make ½ cup ground almonds.

Preheat oven to 375°F. Combine flour, almonds, cinnamon and salt in medium bowl; set aside.

Beat granulated sugar, butter and lemon peel in large bowl using electric mixer at medium speed about 5 minutes or until light and fluffy, scraping down side of bowl once. Beat in egg until well blended. Beat in flour mixture at low speed until well blended. Spoon ⅔ of dough onto bottom of 10-inch tart pan with removable bottom. Pat dough evenly over bottom and up side of pan. Spread jam over bottom of dough.

Roll remaining ⅓ of dough on lightly floured surface with lightly floured rolling pin into 10 × 6-inch square. Cut dough into 10 × ½-inch strips. Arrange 4 to 5 strips of dough lengthwise across jam. Arrange another 4 to 5 strips of dough crosswise across top. Press ends of dough strips into edge of crust.

Bake 25 to 35 minutes or until crust is golden brown. Cool completely in pan on wire rack. Remove from pan. Cut into wedges. Sprinkle with powdered sugar.

*Makes 12 servings*

*Snowman Cupcakes*

## Snowman Cupcakes

1 package (18.5 ounces) yellow or white
   cake mix, *plus* ingredients to
   prepare mix
2 (16-ounce) containers vanilla frosting
4 cups flaked coconut
15 large marshmallows
15 miniature chocolate covered peanut
   butter cups, unwrapped
   Decorations: Small red candies and
   pretzel sticks
   Green and red decorating gel

Preheat oven to 350°F. Line 15 regular-size
(2½-inch) muffin pan cups and 15 small
(about 1-inch) muffin pan cups with paper
liners. Prepare cake mix according to
package directions. Spoon batter into
muffin cups.

Bake 10 to 15 minutes for small cupcakes
and 15 to 20 minutes for large cupcakes or
until cupcakes are golden and wooden
toothpick inserted into centers comes out
clean. Cool in pans on wire racks 10
minutes. Remove from pans to racks; cool
completely. Remove paper liners.

For each snowman, frost bottom and side of
1 large cupcake; coat with coconut. Repeat
with 1 small cupcake. Attach small cupcake
to large cupcake with frosting to form
snowman body. Attach marshmallow to
small cupcake with frosting to form
snowman head. Attach inverted peanut
butter cup to marshmallow with frosting to
form snowman hat. Use pretzels for arms
and small red candies for buttons as shown
in photo. Pipe faces with decorating gel as
shown in photo. Repeat with remaining
cupcakes.          *Makes 15 snowmen*

## Pineapple Lime Tartlets

**Crust**

6 to 8 graham crackers

**Filling**

¼ cup lime juice
1 envelope unflavored gelatin
1 container (8 ounces) low fat ricotta
   cheese
1¼ cups nonfat plain yogurt, divided
½ cup sugar
1 teaspoon coconut extract
1 teaspoon grated lime peel

**Pineapple Topping**

1 medium DOLE® Fresh Pineapple
¾ cup water
¼ cup sugar
1 tablespoon cornstarch
1 teaspoon grated lime peel

**CRUST:** Arrange crackers in 6 (4½-inch)
tart pans with removable bottoms or 1
(9-inch) tart pan. Break crackers to fit.

**FILLING:** Add lime juice to small
saucepan. Sprinkle gelatin over juice to
soften; cook over low heat until dissolved.
Combine ricotta and ¼ cup yogurt in
blender until smooth. Pour into bowl. Stir
in remaining yogurt, ½ cup sugar, extract
and 1 teaspoon lime peel. Stir in cooled
gelatin. Pour into pans; refrigerate.

**PINEAPPLE TOPPING:** Twist crown from pineapple. Cut pineapple in half lengthwise. Refrigerate 1 half for another use. Cut fruit from shell with a knife, then crosswise into thin slices. Combine water, ¼ cup sugar and cornstarch in saucepan. Cook, stirring, until sauce boils and thickens. Cool. Add pineapple and 1 teaspoon lime peel. Arrange over top of tarts.
*Makes 6 servings*

# Chocolate-Rum Parfaits

  6 to 6½ ounces Mexican chocolate, coarsely chopped*
1½ cups heavy or whipping cream, divided
  3 tablespoons golden rum (optional)
  ¾ teaspoon vanilla
     Additional whipped cream for garnish
     Sliced almonds for garnish
     Cookies (optional)

*Or, substitute 6 ounces semisweet chocolate, coarsely chopped, 1 tablespoon ground cinnamon and ¼ teaspoon almond extract for Mexican chocolate.

Combine chocolate and 3 tablespoons cream in top of double boiler. Heat over simmering water until smooth, stirring occasionally. Gradually stir in rum, if desired; remove top pan from heat. Let stand at room temperature 15 minutes to cool slightly.

Combine remaining cream and vanilla in small chilled bowl. Beat with electric mixer at low speed, then gradually increase speed until stiff, but not dry, peaks form.

Gently fold whipped cream into cooled chocolate mixture until uniform in color. Spoon mousse into 4 individual dessert dishes. Refrigerate 2 to 3 hours until firm. Garnish with additional whipped cream and sliced almonds. Serve with cookies, if desired.
*Makes 4 servings*

*Chocolate-Rum Parfaits*

# Acknowledgments

The publisher would like to thank the companies and organizations listed below for the use of their recipes and photographs in this publication.

American Dairy Association
American Lamb Council
American Spice Trade Association
BC—USA
Best Foods, a Division of CPC International
  Inc.
Bob Evans Farms®
Borden Kitchens, Borden, Inc.
California Apricot Advisory Board
California Table Grape Commission
The Dannon Company, Inc.
Delmarva Poultry Industry, Inc.
Del Monte Corporation
Dole Food Company, Inc.
Florida Department of Agriculture and
  Consumer Services
Florida Tomato Committee
Grandma's Molasses, a division of Cadbury
  Beverages Inc.
Hershey Foods Corporation
Jolly Time® Pop Corn
Jones Dairy Farm
Kahlúa Liqueur
Kraft Foods
Lawry's® Foods, Inc.
Thomas J. Lipton Co.
McIlhenny Company

Nabisco Foods Group
National Broiler Council
National Dairy Board
National Fisheries Institute
National Honey Board
National Live Stock & Meat Board
National Pork Producers Council
National Turkey Federation
Nestlé Food Company
Newman's Own, Inc.
Norseland, Inc.
North Dakota Barley Council
Pace Foods, Ltd.
Perdue® Farms
Pet Incorporated
The Procter & Gamble Company
The Quaker Oats Company
Ralston Foods, Inc.
Riviana Food, Inc.
Sargento Foods Inc.®
Southeast United Dairy Industry
  Association Inc.
The Sugar Association, Inc.
USA Dry Pea & Lentil Council
USA Rice Council
Walnut Marketing Board
Washington Apple Commission

# INDEX

# METRIC CONVERSION CHART

## VOLUME MEASUREMENTS (dry)

$^1/_8$ teaspoon = 0.5 mL
$^1/_4$ teaspoon = 1 mL
$^1/_2$ teaspoon = 2 mL
$^3/_4$ teaspoon = 4 mL
1 teaspoon = 5 mL
1 tablespoon = 15 mL
2 tablespoons = 30 mL
$^1/_4$ cup = 60 mL
$^1/_3$ cup = 75 mL
$^1/_2$ cup = 125 mL
$^2/_3$ cup = 150 mL
$^3/_4$ cup = 175 mL
1 cup = 250 mL
2 cups = 1 pint = 500 mL
3 cups = 750 mL
4 cups = 1 quart = 1 L

## VOLUME MEASUREMENTS (fluid)

1 fluid ounce (2 tablespoons) = 30 mL
4 fluid ounces ($^1/_2$ cup) = 125 mL
8 fluid ounces (1 cup) = 250 mL
12 fluid ounces (1$^1/_2$ cups) = 375 mL
16 fluid ounces (2 cups) = 500 mL

## WEIGHTS (mass)

$^1/_2$ ounce = 15 g
1 ounce = 30 g
3 ounces = 90 g
4 ounces = 120 g
8 ounces = 225 g
10 ounces = 285 g
12 ounces = 360 g
16 ounces = 1 pound = 450 g

## DIMENSIONS

$^1/_{16}$ inch = 2 mm
$^1/_8$ inch = 3 mm
$^1/_4$ inch = 6 mm
$^1/_2$ inch = 1.5 cm
$^3/_4$ inch = 2 cm
1 inch = 2.5 cm

## OVEN TEMPERATURES

250°F = 120°C
275°F = 140°C
300°F = 150°C
325°F = 160°C
350°F = 180°C
375°F = 190°C
400°F = 200°C
425°F = 220°C
450°F = 230°C

## BAKING PAN SIZES

| Utensil | Size in Inches/Quarts | Metric Volume | Size in Centimeters |
|---|---|---|---|
| Baking or Cake Pan (square or rectangular) | 8×8×2 | 2 L | 20×20×5 |
| | 9×9×2 | 2.5 L | 22×22×5 |
| | 12×8×2 | 3 L | 30×20×5 |
| | 13×9×2 | 3.5 L | 33×23×5 |
| Loaf Pan | 8×4×3 | 1.5 L | 20×10×7 |
| | 9×5×3 | 2 L | 23×13×7 |
| Round Layer Cake Pan | 8×1½ | 1.2 L | 20×4 |
| | 9×1½ | 1.5 L | 23×4 |
| Pie Plate | 8×1¼ | 750 mL | 20×3 |
| | 9×1¼ | 1 L | 23×3 |
| Baking Dish or Casserole | 1 quart | 1 L | — |
| | 1½ quart | 1.5 L | — |
| | 2 quart | 2 L | — |